Praise for *When Nowhere Is Home*

"A riveting and honest page-turner written with vulnerability and heartbreaking truths about one family's experience with international adoption. I highly recommend it."
- Susan Morea MA,
marriage and family therapist

"A gripping narrative of adoption—with all the hopes and heartaches—and most of all, the enduring love."
- Carol Munson JD,
adoptive mom, counselor

"An insightful and inspiring journey of self-discovery as core beliefs are challenged by the limits of a mother's love."
- Chris Tandy LPC, therapist

An Adoption Story

CHARLOTTE FINN

When Nowhere Is Home: An Adoption Story

Copyright ©2022 by Charlotte Finn

Cover and interior design by Antonio García Martín
thisisagm.com

All rights reserved, which includes the right to reproduce this book or portions thereof in any form whatsoever except as provided by the U.S. Copyright Law.

Published by Duende Press
duendepressbooks.com

Family and Relationships / Adoption and Fostering
Self Help / Personal Growth and General
Body Mind Spirit / Healing General

ISBN: 978-0-9915254-5-4

Dedicated to my three children

Preface

Over thirty thousand children were adopted internationally from Guatemala during the small Central American country's brutal civil war from 1960 to 1996. Many of these children were born to parents who were killed or who disappeared during the long conflict. Many more were bought or stolen from desperate Indigenous women and then sold in a lucrative clandestine business operation that made millions of dollars for lawyers, public officials, and private citizens. The scandal was finally exposed in 2007, and the adoption market in Guatemala was curtailed.

In 1987, the year we adopted our Guatemalan daughter, thousands of children were adopted by parents who were ignorant of their children's origins. The underground business of selling children made some unscrupulous Guatemalans very wealthy, left countless biological parents searching for their lost children, and sent thousands of children to live in families who were unprepared to deal with the trauma and loss their children had experienced. These well-meaning families with loving intentions took in children whose wounds were invisible and whose histories had been erased.

This is my story of one such adoption. Mariela came to our family when she was nine years old. We had been told she was seven years old, smart and healthy, and had lost both parents to disease in the highlands of Guatemala. Her real story, told after her arrival, unfolded from her memories, many of them fragmented and blurred. Every attempt has been made to remain true to real events as she experienced them, but memory, even in the best of circumstances, is not a perfect reflection of truth or reality.

In my story of Mariela and my own journey to wholeness through our complex relationship, I have done my best to remain true to my memory and my interpretation of events. The story of Maria, Mariela's Mayan mother, is a composite character of Mariela's memories and the plight of many Mayan mothers gleaned from countless accounts of Guatemalans who have shared their stories during my numerous trips to Guatemala over the years.

In some cases, names have been changed to respect and guard the privacy of others.

Chapter 1

Charlotte

"You can't carry corn in a basket with holes."
Mayan proverb

The tightly packed retired school bus spewed fumes as it roared uphill and around tight corners, carrying us deeper into the highlands of Guatemala. We were the only gringos onboard and considered ourselves lucky to have seats on the brightly painted bus that sent standing passengers careening into each other with each wild turn. I sat squeezed between my husband and a small and somber Mayan woman clad in a worn and colorfully woven huipil, a tapestry of faded colors.

Once carrying American schoolchildren and now splashed with pictures of saints on its sides, the bus was filled with Indiginos heading to rural destinations in the northwest of the country. Their baskets were brimming with goods to sell in the various market towns along the way. The air blowing through the open widows mingled with the earthy aroma of produce, sweat, burlap, and dust. The music blaring from the radio attached to the dash never stopped, making the quiet murmurs in Quiche, the language spoken in the highlands, barely audible. A long and black tight braid of the woman sitting directly in front of us swung against the back of her seat. In the front of the bus, two teenagers balanced themselves as they hung on to the backs of seats, veering left then right with the bus as they whispered and giggled with each other. I suspected they shared many of the maddening and adorable characteristics of our two children at home, fifteen-year-old Chad and twelve-year-old Jill.

I tried to engage with a sweet infant strapped to the back of his young mother who sat across from us. He gazed in our direction with heavy eyes, but he fell asleep before I could make a connection. The babies, always held securely, seemed calmer here in Guatemala. *Had Mariela been a content baby like this one?* I wondered. *Were her eyes slanted, her cheekbones as high as this darling baby's?* A rosary swung wildly from the cracked rearview mirror at the front of the bus and had a hypnotic, calming effect, at least for a while.

My random thoughts and a complex stew of feelings simmered as I looked out the window. "God, I'm nervous," I said to my husband, Chris, who sat quietly beside me. "I keep trying to imagine what she's like and if we'll recognize her from the photo. I don't know if I should throw my arms out and run to her or let her approach us." I was attempting to express my tangle of emotions.

"Let's see what happens," he said, a response I found frustrating.

Wouldn't we be better off planning what to do, given how nervous all of us would be? I thought. When overcome by emotions, I needed to talk and plan. Chris, an engineer, withdrew into himself, walling off, to gather his resources. In the early years of our marriage, I had tried to get through to him by busting through his walls to connect. "What are you thinking?" "How are you feeling?" I frequently asked, trying to force my way through his impenetrable barrier that I assumed was bursting with unexpressed thoughts and feelings. "Nothing much" was a typical, maddening reply. I had learned over our seventeen years together that this tactic didn't work. My efforts tended to make him more insular and left me hurt and frustrated. He believed once something was said, there was no point in repeating it or delving into a myriad of feelings that only led to confusion. He knew I was anxious, and he didn't need to hear about it again. So, I restrained myself and tried to focus on the drama that would unfold at the end of this long bus ride. I reached for my money belt where my passport had been secured earlier that day after going through customs in Guatemala City. I pulled out the photo that I had carried with me for six months.

"We're coming for you, sweetie," I whispered to the photo of the Mayan girl with golden-brown skin and long jet-black hair pulled tightly back who had the slightest upturn of her mouth, perhaps the beginning of an awkward grin. I had imagined Mariela into a sweet and shy girl anxious for a family and eager for love. Largely defining her as young and vulnerable, I visualized her flourishing with our commitment and care. Still, my heart pounded with as much fear as excitement. The adoption, set in motion six months earlier, was my heart's desire, but my trepidation was a force impossible to ignore.

"Of course you're scared—who wouldn't be?" a friend had suggested. "She's essentially a stranger your family is taking on. It's a little like a blind date or even an arranged marriage," she quipped. Her comments, meant to be supportive, did nothing to reassure me. My mother had raised a wary eyebrow. "You have no idea what you're getting yourself into," she warned in the judgmental way that was her habit. "My God, don't you have enough on your plate with a full-time job and two kids already?" she added, returning to a well-worn theme that indicated her displeasure at my being a working mother. Many friends were eager and enthusiastic for our family; others were as full of apprehension as we were approaching the first meeting with our new daughter.

It had all started when Ellen, a coworker, adopted a four-year-old girl from Colombia a few years earlier. The adoption had worked out well for her. Paula, a trusting little girl with a sunny personality, had adjusted well to her new mother and was the joy of her single mom's life. Ellen had shared that there were hundreds of older children available for adoption through a local agency, and it wasn't long before adopting a waiting child in Latin America went from an abstract idea to a hook that took hold and wouldn't let go. *What a wonderful and selfless way to express my deep desire to make a difference in my life and in the life of a child,* I thought. Chris agreed, and with that, the spark grew and spread, creating a flame that would not be extinguished.

My heart pounded with excitement as I called the adoption agency that Ellen had used and talked to Janice, a social worker who agreed to send us an application right away. "If you and your husband are willing to adopt an older child, there are many available, especially in Guatemala."

"Yes, we want an older child, preferably from a Spanish-speaking country," I said, voicing my husband's preference since he spoke some Spanish. "What are the next steps?"

"Come into the office once you've completed the application," Janice told me. "We'll contact your references and your physician and have our social worker do a home study. Then we assign a child to you. Then, you wait, maybe six to eight months, but it could even be quicker with an older child," Janice droned, as if our life-changing decision to adopt, which charged every cell in my body, was an everyday occurrence.

Janice, a plain-looking, all-business social worker who specialized in foreign adoptions, welcomed us to her office when we showed up for our appointment, application in hand. Both of us were nervous about making a good impression. I spoke first. "We say on our application that we prefer a girl between five and eight years because we think that would be the best fit for our family, but we can be more open, if necessary."

Janice turned to a file on her desk, looking for something. "I've been to Guatemala recently," she said, "and there are many older kids there ready to be adopted. You know, there's been an awful war there." She pulled out a photo and handed it to us. "Her name is Mariela; she's about seven or so; she's smart and healthy and is eager to be adopted. The social worker in Guatemala talked to me about her," she continued as we stared at Mariela's photo, barely listening to Janice. "Once kids are over five or six, they are nearly impossible to place, so they spend their lives in orphanages." She shook her head and looked down, indicating how sad she felt.

"That's terrible. I had no idea there were so many orphans in Guatemala," I said, feeling sure that our decision to adopt an older child was absolutely the right thing to do. It was 1987, and I knew a little about the wars in Central America, but I hadn't thought much about the orphans the wars created.

"What do you know about her? How long has she been in the orphanage? Are her parents both dead? You say she's smart and healthy? What's the next step for us?" I stumbled from one question to the next as I clutched her photo, imagination and expectation taking shape.

"I'll try to get more information on her. For now, we only know that she wants to be adopted and has no living relatives," Janice said in a cool and detached voice.

"She's exactly who we're looking for," I said with enthusiasm when presenting her photo later that evening to Chad and Jill. We all looked at the little girl in the photo, and I could imagine my arms around her small shoulders, as if she were meant to join our family. We all agreed that she seemed perfect, and then as my son and daughter went about their busy lives and Chris busied himself with work, I became gripped with a passion to get Mariela out of the orphanage and into our home. Janice told me when I called after a month or so that there was no more information on her, so I filled in the blanks with my vivid imagination. She was a girl eager to be adopted, anxious to be loved, fun-loving and smart, cute and with an open heart. I knew there was more to her story. I was even prepared for some heartache and challenge as we all adapted, but I didn't dwell on that. Nothing in life was perfect, and the unexpected twists and turns, both positive and negative, were part of the romanticized adventure I eagerly anticipated.

Chris and I both read everything we could find on Guatemala. We learned what we could about the current civil war, the struggles of the Indiginos, Mayan history, and current events. It was difficult to find clear, unbiased information. The slant of the media seemed to be in favor of our government controlling the menacing guerillas who were creating havoc in the highlands. We found a few stories in progressive sources that told a very different story of Indigenous peoples being killed by the Guatemalan military, who were trained and supported by our US government, which was also supporting right-wing groups in Nicaragua and El Salvador. We became aware that we had a lot to learn about Guatemala and the daughter waiting for us.

Meanwhile, captivating images of our family creating space, opening our home and hearts, of the joy and fulfillment Mariela would bring us, and her happiness at having a family filled my days. We'd grow and change to lovingly accommodate another child, and I would have another opportunity to mother, a role I found deeply satisfying.

At the time, I had a full-time career at a large mental health clinic that I enjoyed most days. But motherhood surpassed in satisfaction any other endeavors or accomplishments, and ever since becoming pregnant with my first child, I had been determined to be a good mother. I nursed each of my children over two years, rejected store-bought baby food and made my own, and held, rocked, and soothed each of them through their early years. I delighted in watching them develop their unique personalities with awareness that my own childhood had lacked in some of what I now lavished on my children.

We lived in a comfortable home surrounded by large pine trees in a middle-class neighborhood of Oregon City, a small city built on bluffs outside of Portland, Oregon. Chad and Jill caught the bus to school on our leafy block where they stood with friends in the early morning and were delivered home again after full days of school and various sports activities. There was a busy pattern to my days, occupied by meaningful work, daily early-morning runs along the country roads around our home, keeping the house in order, planning social lives for all of us, carpooling to games, and keeping our family running smoothly while meeting everyone's needs as best I could.

Chris and I sat at the dinner table each evening with our kids. We would discuss the ups and downs of our days and listen to Chad and Jill talk about their friends, school challenges, frustrations, and delights. They were often chatty and exuberant; other times it was difficult to get them to say much at all. "Hey, you guys, I really love you. You all bring so much joy to my life," I said one evening as I looked at both of our kids, tears of gratitude pooling in my eyes. Chris and I smiled at each other, then quickly shifted our loving looks to our children.

Being Chad and Jill's mom was immensely fulfilling and met my emotional needs for connection and love. Although it wasn't a conscious desire at the time, I imagined having Mariela in our family would provide another intense emotional connection that was often missing in my marriage. Other motives for the adoption, years from being excavated, were complex and unconscious.

"I expect adopting to be challenging, but life-changing endeavors are never easy," I told a group of running friends when questioned about choosing to add such complexity to my otherwise smoothly functioning life.

"But why not an older foster child from the US?" a friend asked.

"Older kids from the US are almost always emotionally damaged, or they wouldn't be up for adoption," I said, drawing on what I had read about the calamitous effects of drugs in our culture and the foster care system. "An older child from another country is more likely to be available because their parents died or because of extreme poverty." My determination made me feel immune to challenges. I was aware that adoption of an older child was a risky endeavor, but I embraced it wholeheartedly, secure in my belief that our loving hearts ensured success.

If I had been honest with myself, there were distant rumblings of discontent behind my image of a happy family. Something akin to a midlife crisis had crept up on me and begun to erode the delight I had enjoyed about my life. A dissatisfaction, a restlessness, an impulse to do something out of the ordinary, creating edges where smoothness had been. A yearning to move beyond the confines I had created for myself became too prominent to ignore. I wanted to toss out the steady routine of my life and invite in challenges to revive myself.

My children continued to provide great satisfaction and meaningful connection, but they were slowly and unevenly creating distance, as teenagers will do. Instead of basking in newfound freedom right around the corner, I looked for ways to fill up the holes in my life that their distance created. There were other opportunities for challenges in my life, such as accepting an offered promotion to supervisor in my clinic or training harder for the triathlons I was already doing. I could have left my marriage to enjoy the single life I had missed by marrying at twenty. None of those options seemed appealing at that time, but a needling voice told me I needed to do more, to prove something about which I was still unclear.

At my core, yet unexplored, I hoped to show that I was worthy of love myself—a struggle that evolved from my difficult relationship with my mother. My mother had always been difficult to please; she was angry and felt cheated by her own life experience. She had been raised in poverty; her father had died when she was thirteen, and she and her six siblings were divided up when her mother became depressed and unable to care for them. She and two brothers had been placed in a "children's home" to struggle on their own while four younger siblings got to stay with their mother. Resentment toward her luckier, unappreciative younger sisters was a constant refrain throughout her life. I was often the recipient of her bitterness, which I unwittingly carried into adulthood. I shouldered her pain by trying to prove I was good enough, thus proving *our* worthiness. My childhood wish to take care of my abandoned and hurt mother influenced my desire as an adult to take care of an orphaned child, the ultimate demonstration of my goodness. This insight was lost to me for many years.

It had never felt easy to be my mother's child, her only daughter, to whom she looked for devotion and admiration. What she demanded of me, she had little ability to give back, and I couldn't understand that as a child. She was a puzzle that I worked hard to figure out. At times she could be loving, and other times she was critical and rejecting, and I couldn't fathom how to get what I needed from her. I was never clear what I had done to displease her. Her mood shifts left me, a sensitive child, unsure of myself and feeling like there was something wrong with me. I heard so many times how lucky I was compared to her that I felt guilty and undeserving of any good fortune that passed my way. She often compared me to her unappreciative and self-centered sisters, the younger ones who weren't sent away like she had been. I spent a lot of energy as a child trying to convince her I was different and worthy of her love, that she was wrong about me. My value came from being caring and helpful to others, a skill perfected in my family that transitioned easily to my marriage and then to a profession of being a paid caregiver, a social worker.

Chris and I had been inseparable when we met in high school, but I had gone off to college intending to break up with him to expand myself beyond my narrow teenage focus. However, I hadn't found the social scene in college easy to navigate and didn't meet anyone special. Chris continued to contact me in heavy pursuit, and finally I convinced myself that his love was a precious resource, not to be squandered. Our relationship had been exciting, fun, loving, and easy, and I became doubtful I'd be loved like that again. I often thought later that had I waited only a year or two and gotten through a particularly insecure stage, I wouldn't have married Chris at all. But that thought wasn't shared or explored. By the time I had this realization, I had a baby, and there was no turning back.

Marrying at twenty dealt with a dilemma I couldn't put into words at the time. My parents provided little support or affection, and I was fearful of being on my own in the world. Settling down to married life had little appeal, but joining with Chris for an adventurous life together sounded great. We vowed to embrace life fully, travel, and move west from our East Coast colleges. Each of us believed, mostly unconsciously, that our love would repair our fragile selves and create a family different from the emotional wastelands in which we were raised.

When I looked at my nursing newborn son—our first child—through the dim light cast by a small lamp, I vowed to do everything possible to demonstrate my love. I wanted to get it right. At twenty-one-years old, I knew mothering would be the most important role in my life. I read countless books on parenting, child development, and helping children develop healthy self-esteem. I swore that my children would always know they were wanted. I wanted them to relax into the full embrace of unconditional love.

For the most part, I lived up to the expectations I put upon myself to be a loving, connected mother. When I became frustrated, impatient, or bored with the inevitable tedium of mothering, I was a harsh critic who vowed to do better. I was equally determined to create a solid relationship with Chris, but our marriage couldn't carry the weight of the expectations we'd placed upon it beyond a decade. By then, however, the lives of two kids were riding on our finding enough satisfaction to sustain it. For years, our marriage was held together by our commitment to our kids, and because it really wasn't bad enough to leave. Besides, breaking up a family would destroy the "good girl" image I had worked so hard to maintain. It was unthinkable to leave, and it simply didn't surface as an option.

All these years later, my attempts at talking with Chris about our relationship were still met with withdrawal that only increased my sense of alienation. I imagined that the investment and commitment to an adopted child would seal a bond between us, and our efforts would cultivate a new sense of purpose and closeness. Adopting a child was like putting my feet in concrete, creating a solid reason to stay in an ailing marriage with hope that our marriage would be enlivened—again, the faultiness in this reasoning was beyond my awareness at the time.

Now that our own children were older, rescuing a motherless

child and loving her fully and unconditionally seemed like the ideal solution to demonstrate an altruistic expression of the virtue I still hoped to prove. With only a flicker of this unconscious need, I jumped headlong into adopting a child, determined to give the love I had struggled so hard to obtain for myself, secure in my belief that adopting Mariela would be an anchor for all of us and a gift to a child who needed a loving home.

Chapter 2

Mariela

"New beginnings are often disguised as painful endings."
Lao Tzu

The first call of roosters roused Mariela out of a fitful sleep in the chilly dorm where she slept with thirty other motherless girls, all between seven and ten years old. Fragmented images of the American mother still occupied her fleeting dreams.

They are coming for me today was her first waking thought as she lay quietly in the small hard bunk, staring at the cracked ceiling and trying to imagine her new mama. How would she look, would she be kind, would she be pleased with her or want one of the cuter girls? All of them wanted mamas.

As she tried to focus on the American woman who would be her new mama, the images blurred with those of her own mama, then floated away beyond her grasp. Memories of Maria, and the other woman who briefly called herself mama, were slipping away, shadowy and elusive. But the nightmares hadn't stopped. Flames, smoke, screams, then running, tripping, holding tightly to her mama's hand as they ran from the burning village. She often woke in terror, breathing heavily, confused and tearful, still smelling the smoke-choked air. She didn't know if the nightmares were actual memories. Maybe she had these terrors as punishment. She had never told anyone about the nightmares, which she was sure were evidence that she was a bad child, not worthy of her mama's love.

The old lady with small cloudy eyes who was in charge of the dorm had not yet blown her feeble whistle to wake the girls, so Mariela stayed in bed and thought of the day ahead. "I'm leaving this terrible place forever," she whispered to herself in Quiche, her first language. The large government orphanage had been her home for three years, and she could hardly remember a time when she hadn't competed with sad, angry, disturbed, and mean kids, all of them trying to get what they needed and sometimes hurting the other children to do so. None of them talked to each other about the horrible things they had lived through. Mariela's abandonment by her mama was a deep wound she kept hidden, and as it was for all the kids, the emotional scars of losing parents ran deep. Although they had all suffered similar losses, none wanted to be part of this group of needy, hand-wringing, head-banging, discarded kids. They sacrificed connection with each other to hide their shame of being discarded.

Still, there was some comfort, if not joy, in Mariela's life, which had a predictability to it. Most of it was a dreary struggle against being ignored or forgotten, but now that she was leaving forever and happy about that, it was also scary to think of not having the familiar kids, the peeling walls, the dusty courtyard she called home. When she was asked many months ago if she wanted to go to the US, she was unsure what to say. How was a kid like her supposed to answer that question? She was old enough to know that the answer she gave would change her life forever. If there had been a trusted adult who cared about her to ask, "What should I do? Should I go to America?" she would have done so, but there was no one to ask, and that was exactly why she alone had decided her fate.

From under her thin pillow, she removed the photo of the American family she'd been given. She wanted to take another long look before she got out of bed and filed in line to use the toilet, the first of many long lines each morning. Yes, the American mom looked kind. She and her husband and two kids, a tall boy and a pretty girl, all had big smiles just like all the gringos when they looked into a camera. They looked like the movie stars she had seen once on a TV inside a small store. She couldn't imagine how she'd fit into their group of four with their grinning pale faces and rows of straight, white teeth. She yearned for a mama to replace the one who left her, but she wasn't sure she needed or wanted the rest of them.

Sometimes when she thought of the American mother, memories of her own lost mama clouded her thoughts. She remembered her mama's worried and sad face and her sturdy body on which Mariela leaned as they sat on the hard concrete in the marketplace. These memories were all she had of the mama to whom she had been born. She ached from the loss. It had hallowed her out and broken her young heart. Anger and mistrust had filled the spaces where her mama had once been.

Would she ever forget the smell of her burning village that seemed caught in her nostrils or the terror of running from soldiers that still made breathing difficult when she remembered? She could feel her mama's heart pounding wildly as they ran, she remembered bouncing on her mama's hip, trying to hold on as they tore through the jungle with other women and children. She remembered running in the dark and stumbling, getting up, ignoring the pain, and her mama's whimpering. Why had her mama held her so tightly like she was a cherished child, then discarded her like she was nothing? It didn't make sense. Pieces of her life that didn't fit together were all she had of the days when she and her mama were together. Soon it wouldn't matter. She'd be far from her mama, and whatever her real story was would remain her own sad mystery.

What if my mama finally comes looking for me after I've left for America? she fretted, but she'd been in the orphanage for three years and her mama hadn't come. Her fantasy, played out hundreds of times, of reuniting with her smiling mama who threw her arms around her and offered a good explanation for why it had taken so long, wasn't going to happen. She planned to bury the memories of her mama and wipe clean all that had happened to her in Guatemala. She'd start new, leaving behind the girl who was discarded to become a child wanted by rich people who paid for her like she had value.

Her eyes filled with angry tears as she imagined it. She had to leave everything she knew to find a family who might love her. And what if they didn't love her? What if they discarded her too? She had heard so many times that she was lucky to have a chance at a better life. But she knew she wasn't a lucky girl; she had never had luck. Now she was heading recklessly into a future she couldn't imagine with people she didn't know or trust.

She thought of the early months after arriving at the orphanage. She had gotten on her knees, crying softly as she prayed for her mama to come for her. "Dear God, please show my mama the way to me; please make her come to get me. I promise to be good forever if you will just make her come." She had made so many promises, but God turned his back on her just like her mama had. She wondered what good a God was who wouldn't help a poor and lost Mayan girl. But she dared not be angry at God and figured he must have his reasons. She saved her anger for her lost mama. *I'll never forgive you if you don't come for me. I hate you for leaving me... Please come, mama, I need you... You better be dead, or why else wouldn't you come for me? Please don't be dead. I don't want to be alone in the world.* Confusion, yearning, and rage mixed with her tears. What kind of girl has such hate-filled thoughts toward her own mama? She wondered if this was why God hadn't answered her prayers.

She gathered the thin blanket around herself and remembered the last time she saw her mama, a memory that although replayed many times, never sharpened. Her life was like a jigsaw puzzle donated by neighborhood kids, full of missing pieces. She had only scraps of memories to keep alive in case they contained clues about who she was.

She recalled being a small girl in dirty clothes she wore for months without washing, sitting on the hard pavement in the busy marketplace of Guatemala City surrounded by the smell of frying chicken that was too expensive for them to ever buy. She kept flies off the tamales they were trying to sell with a palm frond. Shoppers stepped around them as if they were invisible. Occasionally, someone would buy a tamale or two. Other vendors yelled to the crowds, urging them to buy, but Mariela and her mama were quiet, too sad or was it too weak to say much even to each other. Her mama's eyes were often glassy and looked right through her.

Once in a while, she remembered mustering the courage to speak up when a friendly-looking woman walked by. "Se vende tamales," she said in accented Spanish. Most ignored her and kept walking. Her mama sat silent beside her, bent in sadness that Mariela felt helpless to fix. Mariela remembered trying hard to make her mama happy. "Look, mama, I think this woman will buy..." "Look, mama, we have ten quetzals now..." Yearning to be seen, trying to please, unsure of the bond between them, afraid of being useless. Her gnawing hunger was constant, but she never mentioned it, not wanting to be a burden.

What happened on that last day? She thought she had been five or six years old but couldn't be sure. That was the beginning of a sadness and confusion that never lifted. She thought her mama told her to watch their belongings, to try to sell a few tamales without eating any. Her mama told her she'd return soon. Did her mama walk away with someone? She couldn't remember. She watched her mama's long braid swishing against her back as she walked farther away. Mariela wanted to shout for her to come back, to say she was scared to sit alone, but she didn't dare. Then her mama disappeared into the crowds of the hectic market. For a long time, she wished she had been brave enough to run after her mama, grab her hand, and promise to be a better daughter, believing she was to blame for her mama leaving.

She sat there, afraid to move, until the sky darkened and the air turned cool. Mayan women with straight, black hair pulled back and cascading down their backs in similar woven huipils just like her mama's passed by, leaving in the frenzy of closing time. Mariela watched for her mama, willing her to return, "Please come soon, please come soon, mama." Tears rolled down her cheeks, but she dried them quickly, not wanting to draw attention. Then the scene she played over and over blurred. She tried, through her tears and fear and heartache, to recount what happened next. An image remained of the tattered basket left on the pavement where she and her mama spent their long days. She fretted about how angry her mama would be about her leaving the basket, one of their few possessions. A Latina took her hand and led her out of the marketplace, saying she would be her new mama. She let herself be led away from the blanket and the basket and the place where her mama would return. This part didn't make sense. *Who was this other woman, and why she did she call herself mama?* The new "mama" said that her real mama would come for her soon; then they walked a long distance to an apartment, which had toys and food and even a bird in a cage. She couldn't remember how long she stayed in the apartment with the nice woman who called herself mama, but she remembered the caged parakeet and sleeping on a couch. Then, as quickly in her memory as her real mama left and this new mama appeared, there was a memory of a large, gruff policeman with a rifle slung over his shoulder walking through the market at closing time. And she was back in the market. Was the apartment memory false? How had she been in both places? The officer reminded her of the soldiers who had hurt her mama, and she tried to hide from his gaze. "Where's your mama, little one?" he said.

She cringed when he addressed her and cried when she told him that she didn't know where her mama had gone. She was mad at herself for those tears for a long time. Maybe if she hadn't cried like a baby, the policeman might have thought she was OK and left her there; then her real mama might have returned to the market to find her. She remembered the large hand of the policeman leading her silently into what she would learn was an orphanage. People she didn't know cursed under their breath as they cut her long, tangled hair filled with lice, leaving little more than a few inches of straight black hair. They gave her a lice treatment and deworming medicine that made her run to the bathroom over and over. Then they dressed her in old but washed clothes, assigned her a bunk, and expected her to fit in and not cause trouble. She became invisible in the crowd of orphans.

She asked many times a day in Quiche mixed with Spanish during the early weeks at the orphanage, "Has my mama come looking for me? Her name is Maria. She doesn't speak much Spanish, but she's very smart and beautiful. I think something happened to her. I know she wouldn't leave me."

"No one has come for you" was always the weary reply from the women who cared for all the orphans. She started to doubt if they would tell her the truth or if anyone even cared if she found her mama. The few old women who cared for the hundreds of kids always looked exhausted and disinterested, so she stopped asking about her mama.

She ceased to be important to anyone. So many people were lost or disappeared—what was one kid to anyone? She had no idea why people in her country were fighting, but she had seen the desperate people on the streets, all the orphaned children, the soldiers patrolling everywhere with rifles slung over their shoulders, and she had her blurry memories of the fires that burned her mama's village and the screams of women and children, like her, running for their lives.

Days turned into weeks, then months, and her mama never came, creating a hole in her heart, an emptiness that couldn't be filled. She adjusted to the ache of lonely despair, but she rarely smiled or felt happy.

Six months later, for no reason she understood, she and twenty-five other orphans were put on a bus with one caretaker and transferred to the large government orphanage in Quetzaltenango, five hours from the capital city. Here she joined a group of more than three hundred in an institution where they were supposed to live until they either ran away or turned fourteen and were released. "How will she ever find me now?" she had cried quietly in the crowded dorm room. She never imagined then that someday she would be adopted by an American family. Babies and toddlers were sometimes adopted, but not older kids like herself. She had always thought no one wanted her, and now they did. She didn't understand why. It was a miracle that she was going with a family and starting a new life. Her heart, accustomed to beating loudly with fear and dread, pounded now with a rhythm of fear mixed with excitement.

The birds were starting to make their usual racket outside the open windows in the chilly dawn. She recited to herself all the numbers she had been instructed to remember, including her assigned birthday, which she was told would be celebrated when she got to the US. "They will give you presents and make you a cake, so remember your special day." She knew it wasn't really a special day for her. All the orphans were given the same birthday, February 14, and Valentine's Day would forever remind her that her real history, like her real birthday, was forever lost. In the orphanage, on the shared birthday, all the Mayan children who had no idea when they were born or what happened to their parents celebrated with a small piece of donated cake. For the rest of her life, she would feel loss instead of joy when her birthday was celebrated. She had no memory of birthday celebrations with her mama. No one ever asked her about her mama, what happened in her village, what she remembered, what she tried to forget.

She looked over at the sleeping girls huddled under their tattered blankets and realized she would miss a few of them. She didn't really trust them or allow herself to depend on them, but they were all she had, and it would be sad to say goodbye forever. She was used to the routines here, and they were a small comfort. The daily food rations wolfed in silence at long tables filled her belly and made stabbing hunger pains a thing of the past. School was a chance to get away from the orphanage five mornings a week, learn new things like Spanish, and see Señora Lopez, her beloved teacher. The orphans came to school in tattered hand-me-downs—there were no uniforms for them—so they were easily identified and often ridiculed by the neighborhood kids. They were kept at a distance as if their parentless condition was contagious. The orphans clung together while at school but fought among themselves on the walk back to their orphanage home. Mariela knew that an orphanage was no place to show weakness and had learned to be tough.

Her friend Marta, a few years older and sleeping in the bunk next to her, had warned her a year before to watch out for boys prowling in the night. "Sleep with one eye open. Boys try to do bad things when they sneak in at night while the old ladies sleep. I pretend to be asleep. I don't know what else to do." The boys had tried to get under her covers just as Marta had predicted, but she had screamed and kicked, making too much noise for the boys to stick around. She worried that her luck would run out. She had heard that soldiers did things to women and even girls and had to protect herself from that, whatever it was. She heard that if she let it happen, she was dirty and shameful.

She turned in bed and forced the frightening thoughts of soldiers away by thinking of Ana, the nurse who visited the orphanage every month. Mariela thought she was the most beautiful woman in the world with her rosy lips that formed words sweetly and the soft, brown eyes that looked straight into hers. "Look what I drew for you." Mariela pressed closer, vying with the other girls for Ana's attention. "Thank you, Mariela, you draw beautifully," she said, smiling like an angel. She often stroked the girls' hair, hugged the children, laughed, and sang with them. Mariela liked to pretend Ana was her mama and finally got the courage one day to ask in her sweetest voice, "Tia Ana, will you adopt me and let me live in your home with you?"

Ana smiled kindly as she put her delicate hand on Mariela's shoulder, "You know I love you, precious, as I love all the children. You are a very special girl. An American family will come for you, and you'll get to live with them in the US, you lucky girl." But Mariela didn't feel lucky. If Ana had wanted her, she thought, then she would be lucky. Leaving her country with strangers who didn't even look like her was not lucky.

She had seen babies and toddlers leave the orphanage in the arms of North Americans and, very rarely, an older child holding the hand of a happy North American. An excitement hung over the courtyard on those days. Those children waved goodbye and were never heard from again, and no one really knew what happened to them. Every orphan dreamed of having a family of their own, but they all feared what America really held for them. Mariela thought it sounded like descriptions of heaven. It was supposed to be wonderful, but no one came back from heaven to describe what it was really like there.

Mariela recently said goodbye to a one-year-old girl for whom she had fed and cared since the baby's arrival shortly after being born to a mother who didn't want her. Mariela had run from the courtyard to keep from crying as the smiling, blond North American parents snuggled their new child. Other babies would be assigned to her for care, but she had loved this one little girl who was now forever gone.

Mariela thought back to the social worker's last visit and what she said about America. "In America, you eat ice cream every day, and there are warm showers, not ice-cold buckets poured over heads once a week, and there are toys and clothes for each child, and kids get to do what they want," the social worker told the orphans. These declarations were the source of many stories that entertained the children with wide-eyed amazement. In Guatemala, kids worked with their families in the fields, or in the orphanage, they were assigned chores. Mariela and other girls her age washed dishes and clothes and helped care for babies. "In America," older kids often said, "kids are treated special and don't have to do a thing. There are machines to do everything: one to wash dishes, one to wash clothes, one to clean the floors, even one to clean you after you use the toilet." The children laughed and begged to hear more. Mariela laughed along with all the children. It sounded both scary and exciting, and now she was the one going north to have that kind of life.

"When I get to America, I will be done working forever and will just snap my fingers for people to bring me ice cream," she boasted to the friends she'd soon leave behind. Mostly, Mariela imagined a life surrounded by the love of a perfect mama who would never leave or disappoint her. She'd have to leave her country and all she knew, but that was the price she'd pay for another mama.

"My American family picked me—they want me," she boasted, but she never added that it was a complete mystery to her why they did. She couldn't figure it out. She heard that a couple in a state called Oregon had seen her photo and thought she was perfect for them. "They must be desperate," she reasoned. "My own mama didn't want me." She heard that Americans liked foreign kids and had so much money that they needed more kids to spend it on. But it still didn't make sense, and her suspicions were deep. Why would this family of strangers want her? *They must think they are getting a perfect kid who will work for them.* If they knew she had taken things from the market when she lived on the streets, what would they think? If they discovered she had gone months wearing the same dirty clothes, would they be disgusted? And they must not find out about the worms that slid from her body into the toilet after the orphanage doctor gave her pills, and the lice, and the bad boys who messed with her, and how she prayed for awful things to happen to people. She felt ashamed thinking of all she had to hide from the rich and perfect Americans. She was good at pretending and planned to do what was necessary to get the Americans to stick with her.

She couldn't imagine having a father and felt no yearning for one. She had no memories of her own father and suspected that he, like so many village men, had been killed by the soldiers when she was small. She had never imagined being rescued by a whole group, a family. She didn't want other kids to compete with her for the mama whose total love was all she could dream about.

Her thoughts were interrupted by the sound of the wake-up

whistle. The others yawned and stretched, then began their sleepy chatter. Before breakfast, there were beds to make, babies to change, and clothes to fold. Her plan was to do her chores, grab a tortilla from the kitchen, and hurry alone to school before the other children arrived. She sat on her cot rehearsing for the final time what she'd say to Señora Lopez, her beloved third-grade teacher to whom she planned to appeal. This was her last chance to stay in her country, and she thought it might work.

The teacher's kind eyes shone from her deeply lined face when she noticed Mariela standing at her classroom door. She touched Mariela gently on the shoulder as she always did and leaned down to talk to her. "Good morning, precious, you are here early. My diligent student." Her words were like a warm embrace.

Before losing her courage, Mariela tossed out what she wanted to say. "Good morning, Señora Lopez, this is my last day at school. They are sending me with my new family to America today, and I'll never come back here." She hoped to see a look of distress take over the smile on Señora Lopez's face.

But she nodded. "Yes, Mariela. I've been told, and we will miss you. You are a smart girl, and you deserve a good family to take care of you. You are brave to go so far away from all you know. May God bless and keep you, precious." Mariela's eyes brimmed with tears. She had hoped Señora Lopez would say that she would adopt her rather than see her leave forever. She immediately felt stupid for thinking someone like Señora Lopez would want her, then quickly replaced the gut-wrenching familiar sensation of rejection as she turned and walked back out of the classroom. "Who would want you for a mother, old woman," she mumbled to herself while wiping her tears just as the neighborhood children, in crisp and clean uniforms, pushed their way into the classroom, straight from their mothers' loving arms, Mariela imagined. Hurt and anger coursed through her body.

The American family was her only hope. A stab of fear and resignation made her fingers tighten on her pencil stub when she took her seat and wrote her name on the blank page in front of her. So, this was it. She'd leave with the Americans. The whole morning stretched ahead until classes were dismissed at 1:00 p.m. Then, the Americans were due to arrive. Leaving Guatemala meant giving up on the dream of being adopted by Ana or Señora Lopez, and it meant giving up hope that her mama would ever find her. She had pretended that she was happy to leave the orphanage for America, but she wasn't. But she didn't want to be an orphan anymore, either.

Later that day, while Mariela sat at a long table in her assigned seat in the sparce dining area eating her soup with tortilla, Señora Inez Hernandez, the visiting government social worker, dressed like a rich city woman with heels that clicked on the floor, approached the throngs of boisterous orphans with a clipboard in hand. Her thick hair was stacked on top of her head, her lips were ruby red, her rosy cheeks glistened, and she smelled of rose petals. Señora Inez found Mariela sitting tightly packed among the others slurping their soup. The girls put their spoons down and quieted to ensure they could hear everything. All eyes were on the social worker, so polished and beautiful, as she hesitated then laid her hand with bright-red fingernails lightly on Mariela's shoulder.

"Your new life will start soon. Are you nervous, sweetheart? Well, of course, you are," she said in the same breath, "but you are a lucky girl to get to go to the US with a new family. It is normal to be nervous, but don't worry. They seem very nice and will take good care of you, I'm sure."

Señora Inez was the important Latina from the capital who came every few months to find children to be adopted by rich North Americans. She had talked to Mariela many months earlier. She had asked Mariela a few questions and scribbled some notes, saying she thought she was a good match with this family from someplace called Oregon. "This family has a nice house and two other children. They want a little girl just like you."

Mariela knew they had made up a story about her, as they did about all the orphans. Rich North Americans didn't care about the lives of poor Mayan orphans, she'd been told. Neither Latinos in Guatemala nor North Americans were interested in what the war in Guatemala did to Mayan families. Señora Inez had taken a hard look at Mariela and made a quick assessment; she was short, cute, and healthy looking, and fortunately able to pass for seven years old, although it was likely she was nine. It was not in Mariela's best interest to be any older than seven; everyone knew that adoptive parents preferred younger kids. No adult had ever asked Mariela about her history or her age, assuming those details were lost to her and unimportant and could be replaced by "facts" more to the liking of an American family. "The report we have here," said Señora Inez, coaching Mariela on the facts of her life for the final time, "says that your parents died due to common illnesses in their rural village. Then your grandmother brought you to the orphanage when her health prevented her from taking care of you." Señora Inez smiled, pleased with her story and secure that Mariela would not dispute it.

"Remember, your birthday is February 14, 1980, and you're seven years old." Mariela didn't mind the story about her family because it was much better than the truth, but she wasn't pleased about having to pretend she was seven. *I bet I'm at least nine, maybe even ten,* she thought. One more thing she'd have to pretend.

After Señora Inez left, Mariela checked to see if all adults had left the area, then asked, as she often did, if anyone wanted their homework done in exchange for a portion of tortilla. Her reputation for getting homework done quickly and correctly earned her extra portions. Hunger, while a thing of the past, was still a constant fear. After doing some simple math problems for a younger girl, she buried the earned tortilla in her sleeve and hurried back to her bunk. She lifted her mattress and grabbed the photo of her new family, tucked it in her notebook, and went outside where she could sit beneath a tree. She knew her time was limited before others joined her or she was told to start hanging laundry. She settled herself and took out the photo, careful not to crease it. Her American family: proud, happy, secure. Indiginos never looked like that.

The father, with his pale skin and blond hair and beard, looked strange but exotic. She had seen foreigners who looked like him when she was living on the streets of Guatemala City. Most spoke awful Spanish as they tried to bargain at the markets, but they still looked confident. And the mother: she smiled at the camera and looked friendly and nice. She had long, dark, curly hair and pale skin and blue eyes. Mariela wished she could curl her own hair to look more like her new mother. The daughter had curly hair just like the mother, and she was pretty. She was as tall as any adult in Guatemala but was only twelve. She wondered how they grew so tall and if she'd also grow tall when she moved to America. The boy, who was fifteen, wore a sports uniform and looked very proud. "Will you be nice to me?" she asked the tall boy in the image. "Why would you want to share your mother with me?" She looked at the girl, her new sister. She was deep in thought when a few children ran toward her kicking a partially deflated ball. She quickly tucked the picture into the book and went back to her bunk to wait for the Americans to arrive.

Chapter 3

Charlotte

"Your task is not to seek for love, but merely to seek and find all the barriers within yourself that you have built against it.
Rumi

Exhausted from an early-morning flight followed by a night in a hotel where a mariachi band played until dawn, I struggled to keep my eyes open as I gazed at the verdant hills out the grimy bus window. Our six-hour bus journey had taken us from the capital into the highlands, through lush countryside and small towns, and finally to Quetzaltenango, Guatemala's second-largest city, where Mariela lived with three hundred other orphans. Graffiti was painted and splashed on buildings and on large boulders on the side of the Pan-American Highway on which we traveled. Soldiers clad in ill-fitting fatigues with rifles dangling from their thin bodies looked bored as they stood on street corners of the small pueblos our bus roared through.

"I can't believe there's a war going on in those hills and people are dying as we go on with our plans like all is well," I said while shifting infinitesimally, trying to stretch my tired body in the cramped space. "Such a beautiful and troubled country," I added with a sigh. "If not for all the slogans and soldiers, it would be easy to miss that this country is at war." I hoped to express some of what I was thinking, trying to connect with my husband and pass the time with conversation.

Chris nodded but remained silent, as he often did. The ride was becoming a test of endurance, and we each had our own way of coping. We had unfolded and folded our map several times, checking our location. We'd practiced our Spanish and exchanged a few thoughts about what we'd do on our first night in the hotel with Mariela.

I talked about the book I had recently read by Rigoberta Manchu, the Nobel Peace Prize winner who wrote of the brutal Mayan struggle against the Guatemalan military. It had opened my eyes to the complicated civil war that left innocent Mayan villagers trying to survive being caught between the government, supported by North Americans, and the guerrillas who fought to protect their rights. I imagined that Mariela's life may have been affected, at least indirectly, by the violent war.

"I can hardly wait to get her out of the orphanage and into our family where she'll be safe."

Chris nodded in agreement, patted my thigh, then stared out the hazy bus window before shutting his eyes. The blur of small, thatched houses surrounded by cornfields and trees hid the realities I imagined were just beyond my view. I wanted to believe that somehow Mariela's life had not been troubled by brutality and deprivation. It was possible, I told myself, that she had not been traumatized and had been under the protection of good people in a caring orphanage. The bus roared farther into the highlands, we hung on tight, and I tried to quiet my mounting apprehension by focusing outside.

Mayan women, in hand-woven textiles with huge loads secured to their backs or with woven baskets balanced on their heads, ambled together along the pot-holed roads leading off the highway. Avocado trees heavy with ripe fruit grew among the many shades of green that dominated the landscape. Small boys worked alongside their fathers, and young girls helped their mothers haul, plant, and pick while caring for smaller children. Industrious Indiginos worked their rich land the same way they had for centuries, I thought. Now more powerful Latinos wanted to take the land from them, creating the struggle and bloodshed about which we had so recently learned. I imagined it wasn't that different from the aggressive campaigns of our early settlers who stole the land and killed the early inhabitants of our country.

The bus screeched to a stop often, letting Mayans, laden with their wares, board or squeeze past others to get off the bus. When the stoic Mayan woman we had sat next to for hours got off, a new one slid in quickly to take her place. I smiled at the young woman who gathered a young child onto her lap, but both looked straight ahead, neither willing to look my way.

Straining loudly as it climbed, the bus came to an abrupt stop and let on a young, bewildered-looking soldier with a rifle slung over his shoulder. Passengers froze, eyes averted, and we felt their fear. The thin teenager, his face pockmarked, stood at the front of the bus and occasionally looked back among the passengers. His chiseled Mayan face took on a menacing look when he did. I wondered if he was one of the soldiers I had read about, recruited from distant rural areas, and willing to brutalize fellow Indigenos for a pittance of military pay. We had read that visiting Americans and Europeans weren't at risk, as long as we kept our noses out of the conflict and went about our business without drawing attention. We bowed our heads, looked at our laps as our fellow passengers did, and held our breath. Finally, the soldier got off the bus at a busy crossroad, turning to give a final threatening look to no one in particular. We breathed a collective sigh of relief as the bus pulled away, leaving him in a cloud of exhaust.

Now more relaxed, the passengers sat passively and gazed at a middle distance. No newspapers or books distracted them, and I marveled at their ability to sit quietly, lost in thought. A tiny, plump-cheeked baby with glistening, black, straight hair interrupted the silence by whimpering, and his mother gently shifted him from back to front to offer her breast. Older children sat securely among their families with small hands touching their parents. What if any of these children didn't have the protection and care of their parents and ended up in a large government orphanage? What would their fate be in this war-torn country? I tried to imagine what harsh realities led to Mariela's abandonment, with a realization that I knew very little. Where was the mother who strapped Mariela to her back and nursed her? And what about her father or siblings?

I knew only the brief and sketchy story offered by a social worker that Mariela had lived with her mother for the first several years of life before a vague illness led to her parents' untimely deaths. *Was this even the real story?* I wondered for the first time. The unsettling thought arose and then just as quickly receded as I focused on my eagerness to embrace and comfort her. I dozed on Chris's shoulder with images of Mayan children streaming through fitful dreams.

I woke when standing passengers were thrown forward as the bus came to another screeching halt to let on a few more travelers. I gasped, "How in the world can they fit any more people on this bus, for God's sake?" I was exhausted and impatient with the trip that seemed to be taking forever. Stoic and quiet, passengers squeezed tighter to make room for others.

"We're almost to Quetzeltenango. Only thirty more minutes, I figure," Chris said, trying to reassure me and holding on tight as the bus lurched forward again. A picture of the Virgin Mary taped at the front of the bus looked down at us, her serene face modeling the patience and tolerance necessary to endure this cramped, bone-jarring ride.

Now fully awake, my anxiety kicked in. "We're getting so close. I wonder how she is feeling, if she's scared. What if she's scared of us? What if she changes her mind and doesn't want to come with us?" I fretted.

"She won't change her mind. Settle down. Why not try to take a nap?" he urged.

"You've known me seventeen years—you know I can't sleep when I'm nervous!" I scowled, then apologized quickly. "I'm sorry, I'm just so damn nervous."

"Well, it's not helping to worry. Let's look at those directions to the orphanage one more time so we know where we're going when we get off the bus," he suggested, always practical and trying his best to help relieve my anxiety.

I was accustomed to his sparse conversation and few expressions of emotion, and I rarely relied on Chris to help sort out feelings. Girlfriends helped with that. Chris's linear, analytical style, so different from my own, provided a nice balance, I reasoned. The connection I felt with Chad and Jill filled the emotional gaps. Soon I would have Mariela to focus upon, and the disconnect I sometimes felt with Chris would be less important.

My mind turned to the outfit we had with us that Mariela would wear when we left the orphanage. Even the clothes on her back would be passed on to other orphans, we'd been told. I tried to imagine her in the cute jeans and blue sweatshirt that had seemed so perfect weeks earlier when Jill and I picked them out. Now I was unsure. Would I help her get dressed, and would she allow herself to be mothered? And would I feel the maternal care toward Mariela that came so readily with Chad and Jill? Would an older child, one of seven or eight, as we'd been told she probably was, illicit the same kind of tenderness? My eagerness and idealism had overshadowed the truth that I would be meeting a small stranger, a girl already formed. The reality of what it would mean to mother Mariela began to take shape, and the fantasy, so dearly held, blurred, but only slightly.

I blurted out my doubt before I could screen it, "I'm worried about how it will feel to be her parents so suddenly. What if it isn't a good match? What if it just doesn't feel right?"

"You'll be a great mother to her." Chris tried to sound sure, but I wondered how he could say this with such certainty. "It's just nerves. Try to settle down. Everything is going to be fine." Then he went silent, apparently hoping he had quelled my anxiety.

"OK, I'll try." He was right. The anxiety wasn't helping anything.

Chad and Jill, whom I loved deeply and without reservation, were waiting at home and excited about meeting their new sister. Whoever she was, we were capable of loving her, and we would embrace her fully and unconditionally. Chad was an outgoing and popular sophomore in high school who, while excited about the adoption, would be minimally impacted by a new younger sister. Jill, a quiet and studious seventh-grader, was excited to have a younger sister and imagined braiding her hair, teaching her new things, and proudly introducing her to friends.

"You'll no longer be the baby of the family," I teased Jill while trying to illicit conversation about her feelings.

"I'm tired of being the youngest. It will be fun to be a big sister." She laughed. Both Chad and Jill were well-adjusted and kind, and I had few doubts about their willingness to accept Mariela into the family. My heart filled just thinking of them.

I picked up a Spanish phrase book, intent on learning some important phrases. "Estamos muy emocionados de conocerte finalmente," I said softly, turning toward Chris with a smile. (*We are so happy to finally meet you.*) "Te vamos a cuidar muy bien." (*We will take good care of you.*) Chris corrected my pronunciation; his Spanish was far better than mine. "Estamos muy felices que seas parte de nuestra familia," I repeated under my breath several times. (*We are so happy that you are part of our family.*) Chris smiled, apparently endeared by my attempts at Spanish. "Let's see—what else could I say that would let her know how much she is loved and how safe she is with us?"

Chris interrupted to point out the sign: "Bienvenidos a Quetzaltenango."

"Oh my God, we're here. I thought I couldn't wait for this, and now…I'm so scared…" I gathered my things with shaking hands.

"I hope these directions will help us," Chris said. We filed off the bus with the other weary travelers, stretching our stiff backs while taking in the chaotic scene. We were approached immediately by several men outshouting each other, and in our faces. "Taxi!" "Taxi!" "Where you go?" "I take you."

"Let's just take a taxi—it will be easier. I don't know if I can handle getting lost," I shouted above the din.

"No, I've got it under control. Let's just walk. It's less than half a mile."

Too anxious to bicker, there was no argument from me.

"No gracias, no gracias," I yelled to the disappointed taxi drivers. We hoisted our backpacks and set off through congested streets in the general direction our map indicated. Walking quickly and deliberately, we were conspicuously tall and surely impossible to ignore, but locals didn't stare. We walked past women in vibrant, multicolored woven skirts sitting by baskets brimming with plump tomatoes and stacked precariously high with avocados.

"Dos por un quetzal," they yelled, lowering their voices when we passed. Small children chased each other with corn stalks, skillfully avoiding the piles of fruit. Babies were strapped securely as their mothers moved freely, buying and selling in a frenzy of commerce, stashing money into their aprons as they looked for their next customer. Mayan men pushed, pulled, hauled loads, and coaxed animals. Older women and men, their leathery skin etched, worked quietly to sort and fix small things, keeping a trained eye on the toddlers who were too big to be secured to their mothers. Aware of our intrusion into their lives, we nodded and smiled as we passed, but the locals seemed untroubled and made no eye contact. Did they know we were here to take one of their children? And how did they feel about it? I had no idea. I wondered if they were grateful to us for giving an orphaned child a home or resented us for being rich Americans who could essentially buy one of their children.

"Their lives look simple and tough, but connected and..." I searched for the word to express my conflicted feelings, coming up short. "Are we doing a good thing to remove her from her culture and all she has known? What if her life is more challenging with us? Do we really have something better to offer her?" I asked as we passed several grimy children in rags, laughing as they tossed a mango pit over each other's heads. The questions spilled out as we kept pace with each other in the direction of Mariela's orphanage.

"Of course we have something better to offer her...an education and a future that she couldn't possibly have here," Chris responded as he stepped around an emaciated dog asleep in the street. I wanted to believe it, and it made sense that being adopted into an American family would surely be better than being an orphan in Guatemala.

"We should plan to bring her back to Guatemala to visit regularly and teach her about her people and culture," I offered, trying to soothe myself.

"Yes, we can do that for sure," he added as he readjusted his heavy backpack. We walked by a young boy who swung several stunned chickens upside down by their feet. I flinched, thinking of their imminent fate; the boy flashed a bright smile, and I smiled back, eager for some connection. A young girl carrying a baby on her waist, her hip jutted out to support the weight, walked by. She was about the size I imagined Mariela would be. A sudden thought: *How do we know for sure that Mariela doesn't have siblings?* We'd heard she was an only child, and yet everyone seemed to have many children. Again, anxiety coursed through my body. *Who is she? What has she been through? What happened to her family? Will we ever know?*

Scanning our map frequently did little good because there were no street signs. We greeted the few locals who looked our way and asked directions to the orphanage. They urged us on with a flick of the chin in the general direction we were heading. Most looked away as we walked past, and I couldn't interpret how they felt about us. I was hungry for approval; it may have helped subdue the anxiety gripping me. My notion of being here to rescue a child now seemed naïve and idealistic.

The bright sun slanted in the sky as we walked the dusty, twisting street that finally led us to a dilapidated and faded turquoise building sitting forlornly where the street ended. We were lost in our own thoughts when we spotted a wooden sign with fading letters hanging above a large metal door: Hogar Temporal (Temporary Home). We had arrived at the orphanage where Mariela and hundreds of other orphans lived.

Chris pushed the bell high on the wall, and we waited several minutes. "What's taking so long? I thought they were expecting us." He impatiently pressed the bell a second and a third time.

"Let's not be ugly Americans. Be patient," I said in the tone I was certain he found dismissive. Just then, the heavy door swung open, and a stooped old woman in a filthy, long skirt motioned us in, securing the door behind us. She shuffled away without a word, leaving us in the sparse outside play area. "What are we supposed to do now?" I whispered as I scanned the play area for a girl who looked like Mariela.

"Just hang tight. I'm sure someone will come talk to us."

Several children dropped the old tire they had been rolling and rushed toward us. "Están aquí para llevar a Mariela a Los Estados Unidos!" one shouted with excitement. I looked to Chris, and he translated the rapid-fire Spanish spoken with a thick accent, "They are here to take Mariela to the United States."

"Son los padres de Mariela [They are Mariela's parents]," another repeated playfully. "Llevenme, llevenme [Take me, take me]!" begged a wiry girl of five or six as she pushed past the others and grabbed my hand, holding it tightly. Another girl with sad eyes and dimples on her small, grimy face, took Chris's hand, moved close to him, and looked up. Her grave, dark eyes matched her pleading. "Puedo irme contigo; no tengo padres [I can go with you; I don't have parents]."

Struggling to maintain composure in the face of all these orphans and with Mariela still nowhere in sight, I tried to be lighthearted. "What a relief we don't have to choose!" I let out an anxious sigh, touched the small girls tenderly, and searched the area again for Mariela, whose photo I had carried for months. Then I turned to Chris. "Where is she? Where is Mariela? Oh my God, I can't handle this." Everything felt out of place, and the timing was wrong. I hadn't expected to see all the other orphans vying for attention, and I had always imagined Mariela standing ready and waiting with a smile and open arms, rushing toward us.

More children joined us, grabbed our hands, and started to circle around and around, singing a rhyming song. The children were darling even with their ragged clothes, oily hair, and dirty hands and faces. Smiling at the kids who competed for our attention, I tried to join in the song, but my stomach tightened, and I felt lightheaded. Many of the little girls were very young, no older than four or five, and seemed eager to please us. I wondered for the first time how Mariela had been chosen specifically for us.

I had believed that the process was ordained by fate and had trusted it. Now I realized it would have been wonderful to make a choice after seeing the kids and intuiting which one felt right for us. But it was too late for that. The chaos in the courtyard was knocking me off a delicate balance. Then, one of the little girls shouted excitedly, and the song stopped, "Mariela, Mariela, tus padres están aquí [your parents are here]." We turned and looked toward the dark corridor where a small, attractive woman approached, holding the hand of a scruffy, dark-haired girl with downcast eyes. As they came into the sunlight of the courtyard, I searched the young girl's features. Her slanting eyes set over high cheek bones and full lips were familiar, but something wasn't right. Then I sensed it. This young girl was wary, untrusting. She seemed to have a lifetime of troubles behind her eyes and a hardness that made her wrong for the part in which I had cast her. Where was the eagerness, the softness, the cuteness I had imagined? And why wasn't she rushing to us? Coaxed by the social worker, Mariela moved reluctantly in our direction. The long, black hair that Jill had imagined braiding had been cut short and blunt. Her dress was a faded rag, and her shoes were tattered. Her thin shoulders were slumped as she walked slowly toward us on skinny, bruised legs. Suddenly aware of holding my breath, I exhaled deeply and tried to steady myself.

"Here's our girl," Chris stammered.

I hesitated. "Is it her?" Then I feigned a smile in her direction, hoping to cover all traces of disappointment. The long-anticipated drama, played out in my mind hundreds of times, collapsed into this one frame, and time stopped. Visibly trembling, Mariela stood before us and finally looked up, her face expressionless. I had visualized reaching lovingly for her, smiling, and holding her tightly. I'd expected to feel connected to her and filled with tenderness. Instead, I stood frozen. Mariela looked to each of us, then down, then back up, her face unyielding. I willed myself to kneel and embrace the sad stranger, then nervously spilled out practiced Spanish phrases, hoping to cover my feelings. Chris got on his knees level with her and spoke in Spanish. Only then did a small and timid smile soften her face. Then, the smile left as quickly as it had come.

Señora Inez Hernandez introduced herself as the social worker in charge of adoptions. She seemed quite pleased with herself, as if she had managed to pair American parents with the child they would take out of the orphanage and love, a win for everyone involved. "Here is the girl you want," the attractive, heavily made-up social worker said as she let go of Mariela's hand, urged her toward us, and stepped back. She had observed our awkward meeting without comment; then she waved the noisy young onlookers away and followed them out of the courtyard. Suddenly alone with Mariela, I staggered to my feet, dizzy and disoriented. She was not who I had imagined, anticipated, and created. I had expected to feel an instant bond. Instead, here was a girl I didn't know, with hurt and confusion etched on her small face, and a hardness that her forced smile couldn't mask. I kept a hand gently on Mariela's thin shoulder, still trying to override the uproar in my head and heart.

"She doesn't look like her picture," I whispered and looked to Chris, desperate for support. His expression gave no hint of how he felt. He spoke simple Spanish and joked with the frightened girl. She hesitated, then smiled shyly, and Chris turned to me, seeking my approval. I couldn't give him what he wanted. I was bewildered and scared but took a deep breath and tried again to engage her.

"Soy tu mamá ahora." *I am your mama now.* The words caught in my throat as I embraced her lightly and she leaned stiffly into me. Hesitating, she looked up and said, "Ello," her only English word. I hugged her gently, then closed my eyes and willed the frightening grip on my heart to loosen and open.

Other orphans, who had temporarily been denied access to their only play area, drifted back, circling around us, and their antics provided a welcome distraction. Our introduction to our new daughter, contrary to my anticipated heart-warming expectation, had been baffling and tense. When Señora Inez returned and announced that Mariela would have to stay at the orphanage for the night until paperwork could be signed and completed the following day, I felt relief. "That's fine, no problem. We can come back tomorrow." I gave Mariela what I hoped was a reassuring hug, promised to see her the next day, then turned quickly toward the heavy metal door that, when opened, would release me from this bewildering drama. When we turned to wave to Mariela, she stood in the same place, eyebrows furrowed as she passively watched us leave. "Hasta mañana." I tried to sound enthusiastic. Chris followed me out of the orphanage, seemingly oblivious to my turmoil. A stew of frightening feelings cascaded inside me, and I had no idea how to share them with Chris, so we simply walked to our hotel without saying a word.

That night as I pulled a nightgown over my head with tears brimming in my eyes, I tried to put the feelings into words. "She just isn't what I expected. I didn't feel what I thought I would. I wonder if this is what we want to do. I mean, what if this is all a mistake? What if it just isn't a good fit?" I struggled to convey my doubts and fears without fully expressing my panic. Exhausted from the restraint required while visiting Mariela, I collapsed on the hard bed and looked at Chris, who was looking at a map in our Lonely Planet travel book. I waited for a response from him.

"How can you seem so OK? Don't you have any hesitation?" I pleaded for understanding. "How can you not feel anything?" I accused, remembering Mariela's steely, sad eyes and the resolute hardness to the set of her jaw. "She looks older than seven and seems heavy and distant, not sweet and cute like I imagined." I desperately wanted Chris to join me with a shared experience of trepidation and fear, then to find a way together past these feelings so we could open our hearts.

"You're just worried and tired. Everything is going to be OK. I'm sure she's as scared as we are and not at her best." He tried to reassure me. His attempts at encouragement helped a little. Maybe the next day's meeting with Mariela would go better; maybe it was too early to assess how I felt, I told myself. Mariela was a vulnerable child, I reasoned, nervous and unsure of her future, but we would show her that she was safe. Surely, she would seem softer, younger, and more accessible when she felt secure. Finally, I fell into a fitful sleep. Our plan was to arrive at the orphanage early in the morning, meet with Señora Inez and an attorney, sign paperwork, then leave with Mariela.

When I woke up the next day, I wrestled with my ambivalence of the day before and prepared myself emotionally for the day ahead. "I was exhausted and nervous yesterday. I think things will go better today." I tried to be optimistic and denied my unease—personality traits built on childhood necessity.

We walked the fifteen minutes from the hotel to the orphanage. Waves of excitement collided with equally strong feelings of foreboding that threatened to tip a fragile balance I was determined to maintain. Señora Inez met us at the orphanage door with a look of concern. Mariela was nowhere in sight. My first thought was that she must have sensed my hesitancy the day before. Then I wondered if Mariela had bolted from the orphanage, if she was as scared as I was.

Señora Inez motioned us to a small, shabby office located at the end of a dark hallway and introduced us to a waiting attorney. "I'm so sorry, but Señor Martinez has found a mistake in the paperwork. You cannot leave the country with Mariela until it is signed properly by the judge in Guatemala City," Señora Inez announced with graveness and apparent empathy for our plight. The attorney, short, stout, and dressed meticulously with a helmet of thick dark hair, shook our hands, addressed us formally, and explained our options. We could wait for three to five weeks in Guatemala while our paperwork slowly moved to the top of a pile for a judge to sign or go home and return for Mariela when the attorney notified us that things were in order.

"We have other children at home. We can't wait here. We're going to have to go home without her," I said flatly, unsure how I felt about this new development. Was it a sign? Was I relieved? Disappointed? Had the attorney just handed us a reason not to proceed? Then the attorney, reeking of cheap cologne, took a few steps closer to us and interrupted my internal dialogue. "For $500 more, I may be able to get the judge to sign quicker." We had been warned that this was a common ploy: get the adoptive parents primed to take their child, then mention a holdup that could be solved with additional money.

We looked to each other, confused and dismayed. Chris spoke first. "We've already paid $5,000—what's $500 more?"

"How do we know they won't ask for more when we return to get her? How do we know this is even the right thing to do?" I risked saying out loud in English, hopeful that Señora Inez and the smug attorney couldn't understand.

Chris's response was immediate. "Of course it's the right thing to do. This is what we've planned for a long time. We can't let a small obstacle get in our way."

I wanted to snarl at him that my intuition was no small obstacle, that I was scared and this snag in the process may be a way to stall our decision until we could figure out what to do. But self-doubt and guilt seeped in, and I wondered if I could trust my feelings; I was as unsure of my feelings as I was of her.

My wavering felt immature and self-indulgent. What kind of mother looks for an escape? Chris seemed so sure, so steady, and I wondered what was wrong with me that I didn't. I looked to him for the answer and saw in his determined jaw and positive engagement with the attorney that he intended to proceed. I wanted to get off this fast-moving train and declare my feelings, but I felt paralyzed. By admitting my reservations about Mariela, I would expose myself as selfish and uncaring, a criticism frequently lobbed at me by my mother, and one I had worked hard to dispel. Mariela, a vulnerable child, would be shattered by my ambivalence, and my adoption fantasy would be destroyed. But failing to speak up now and declare how I felt would move us to an irrevocable decision.

We sat together in the small, cluttered office to discuss the options presented by the attorney, and I frantically rehearsed my responses. "We met her, and now we've changed our minds." "We can't adopt her; it just doesn't feel right." I winced as I imagined saying these words out loud. We had come so far in this process; we had looked into her eyes, touched her. Could we live with ourselves if we walked away from this orphan girl? Would we regret it the rest of our lives?

The attorney, glancing at his watch, appeared disinterested in our dilemma, but continued to wait for our response about paying the additional $500. Unable to speak, I stood silently as Chris nodded his agreement to what amounted to a bribe, and the two men shook hands, sealing our deal to adopt. The attorney nodded in approval as Chris counted out $500 in traveler's checks brought for emergencies, or palm greasing. He spoke in heavily accented English. "I will hurry up the papers, and you can take the girl to your country when all is ready, maybe two weeks." I hadn't known he spoke some English and was unclear if he understood me when I voiced my reluctance about adopting earlier, but now it didn't matter. He showed his pleasure with the outcome as he tucked the checks into his leather satchel.

Mariela was in the courtyard, swinging a frayed hula hoop around her waist, when we arrived. She looked up at us and smiled shyly, with a little less reserve than she had the day before. Señora Inez went with us to help explain that we wouldn't be taking her right away. Chris told her she would have to stay in the orphanage to allow paperwork to be completed; then one of us would return for her in a few weeks. The explanation sounded weak, and I wondered at the plausibility of it when heard through her filter of loss and rejection. *We are not rejecting her,* I told myself when I saw her dejected look, yet I had entertained the idea of it only moments before.

Mariela's face went blank and was impossible to read when she heard we were leaving without her. Did she expect to be rejected? Was that relief on her face? I felt compassion for her. We were irritated about what we assumed was the graft of the Guatemalan legal system, but we covered our annoyance and tried to simplify our explanation and reassure her that we wanted her and would come for her as soon as possible. It was our first act of love, putting our feelings aside to provide support to her.

Both of us were tearful as we stammered about in Spanish, interrupting each other with corrected words, but Mariela's eyes remained dry with a stony silence that we would come to know well. We took turns hugging her and saying goodbye, then retraced our steps out of town and onto a bus bound for the capitol. I was furious with the corrupt system that had ensnared us and forced us to pay what amounted to a bribe while they held our promised daughter hostage. Sick to my stomach with confusion, exhaustion, and guilt about my reaction to Mariela, my eyes stayed filled with tears on the six-hour bus ride back to the capitol where we caught a plane back to the US.

Chapter 4

Maria

> "In peace, sons bury their fathers. In war, fathers bury their sons."
> Herodotus

"You need time on the ground," said Josefa as she unstrapped Maria's small body and gently sat her in the field beside other village children. "I can work faster now that she is old enough to be on the ground with the other children," Josefa said to another mother as she smiled and wrapped her hands around an ear of corn and yanked quickly, dropping it in a basket that sat beside her. It was harvest time, and the villagers were blessed with a good crop. Maria's days of being tightly secured to her mother's back and breastfed at her whim came quickly to an end.

"Our children won't go hungry this season," the other mother said happily. When food was plentiful, they feasted on tortillas, corn, beans, bananas, mangos, and avocadoes.

"Next week, we will kill that old chicken that no longer gives us eggs and celebrate this harvest," said another mother.

Back at home, Maria played with a corn husk that had been made into a doll while sitting at the skirt of Josefa as she cooked. The rhythmic *slap slap slap* of tortillas being made was like a comforting lullaby. Then, one day when Maria was about four, her mother turned to her and said, "You are old enough to carry wood for our fire now." Josefa handed her two sticks. Maria began to haul wood, stalks, water, and anything else her sturdy body could carry and was proud to be helping.

"Four of our children have lived to work beside us," said Maria's father as he stoked the fire and looked around at the faces of his family in the flickering light of their one-room thatched hut. There had been six children, but it was an accepted part of life that young children often died. Villagers grieved together the loss of so many of their babies, then stoically went back to the hard work that sustained them.

Maria's mother and father and their Mayan ancestors before them had large extended families who relied on each other in tough times and celebrated together with gratitude when they were blessed with abundance. There was a comforting rhythm to the routines of daily life that they had known their whole lives.

Maria was soon able to take her place among the women in the endless chores. She made the daily walk to a one-room school with other children for a few years, but her father announced one evening that she could not continue. "Things are difficult, my daughter, and we don't have the money to pay those school fees. And we need you at home to help your mother," he announced unapologetically. It was useless to argue. Most children in the village didn't go beyond third grade, which gave them the ability to read and write and do simple math, which were skills needed in the large marketplace, a day's walk from her village.

Maria daydreamed of a different life as she picked beans or scrubbed pots, but her imagination was limited by a vague idea about life outside her village. She was happy in her village, but as she got older, she wondered if there could be more for her.

"That girl is a beauty and will have plenty of boys wanting her," said one villager to Josefa, who had heard similar comments for years. When Maria became a young adolescent, Josefa harbored a fantasy that Maria would be spared the drudgery of village life because of her beauty but dared not put such ideas into Maria's head. "That girl is already brazen with boys, flashing her smile as she walks past, secretly enjoying their hungry looks," she said. Maria knew the boys were captivated by the curves visible in her huipil, the woven skirt tied snug over her shapely hips. Her long, black braid swayed to the tempo of her graceful walk as she carried a basket on her head. They desired her, and she enjoyed their attention.

Headstrong and vain, Maria's personality was tempered by the constraints and limitations of village life. By the time she was fourteen, she decided on Carlos, a boy a few years older and far more muscular and assured than the others. She expertly played the part of the sought-after, hard-to-get beauty, and just as she hoped, Carlos's focus turned to her, and he no longer looked at the other girls. "When your work is done today, come join me to watch the sun set from the hill," said Carlos. Then they began to look for each other when the day's work ended and sat quietly together before sunset, when they would go to their separate huts.

"He is so handsome, so sweet, so strong and hardworking. I want to marry him someday," Maria giggled to Yesenia as they worked long hours in the fields together.

"Of course you will marry him. Neither of you even looks at anyone else." Yesenia grinned at her dearest friend as she wiped her brow. They had played together since they were toddlers.

When Maria was sixteen years old and Carlos was nineteen, a simple ceremony united them in marriage in front of the whole village. Carlos built a small, thatched hut for the two of them, and they were blissful to share a small straw bed together at the end of each long day. Within several months, Maria consulted with the village midwife and learned she was pregnant.

"Carlos, we are going to have a child, a family. We must celebrate with the village," Maria said as she stirred a pot of beans over the fire.

"Our life together is beginning," said Carlos as he embraced Maria, and she allowed herself to feel true happiness. A healthy baby girl joined the village in the spring of the year following their marriage.

After Mariela was born, Maria worked with others in the field with her young daughter strapped on her back, rotating her to her breast when she whimpered. As they worked, villagers shared rumors from distant villages.

"There are soldiers killing our people, grabbing our lands, taking our children and women. They are powerful and have weapons and work for the government," a man exclaimed breathlessly as he bent under a heavy load of wood.

"But there is also a guerrilla army made up of village peoples and educated students from the cities who want to help us," said Maria's father as he looked to others for encouragement.

"The guerrillas are no match for the government's soldiers. There are rumors that North Americans are sending dollars and guns for the soldiers to fight us," said Paco, Maria's older brother.

"That can't be true. Why would Americans want to hurt us? What have we done to them or to our own government?" said Maria's uncle as he hoisted a burlap bag of pumpkins onto his back. The talk went back and forth, and none of them knew what was true and what were stories meant to frighten them. The green hills of their homeland seemed far removed from the rumored fighting, but still, many no longer felt safe.

"The soldiers will rape our women, take our children, and kill our men. We have to be prepared to fight." Carlos raised his voice and squinted, looking intently to the other young men one evening at a village gathering.

"We are too poor and too far from cities to be a problem to anyone," scoffed an elder. Others nodded in agreement as they gathered their tools and trudged back to their huts, exhausted after long hours of heavy labor.

Maria was almost eighteen when her quiet and predictable life in the secluded village changed. Angry young soldiers clad in baggy, camouflaged uniforms exploded into the village one sunny morning. "All of you, move to the center of the village now," a soldier who seemed to be in charge yelled. They spoke Spanish, a language that most of the villagers didn't understand, but the menacing looks and rifles didn't need translation.

"Have any guerrillas come to your village wanting food or help?" One of the soldiers looked at the village men standing mute in front of him. "This is a warning to you," he seethed, "that if you cooperate in any way with those sons of bitches, we'll burn your village to the ground. Those snakes are crawling all over these mountains, and they will want your help. This is your only warning." He shot his rifle in the air to punctuate his aggression.

Maria watched as the soldiers, their faces chiseled into hard lines, looked over the village men who were simple farmers whose frightened faces told of their confusion. How had they offended these enraged men who were ready to hurt and kill? As far as they knew, their lives had nothing to do with the government in Guatemala City. The government didn't pay for schools, medical care, or give assistance to poor villagers. The Mayan people asked for little and were content to live on their land as they had for generations. Their land was all they had, and the best they could understand was that the government was trying to take it from them, and the guerrillas were fighting to defend their rights.

Maria stood with other villagers, silent and afraid to move other than swaying her body gently to keep her little daughter asleep. She watched as soldiers yelled threats and waved their guns. Her fear turned to terror as Carlos and a few other men were singled out and told to stand still while their hands were bound behind their backs.

Yesenia, Maria's lifelong friend, knew that Maria might try to defend Carlos. She wrapped her arms tightly around Maria, whispering for her to remain quiet. "Shhh, don't say anything. Carlos is strong."

Maria cringed as Carlos and the other men were kicked mercilessly by the soldiers in a warning to the others. A mother of a bound young man protested loudly as blood poured from her son's nose and mouth. The soldier in charge commanded another man to silence the woman. She was dragged off to a nearby cornfield, screaming and kicking. They had all heard stories of village women being raped by soldiers but had never imagined they would see it on their own land.

Heavy boots pounded into Carlos repeatedly while he writhed on the ground, his blood mixing with dust. Every instinct Maria had ached to express rage against the soldiers and urged her to run to Carlos. Instead, Maria rocked gently to hush the infant strapped on her back and prayed for Carlos to be able to withstand the blows.

"Enough, leave the idiots," barked a commander, looking on in impatient disgust as Carlos and the others writhed on the ground. With a flick of his chin, he signaled his soldiers to take the winding trail out of the village, satisfied that the villagers had been intimidated. A few soldiers fired off angry shots and yelled more threats as they rounded a corner into the dense vegetation.

The villagers stood speechless until they were certain the soldiers were gone, then ran to their young men. An older woman tended to the disgraced mother left half-dressed in the cornfield. Maria rushed to Carlos.

"My sweetheart, my life, are you OK?" She wept while cradling his head, her tears flowing onto him. He couldn't answer her except with his eyes, which spoke of his helplessness. He was alive but badly wounded and gasping for air. The beaten men were taken inside a small hut and attended to by older women. Mariela, Maria's five-month-old baby girl, was awake on Maria's back. She had absorbed the violence in wide-eyed silence before joining the chorus of inconsolable wailing of the other children of the village. In the following weeks, some villagers told the story over and over of the day the soldiers came, reliving the trauma. Others walked in numb terror and dared not mention it. Most tried to resume their daily lives, believing that staying clear of both sides of the struggle and simply tending their plots of land as they always had would keep the soldiers away. Some young men, including Carlos, talked of joining other men from nearby villages who were hiding in the forested hills training to join the guerilla forces.

"We cannot stand by like nothing is happening," urged Carlos one evening as villagers met in the central square where the soldiers had been only weeks before.

"What can you do, Carlos? You saw those guns!" said Juan, his short, muscular friend since early childhood. The men were divided on how best to respond. Later that same evening, after Mariela was asleep and Maria and Carlos held each other in their small bed, Maria broke her silence.

"Your place is here in our village," she said, afraid she was losing influence over him. "We will be good if we stay out of the conflict and go about our lives." Maria rubbed his broad chest as she spoke. But he didn't respond to her, and she had reason to suspect Carlos was already meeting with the guerilla group. He and many of the young men had started to leave the village and return days later exhausted and dirty, spewing angry slogans and full of bravado. Maria had begged Carlos to stay clear of the fighting and remain with her in the village, but Carlos responded by wrapping his arms around her and their child, saying little, his face etched with angry determination.

Weeks later, a band of thin, dirty, exhausted guerilla fighters arrived at the village one late afternoon asking for food and a place to sleep. "Please, friends, we are fighting to help you stay on your ancestors' lands, to protect your children and women, and we need your help," said a young man who wore glasses and stumbled as he tried to speak rudimentary Quiche.

"He is not one of our people—why does he want to help us?" whispered Maria's father.

"Father, he is educated and good and knows what is right," Carlos whispered to his skeptical father-in-law.

"They are helping our people. We should help them," added a muscular young farmer as he wiped his dirty hands on his pants. Villagers were divided and fearful of helping due to the soldiers' angry threats, but many were persuaded by the brave young men who wanted to fight for what was right.

"It is the right thing to do," Carlos spoke finally to end the debate as he gestured for the guerrillas to sit. Maria and several other young women hurried off to grab a few chickens. Maria lopped off their heads with skillful speed as another woman started the fire.

"Our chickens are raised for special times when we celebrate. We will eat together now to celebrate your fight for us," said Hector, a strong, young father of four who was admired for his ability to fix anything and his quick humor.

"This food will give us the strength we need to walk the hills by night and set up daytime ambushes of our enemy," said the heavily accented man with glasses, looking directly at Carlos, who had already assumed the role of spokesman.

Maria watched Carlos's handsome, expressive face with pride as he encouraged involvement from the men of his village. At the same time, her heart ached with fear of the reprisals that could await them. Carlos and the other men readied themselves to leave for a night patrol by the light of the moon, which lit up the hillside. "My sweetheart," said Carlos when he saw the panic on Maria's face, "don't worry; we will be careful, and we are strong and sly. I love you and Mariela deeply, but I must protect my village and the ones I love."

"There is no use in arguing with you, Carlos, I know that, but I'm so afraid for all of us after seeing the wickedness in those soldiers' eyes," Maria said as she kissed Carlos and removed Mariela from his leg where she was holding tight. Carlos picked up the giggling two-year-old girl who braced herself to be thrown up into the air. He caught her and hugged her tightly, kissing her head before handing her back to Maria. Mariela was secure in the love of her mama and papa and the many other villagers who watched her grow. She was either being carried by Maria or an older girl if Maria was busy with the harvest. When she was hungry, Maria swung her to the front and nursed her, then released her from the sling when she squirmed and whined for freedom. Demanding, willful, and clever, she challenged

Maria, who benefited from the support of other young mothers. "That girl is as stubborn and willful as you were," they good-naturedly teased her as they worked together in the cornfields.

Carlos and the other young men routinely ventured away from the village to join guerillas who taught them how to defend their village and even ambush small groups of soldiers. They were often gone for days, and the women anxiously awaited their return, overjoyed when they appeared through the dense vegetation. It was during the rainy season about a year after the soldiers' burst into the village that Carlos and other men failed to return through the soaked underbrush.

"We can't wait any longer. It's been two weeks, and they may need our help. We must find them," said Maria's father, who looked older than his fifty years after years of hard work in the sun. He was addressing a group of older men who felt helpless waiting behind while young men were missing.

"We will pack food for the trip right away," said Maria, frantic with worry about Carlos and the other missing men. The men took the cloth sacks of food and headed out of the village as the women and children who were left behind stood stone-faced and anxious.

The older men had lived through rainy seasons that turned the village to mud and debris and droughts that shriveled their corn. They had seen babies' listless bodies felled by disease, hardy youngsters succumb to ailments, and women die long and painful deaths in childbirth. This was the natural and often tragic rhythm of village life and death. But nothing prepared the men for the mass graves they discovered on their second day deep in the forest off a trail beaten back by soldiers' boots. Seeing a large, hastily dug hole, they approached slowly and found Indigenous men with hands bound and throats slit, their bodies tangled in a grotesque heap. It was difficult to determine if their own young men were among the dead.

The men stumbled on in shocked silence and found several more mass graves littered with the bodies of strong young men killed hastily with no waste of bullets. In the third discovered mass grave, clothes belonging to their village men were spotted. "Oh my God, it is our boys," gasped Maria's father as he reeled with shock. Several men gagged and threw up. They left gifts of food for the departed souls of their village youth, then began the long walk back to their village. "Let us remember where they are, so we can return with our women and children to properly respect them," said a grandfather as he walked away from the site and into the forest in the cover of night. Without the older men's search, the bodies would not have been discovered, and the missing young men would simply have become some of the thousands of "disappeared" villagers who vanished during the decades of brutal Guatemalan civil war.

The older men returned to the village with stricken faces and slacked shoulders. Villagers stopped their work in the fields and ran to them. The elders hesitated and breathed deeply, then mumbled and swore under their breath, knowing they must deliver the horrible news. Maria stood frozen in terror, but she quickly discounted the possibility that Carlos could be among the dead. Her Carlos was not like any man; he was stronger than most and a clever survivor. She scooped up Mariela and rushed to her father's side for reassurance.

"Popi, did you find Carlos? Is he OK?" Her father said nothing and looked into the distance. This was the way of the Mayans when there was only bad news to tell. He put his strong arm around his daughter to comfort her. Large tears made trails down his otherwise stoic, weathered face as he spoke of what he had seen. Maria collapsed in disbelief at her father's feet. Mariela patted her mother's face, not understanding but sensing something terrible had happened.

For days after the awful news, women and children old enough to understand what had happened wailed for their husbands, fathers, and brothers, and the remaining men vowed to avenge the deaths. Maria's adolescent brothers were among the dead, and her parents were inconsolable. Maria, still unable to accept that Carlos was among the dead, held on to hope that he had lived and would walk into the village one day. But weeks and then months went by, and he did not return. Her waking and sleeping hours were filled with the memories of his tender face looking at her, his strong arms holding their child, his sensuous smile as he took her in his arms. She ached for him and after dreams of him, prayed his death was only a nightmare.

Mariela was demanding and moody as the spell of grief and loss hovered over the once-serene village. "Where is papi? Where is papi?" she demanded, but Maria was sullen and withdrawn and had little energy for her beloved daughter. Mariela began to seek comfort from other village women.

The villagers believed the soldiers had punished their village by killing their young men and would not return. They went about their lives stunned by sorrow and found it difficult to enjoy the simple things that once brought them joy. Then one hot afternoon as the sun beat down and they thought of nothing but the brief siesta they would soon take, soldiers burst into their village again, ordering the remaining men, mostly old men and adolescent boys, to stand together.

The soldiers' rifles flashed in the bright sun as the terrified villagers waited to see what would happen next. The men and boys were bound and led away unceremoniously; a few soldiers stayed behind with the women and children, who stood helpless and weeping. Maria and Yesenia, both holding their young children, leaned on each other and shared the terror as their fathers and young brothers were pushed out of the village with rifles at their backs. Maria's father turned to her and flicked his chin up toward his wife, who was frail and weak with grief, indicating that Maria should watch over her. He seemed to understand his fate would be the same as the young men he had found. This was the last time Maria saw her adored father.

"Women and children, this is a warning, come away from your huts. You idiots were warned not to help the guerillas," a khaki-clad soldier screamed at them. "We have no choice but to punish you as an example to others." He looked at them with contempt. The soldiers started to work quickly, pouring a liquid around the huts and lighting torches. Maria turned to see her mother run toward her hut to gather her woven textiles, her pride and a source of income, into a basket. The easily combustible huts burst into flames as Maria shouted, "Mama, mama, quick, come out!" Maria screamed as she saw the hut burst into flames with her mother still inside. She started to run toward it, but Yacenia grabbed her. Maria broke free but was stopped by a soldier's gun pointed at her. There was nothing she could do; the hut was engulfed in flames, her mother inside. She heard screaming, shrill and terrible, and realized it was her own voice, raised in torment as the fire consumed the hut and her precious mother.

Maria and the other shocked women and children held each other and wept as their homes, belongings, and crops crackled and hissed in the dry wind until there were only ashes. Their faces were swollen from tears, red from heat, and smudged with smoke. The women stumbled through the smoldering debris of their destroyed village that had sustained their people for centuries. Maria stepped into the remains of her parents' hut and saw the charred remains of her loving mother clutching the basket with the once-colorful textiles, now burned beyond recognition. At that moment, Maria wanted only to be with her in the land beyond, where there were no soldiers and no suffering. Had it not been for her whimpering daughter clutching at her tightly, Maria would have taken her own life that day. "I can't bear it. I can't go on," she cried. "It's only for you that I go on," Maria said to her bewildered child as she stroked the child's hair. But after that terrible day, the light in Maria was extinguished, even for Mariela.

"Mama, mama." Mariela stretched her arms up to be lifted off the ground and comforted. But Maria, now disconnected and numb, stood stiff and silent and seemed hollowed out. Unable to elicit a response, Mariela gave up and sat on the ground, whimpering. Maria, at nineteen years old, had lost her father; her two adored brothers were disappeared and without a doubt murdered; her mother had been burned alive; and Carlos was dead. She floated in a cloud of grief; her nostrils filled with the smoldering remains of the life she had been powerless to save. Her will to go on against such odds and without her loved ones collapsed. Utterly defeated, she looked around and saw the other bewildered women, all stunned with disbelief. Mariela held on to her mother's long skirt and again cried to be picked up. Finally, without a word, Maria reached down and hoisted her onto her back, failing to console the distressed child.

Maria followed the long line of women and children who left the ash-strewn village to walk across the hills, going east to flatter land and the cities beyond. Most had never been out of the village of their ancestors, and none knew where they were going. And so, Maria with Mariela on her back, stumbled away from the only life she knew, following the others, too stupefied with grief to comfort her terrified child.

They walked up and down hills thick with vegetation that tripped and snarled them. Terrified about getting too close to military-occupied towns, they made long detours. After seeing soldiers feasting on chickens and drinking chichi (corn beer) in one village, they quickly detoured to avoid the men who looked drunk and menacing. Despite hunger and exhaustion, the women walked the longer route while suckling their babies and hushing their children. When they could no longer see enough to go on in the moonless tangle of vegetation, they stopped and shared the tortillas they had tucked into their skirts when they fled.

The women flattened a small piece of ground, released their small children from their backs, laid them on the ground next to the exhausted older children, then joined them, all shivering quietly together in the cold mountain air. The women sang quietly to comfort the children but said little to comfort each other. Yesenia broke the silence and talked of her dread of what lay ahead. "We have to stay awake and listen and be ready to run if we hear soldiers."

Another woman disagreed. "Don't run—the children will make too much noise. Just hold your children close and feed them to keep them quiet." The women understood how vulnerable they were to the whims of soldiers and also knew that prolonging the talk deprived them of energy they'd need for the next day's long walk. Maria, who had once shared intimacies and laughed heartily with Yesenia, now ignored her friend and looked at the star-studded sky with glazed detachment. Mariela lay quietly beside her.

Village women were practical and stoic, conserving energy for what must be endured. They wasted little energy reliving the details of the past or talking about future fears. Long days spent trudging in the daylight followed by fitful sleep when the sky darkened turned into weeks of hunger and despair. They plodded on through the verdant landscape farther from their village in the direction they only knew as "the city," where Mayan villagers found places to live on the crowded streets. Sometimes there were bananas, avocados, or corn in fields that they hastily grabbed and fed to the children, who ate with ravenous hunger. Maria's young breasts, once full of nourishment, provided no milk for Mariela, now almost three years old, and the child whimpered and fretted during most of the long days. Maria's despair intensified with the child's fussing, but soon she developed the ability to ignore her much as she ignored her own mounting anguish.

The women accepted the harshness of daily life in their village, but once outside the familiarity of their homeland, they were bewildered by challenges. Tension mounted as they walked farther away from all they knew. Cooperation and affiliation with each other had been a strength in village life, but now they argued. A strong leader didn't emerge despite several trying to exert authority, and the women broke into smaller groups based on agreements about the safety and speed of various routes through the highlands.

"There is another big city before we reach the capital. We can save at least a week of walking if we stop in Chimaltenango," Yesenia urged, remembering her uncle, now dead, talking about the city. As they slogged through the rain-soaked landscape day after day, they argued about continuing the long journey toward the capital, many now agreeing with Yesenia that the shorter route to a smaller city was better. Many women, including Maria, wanted to continue the longer walk to the capital, believing only it offered the safety of true anonymity.

Yesenia, whose young infant slept listlessly strapped on her back, was desperate to stop walking so she could tend to her weakened baby. She urged Maria to join the group going to Chimaltenango, where it was rumored soldiers mostly left Mayan women alone.

"Soldiers won't bother with us. We're a bunch of desperate women and children who pose no threat," Yesenia reasoned. Maria remembered the soldiers' merciless aggression and was too paralyzed to follow Yesenia when her group set off early one morning. Maria's eyes were dry, her tears dammed behind a wall of despair, as she watched her dearest childhood friend disappear into the dense wood on a different path than she would take.

In the haze of morning light as she looked over the desperate women and children who remained, she felt a sickening vulnerability. They knew nothing of the capital but dared to imagine safety in the vastness of it, so they walked to the southeast. The absence of Yesenia and the other women bore down heavily on Maria and the others, but no one was willing to speak of it.

"Let's walk faster now that there are fewer of us. God is with us," encouraged Yolanda, her voice shaking as she tried to maintain her usual positive tone. The women urged their children forward and tightened the knots holding the babies to their backs.

Then, one day, Maria and her group encountered a small group of soldiers. The men stopped the frightened women and questioned them.

"Where are you going? Where are you from?" a soldier demanded but didn't wait for an answer as he motioned his soldiers to take several of the young women aside. These women were instructed to hand over their children to other women, which they did, too afraid not to comply. Mariela shrieked and tried to release the grip of a woman who held her as Maria was led away by a soldier. "Mama, mama," she wailed as she watched her mother being dragged by her wrists.

Maria and three other women were pulled behind an old shack on the side of the road within sight of their children. Mariela could see her mother struggling on the ground with a soldier on top of her, hurting her, suffocating her as she pleaded and cried. Maria cried out in awful choking gasps, and Mariela, held tightly by a stunned woman, howled. Over the years, the scene of her mother's face twisted in pain and helplessness would assault her nights and cause her to scream with the same terror she had felt as a child.

The traumatized group was allowed to continue their journey when the soldiers were finished with them, and they staggered on in silence, not daring to speak of the shame and dishonor they had experienced. Unhinged and floating above the scene of other tearful women and whimpering children, Maria's body moved ahead, but she was not in it. She had disconnected from it and from the little girl on her back. All sensation had been severed. Mariela clung to her mother and stroked her hair, desperate for connection and affection. Occasionally she cried with hunger, but still Maria didn't respond.

They walked in silence until they found a sheltered place among avocado trees laden with fruit. Maria unstrapped Mariela and put her on the ground to pick at avocados. She frantically tried to remove the thick green skin and looked to her mother for help before biting into the bitter tough peel in desperation. Maria sat on the ground and stared off into the distance, leaving Mariela to seek help from another mother, who looked alarmed at Maria who sat unfazed by her child's frantic hunger.

Finally, Maria picked up a single avocado, peeled it, and shoved it into her own mouth. Mariela moved closer to the woman who helped her, confused about her own mother's apathy but determined to get what she needed from anyone willing to provide it. She watched her own mother intensely but from a distance. The others gorged themselves on the velvety fruit then fell into a fitful sleep.

Days later, they could see the capital off in the distance, a smudge of dirty air hovering around lofty buildings that dwarfed the trees. The weary women and children stood in disbelief. Wary of continuing toward this foreboding site, they searched each other's faces, hoping to find the courage they needed to enter the massive city. Most believed survival depended on hiding somewhere among the crowds and chaos of the city to care for their children as best they could. As they entered the outskirts, a woman in the group who spoke some Spanish inquired about where they might stay. The Latina (a woman who is not a Mayan villager and dresses in "city clothes") they had cautiously approached eyed the haggard group and told them how to get to Zone 1 of the city by the railroad tracks where many Indiginos lived in makeshift camps. So, the group of exhausted women and children trudged on, inquiring about the location of the tracks in Zone 1 until, at last, they found the ramshackle camp they would make their new home.

Chapter 5

Maria

"Remember us after we have gone. Don't forget us. Conjure up our faces and our words. Our image will be as dew in the hearts of those who want to remember us."
                                        Popol Vuh, Mayan text

A short, old woman with long, gray braids that reached her waist, a weathered face, and deadly serious eyes addressed the group of exhausted women and children who walked by looking for a place to drop their meager belongings.

"I'm Lupita. You can stop here and make yourself a place to stay, but there are a few things you should know. It won't be easy or nice, but it's better than your other choices," she said in Quiche. "Don't make any trouble. Keep your kids quiet and out of the way. And be prepared to share whatever you have. We've all lost everything. We have nothing but each other. We're your village now, if you decide to stay." With that, Lupita patted a few of the exhausted children on their heads and passed some stale tortillas out for them to share.

Mariela grabbed Lupita's skirt, looked up at her, and begged to be picked up. Maria didn't notice that her daughter had left her side.

"Whose child is this?" inquired Lupita. Before anyone answered, she continued, "Children disappear just like this." She clicked her small, crooked fingers. "They are sold to rich Americans for lots of money, so watch them carefully."

The women listened to Lupita, trepidation showing on their faces as they pulled their children close. Maria looked around for Mariela and saw that she was pressed tightly against Lupita, looking up at her intently as she spoke. Maria was reassured that Mariela appeared to be in good hands and made no move to pull her young child to her side. If she was frightened by Lupita's warning, she didn't show it and remained lost in her troubled thoughts.

Finally, Lupita took Mariela's small hand and gave her to her mother with another warning as she introduced the women to Henrique, the boss of the makeshift camp, who would tell them where they could carve out a place of their own. Henrique was a sad-looking man, bent over and gnarled. He motioned them to a place farther along the vast area strewn with trash, an open sewer running beside it.

Maria walked through the mass of ragged people and thought she saw her father. He turned, and she saw instantly that it was not him but another Mayan man of short stature, sloped shoulders, and beaten expression. Maria winced as painful memories surfaced of her father being led away, her mother being burned alive, and Carlos with his hands tied behind his back. The memories swept over her, making her dizzy and weak until she was able to push all feeling and sensation away and continue walking through the debris and filth.

Maria and her small group laid out their parrajes (large woven cloths used to carry their babies), a few worn baskets, and other meager belongings and sat quietly absorbing the staggering sight around them. There were no fields in which to grow food, no personal spaces or privacy, no places to wash or bathe. Maria recoiled when several rats darted across their path in broad daylight. Older children kicked at empty bottles in the dirt. Desperation was etched in the faces of all of them.

As night fell, some of the people made fires and gathered together. Maria and her group joined and eagerly grabbed a few tomatoes and tortillas that were passed out by Father Jose, a tall, young priest with kind eyes, who walked through the camp saying encouraging things. The Latino priest spoke sincerely of their hardships and encouraged them to stay strong and resist turning to lives of crime "and worse" to support themselves. "Hold on to your self-respect and dignity. You have lost so much. Your bodies and those of your children are sacred. Protect them." He repeated the warning that Lupita gave earlier in the day, "In these difficult times, people make money off children. Many children disappear and are never seen again. Don't take your eyes off your children."

The mothers looked around the circle at each other, trying to understand the message of the priest as it was translated into Quiche from Spanish. Why do children disappear, where do they go, and what happens to them? Danger lurked around every corner in this massive city full of strangers. Maria's breathing slowed as she took full inhalations of the night air. She may never feel safe or happy again, but at least here among other women from her village and with others just like themselves, she could stop running. Maria realized that Mariela had crawled onto her lap as she hungrily sucked the juice from a tomato. For the first time in a long time, Maria wrapped her arms tightly around her child. Mariela responded to this rare affection by putting her hand on her mother's face. Maria lightly kissed Mariela's hand and then resumed her long stare past the others and into the night.

As the weeks wore on, camp life took on a desperate rhythm. Camp dwellers were edgy, hungry, and scared, and no one knew what to expect. They had been allowed to live in the vacant area by the railroad tracks but were unsure how long they would be safe. Each morning large groups walked to the huge city trash dump and spent hours looking for anything to sustain themselves. They sometimes found plastic and metal that could be turned into a small amount of cash. They often found food scraps thrown away by city people. Mariela was too young to safely sift through the garbage, so she was tied securely to Maria's back during the foraging. Maria often grew despondent and untied Mariela, placing her on the debris. Mariela would later recall, as one of her first memories, scraping her teeth against the insides of a banana peel to taste the small sweetness of the meager pulp.

Each day was a test of survival; many were ill, and some young children died. The Guatemalan government blamed the Mayans for their fate, saying they should have stayed in their highland villages. A few priests gave the only assistance the women could depend upon. Maria avoided reaching out to others; her world consisted of surviving from one day to the next. While many mothers clung more fiercely to their children as their reason to survive, Maria withdrew into herself and away from her now almost-four-year-old daughter.

A year into their miserable existence in the city, Maria succumbed to the fate of many of the desperate women. She walked away from the camp in the evenings to be with the men who loitered on the streets nearby. They gave her small gifts and lots of attention. She was young and pretty and pliable. She had her first sip of alcohol with a jovial man who offered her a drink from his bottle. Mayan village women rarely drank, and she learned quickly that the alcohol further numbed all feeling, and the men gave her some relief from her desolation. One after another encouraged her to have sex with him for a small amount of money, but she resisted for weeks, not believing she was capable. Carlos had been her only love, and she felt a fierce loyalty to him. But clearly Carlos was gone, and she was alone to decide her fate.

"Forgive me, my sweetheart, I am desperate," she whispered to herself when she finally agreed to accompany a man to his small apartment after she saw other women come away from their brief encounters with enough quetzals to buy cheese, tortillas, and fruit at the market. Selling her body, her only valuable possession, was a way to ensure survival for her and Mariela on the cruel streets of the capital. Soon, she was leaving the camp each night as the sky grew dark to walk with a few other women, quickly and with heads down, through the seedy streets where the demand for their bodies was predictable.

She learned to pretend to enjoy the sexual trysts with men, most of whom were unshaven, dirty, rough, and brutish. Numb with so much loss and shame, pretending came easily, especially with the help of the alcohol, which was freely given by men eager to enjoy her.

"Mama, please don't go, please…" Mariela cried and begged her mama not to leave each evening. Maria's shame kept her from comforting her child. Lupita cared for all the children of the women who were prostituting for a pittance. Though she was old and stern and overwhelmed with the care of ten or more children, she loved the Mayan children and saw them as the only hope for her people who had been displaced and reduced to selling themselves. "Come collect your children in the early morning and don't be late," Lupita told the exhausted, edgy mothers as they crept away from their crying children.

"You've been gone two days," scolded Lupita one day when Maria finally returned to claim Mariela. "You need to care for your daughter. You act like you don't remember you're her mother," chided Lupita as she handed the sleepy little girl to Maria. Mariela desperately clung to her mama and, at the same time, scowled at her. Maria could barely tolerate the clinging and desperate behaviors that Mariela used to get her attention, and she often pushed the child away angrily. "Can't you see I'm exhausted? What do you want from me? I'm here; now leave me alone!"

Maria was overcome with guilt when she yelled at Mariela, but it was the only time she could safely vent her frustrations. Maria resolved to be more patient and to hold and comfort her daughter but could rarely maintain the steady calm necessary to do so. Soon she'd repeat the angry outbursts at her daughter despite her determination not to. She saw how Mariela grew anxious in her company, not knowing what to expect from her mama, but Maria felt helpless to control her growing distress.

One evening, Father Jose, whom the women called Kind Eyes, approached the women. "You young women, he said in his caring voice, "could make tamales in our church kitchen each evening, then sell them the next day at the market and keep the profit for yourselves and your children." The priests of his order saw it as their mission to help the Indigenous villagers and hoped that the women's increased self-respect would more than make up for the income lost by giving up prostitution. Most of the women, eager to please Father Jose, who had helped them so much, agreed to the plan. It seemed worth a try to regain some self-respect. Several of the young women had been badly injured by violent men and were eager to make money in a less dangerous way.

Father Jose explained, "The children will continue to be cared for by Lupita in the evenings while you prepare the tamales; then you can return home to spend the night with your children, as you should. During the day, your children can sit with you in the market while you sell tamales. By your good work, you will feed your children." The priest smiled in his calm and inspired way, happy to offer a solution to redeem the souls of the desperate mothers. He agreed to get the plan started immediately.

Maria joined the others in the evenings for hours of mixing and forming the soft masa dough into corn husks to steam. The women worked late into the night, then returned home through the streets teeming with men and prostitutes, resisting the catcalls from the jeering men.

They woke early, walked to the market, and struggled to find a small place to sit with their baskets to sell their tamales. They squeezed in among the fruit and vegetable vendors in the busy marketplace. As long as they didn't encroach on someone else's portion of pavement, they were tolerated. Maria sat with Evelyn, another woman involved in the project, and her five-year-old son, Paco. Mariela and Paco sat patiently on the pavement by their mothers at the edge of the busy market on a street corner filled with passing cars and pedestrians. The mothers and their two children smiled tentatively at passersby from their places on the street. "Tamales, fresh tamales," they said in turn, still too self-conscious about speaking their few words of Spanish and fearful of the Latinos' harsh judgments.

Orphaned shoeshine boys called to passing men, encouraging them to get a shine, while other children yelled at the top of their lungs to sell the daily newspaper, which few Mayans could read and which never spoke of the war that had killed so many villagers in the highlands of their country. In every far-off corner of the market, mothers with their children, determined not to turn to selling their bodies again, tried their luck at selling their perishable tamales by the end of the day. Maria managed to sell a dozen or so tamales her first day, giving her enough money to purchase some fruit, a small bar of soap, and a used pair of shoes for Mariela, whose battered shoes had been cut at the toes so she could keep wearing them.

Each night, Maria stood and made tamales until well after midnight, and each day if she was lucky, she'd sell enough to buy a few items from the market. Mariela was eager to help by running to get change for customers, picking up discarded fruit, and trying to cheer her mother with funny antics. "Look, mama, I can make a hat out of old newspaper." Mariela smiled as she displayed the paper hat. Occasionally, Mariela's mama would touch her affectionately, and the physical contact warmed her heart and gave her hope. But despite Mariela's repeated efforts, Maria was lost in her own misery and mostly indifferent to her. Maria missed the relief that the alcohol provided, the company of several eager men, and the income she earned from selling her body. She had promised Father Jose that she'd continue with the tamale project despite the difficulty, and she intended to do so. Despite the voice in her head urging her to go back to the streets for relief from the drudgery, she continued making and selling tamales and getting so little income that their stomachs still growled.

One early morning as the chilly air bit her small hands and hunger gnawed, Mariela eyed the warm, plump tamales and breathed in their aroma with a strong urge to seize one and stuff it in her mouth. She had been warned that the tamales were for sale and not consumption.

Despite these warnings, Mariela grabbed the warm tamale and with the speed of a hungry animal, devoured the tamale, almost choking as she tried to swallow the evidence. Maria found her straining to swallow and hissed at her angrily, "What are you doing? I work hard to support us, and look what you do, you lazy girl!" Mariela blinked back tears of confusion and anger, feeling the satisfaction of food in her belly and sting of the rebuke of her mother. Years later, Mariela's memories of this incident would be sketchy, but the thought of eating tamales would cause her stomach to knot, and she'd feel a familiar but unnamed anger rise in her.

Maria and Mariela sat on the cold ground one day in the rainy season with a sheet of plastic covering their tamales to shield them from the morning drizzle. Mariela sang out to shoppers in her heavily accented, sweet, young voice, "Se vende tamales…" over and over, but shoppers hurried by without looking her way. Maria was pensive and cut off from both Mariela and from the stream of people walking by. Mariela looked to her mama for attention or approval occasionally, but it didn't come, so she played quietly with her corn husk doll.

Maria had been diligent about the tamale project for several months. Each day she and Mariela sat huddled together in their usual spot in the crowded corner near several shoeshine boys and the paper sellers. Evelyn had moved to another area of the market when her Spanish improved so she would not have to share sales with Maria.

"I'm tired of sitting here in damp clothes and with wet feet, waiting all day to sell a few tamales," Maria complained to Mariela, the only thing she had said that day.

"I think people will buy today." Mariela tried to reassure her sad mama.

"There's no use. Why do I keep trying?" Maria sounded so tired, and Mariela was frustrated that she couldn't help her mama. It was early in the afternoon, and Maria was edgy and ready to give up and leave the market.

Fear of the other mothers' ridicule and the priest's disappointment kept her involved in the project, but recently she cared less and less what others thought. If she knew where to go, she would grab Mariela and go toward it, but she was paralyzed by her inability to imagine a different life from what she now endured in the camp and market.

As Maria sat in her misery, a man stopped in front of her, his muddy shoes partly on the tzutes (Mayan carrying cloth) on which she and Mariela sat. Aggravated, Maria looked up and saw that it was Jorge, the man who had paid her for sex many times when she was prostituting. Jorge had more appeal than many of the rough, disheveled men, and the way he looked at her made her soften. "Where have you been, sweetheart? It's been a long time. Too long." He winked. His eyes shifted to Mariela, who sat looking straight up at him. He asked for a tamale, handed her a crumpled bill, and told her to keep the change. She smiled shyly and handed him the warm bundle.

He looked back to Maria. "Can I take you to get a drink and something to eat?" He glanced around the market and back to her with an eager grin. She knew his meaning and understood that while there may be a quick meal and drink, he would want more. She also knew he would give her more money than she could earn in a week of selling tamales. She thought of the soft, dry bed where they would lie and the possibility of some small measure of pleasure in the arms of the strong man in front of her.

Jorge looked at Mariela again. "You stay here, be good, and sell tamales for your mama, and she'll bring you something good to eat," he instructed, using hand motions to make sure she understood his Spanish. Eager to please, Mariela nodded but cast a wary eye at her mother, not completely confident in her mama's devotion.

Mariela watched her mama's back as she walked away, hoping she would turn to wave and reassure her. Finally, she did. A quick turn of the head, a hand lifted, a furrowed brow, a slight nod; was it meant to apologize, reassure, or trick her? Then her mama was gone, following Jorge away from her. Years later, Mariela would replay this scene over and over, straining to recapture the last fleeting glance of her mama and intuit its meaning.

Mariela sat on the pavement and tried to warm herself, humming a song she had learned long ago in the village. The melody and words from their Quiche language comforted her as it had her mother. She looked around the market and saw that it was filling with people, typical for the time of day. She checked her supply of tamales, straightened her back, and forced an enthusiastic call in Spanish, "Se vende tamales!" She knew her mother would be very happy if, by herself, she was able to sell the day's supply. And the thought of her mother returning with a small package of something good to eat filled her with hope as she sat alone.

Maria tried to appear as if it was a natural thing to be walking with a man down the busy street away from the marketplace. She tried to imagine being with a man such as this, who might share his money and provide protection and care. She looked to his face as they walked and allowed herself to believe he might care about her. They walked past the cheap hotel where he had taken her in the past, but he continued to walk quickly through the streets, looking over his shoulder several times. He was taking her farther and farther from the marketplace, but she didn't protest or inquire. She allowed herself to be led by him and willed her mind to go blank as she struggled to keep up with him.

Jorge's muscular shoulders seen from behind made her think of Carlos. The memory stung, and she quickened her step as if to run from the sadness it evoked. Then her stomach tightened with fear as she realized how far from the marketplace they had gone. She had never left Mariela alone in the chaotic marketplace before, and she imagined the fear that might grip her daughter if she was gone too long. Jorge grabbed her hand tightly and pulled her to hurry her, his boyish grin growing intense. After walking what she suspected was more than half an hour, making many turns through the crowded streets into a derelict area with street corners filled with idle men, they came to a collapsing building with a locked metal gate.

Jorge took out a key and winked at Maria. "Follow me, sweet one; we'll go upstairs." She followed without a word, not knowing what else to do. Jorge unlocked another door and led her into a small, shabby room. "It's not much, but it's all ours for as long as we want it," he motioned to the small bed, keeping his intense brown eyes on her.

"When we've had some fun together here, we'll get something to eat and something you can take to your kid," Jorge said, already unbuttoning his shirt. The mention of Mariela startled her, and she pictured her daughter alone in the marketplace. She felt sick to her stomach with an urge to bolt out of the room and back to the market, but Jorge moved closer, his moves insistent. She smiled weakly and tried to calm her fears, reasoning that in a short time she would join Mariela with some delicious food as a gift for the fear her absence had caused.

The sex was rough and hurried, and Maria felt foolish for thinking it could be more. Despite efforts to stop her tears, a few ran down her face and onto the dingy pillow. Jorge didn't notice. He fell asleep quickly and wouldn't budge when she tried to wake him. She thought of leaving, but she hadn't gotten any money from him and realized how naïve she had been not to collect the money before the sex. She was a long walk from the marketplace with no money, her daughter was alone, and she was with a man who was snoring beside her who clearly didn't care about her.

As she reached for her clothes, still unsure what to do, she heard the door handle move. Within seconds, two men burst into the room with a powerful ferocity, guns drawn and aimed. She pulled the sheet up to cover herself as Jorge sat up and reached for his pants. Before he could snatch them off the floor, the men were in front of them, guns pointed at both of them. They saw that Jorge was naked and defenseless, and they both grinned and shifted their eyes toward her.

"You should be careful who you bed down with, beautiful," said a wiry man with a scar under his hard eyes and tattoos covering his neck. The other man, heavier and older, moved closer, his fist tight around the pistol, his eyes angry slits.

Maria tightened the sheet around her, barely daring to breathe, hoping to keep attention from herself. She didn't know what was going on but knew things could unfold horribly. She was paralyzed with fear as she looked at the guns. For a minute she was back in her village looking at the guns of the soldiers. She floated above the scene and away from the unfolding drama, as her body knew how to do.

The older man seethed when he addressed Jorge. "You've been working for the other side. You know what happens when we discover things like that..." He moved the pistol closer to Jorge's face, which was drained of color.

"No, it's not true. I can prove it. I only sell for your group," Jorge stammered. Maria smelled his sweat and fear and the heat of his body inches from hers. Jorge made a quick move for his pants only a few feet away, and a gun went off. Maria screamed, her ears rung, and she felt the warm liquid of Jorge's blood cover her arms and neck. Jorge had been shot at close range in the chest. His full weight slumped against her, his blood soaking the bed. Gasping in horror, she tried to move away from his body, but she couldn't without exposing her naked body to the killers.

The men shoved their guns into their pants, hurriedly searched Jorge's pants pockets, stuffed his gun and a wad of money away in their pockets, and scanned the room for something, yelling at each other frantically. She tried to shrink into the bed, hoping that in their hurry, they would forget about her, consider her unimportant, and leave as quickly as they had come. But the small man stopped his frenzied search and stared at her. "What do we do with her? We can't just leave her here." He deferred to the older man.

"We take her with us. Listen, sweetheart," he addressed her, "we could shoot you, but we won't if you come quietly with us and don't cause trouble."

"Please, please, let me go. I have a daughter. She has no one else.

She's alone. I have to go to her," Maria pleaded softly, afraid to raise her voice.

"You'll get back to her, don't worry. Now, get dressed." He snatched the sheet away from her and paused to look, letting out a vicious growl. With shaking hands, she put on her skirt and blouse, crying softly in terror as she thought about what might happen to her.

The older man grabbed her wrist and yanked her out the door, threatening her to keep her quiet. She glanced back to the bed to see Jorge's splayed, bloodied body, now lifeless. She had been grabbed roughly like this before being raped by the soldier on her journey to the city. Her mind went fuzzy with terror as she was pulled from the building.

She pleaded with her eyes as they passed others, but the people on these streets were indifferent to her. She thought it must be late afternoon; the sky had darkened. She thought again of Mariela, alone and scared. When they arrived at a waiting car several blocks away, she made another plea to be released, promising to keep quiet about what she'd seen.

"Put a blindfold on her; she doesn't need to see where we're going," one said as he shoved her into the backseat of the car and got in beside her.

Maria whimpered as the blindfold was tightly tied. "Please let me go," she cried again. Not being able to see increased her sense of smell, and she gagged at the strong odor of blood, body odor, filth, and her own urine, which had dampened her skirt.

She tried to imagine the options. From their accents, she thought they were not from Guatemala. Many men came from El Salvador to commit crimes and sell drugs on the streets of Guatemala City, then rushed back across the border. They may take her across the border, use her for sex or as a cook and domestic. She could be kept for years under their control. Or they might kill her after they were through with her, leaving her body on the side of the road. She was just a poor

Mayan woman, living on the streets with her daughter. No one would miss her; no one would come looking. The frightening truth was that they could do whatever they wanted. She was at their mercy. And Mariela's fate was in the hands of those who found her, who could sell her for profit, as Maria had been warned.

She listened intently as the car slowed on the crowded streets. She could hear a newspaper boy shout and shoeshine boys yelling to customers. They were by the market. Mariela would be close by. She screamed her daughter's name out the car window until a man's hand tightened around her braid and yanked her to the floor of the back seat before delivering a blow to her head.

Chapter 6

Mariela

"Only here can we feel whole; nowhere else would we ever feel complete and our pain would be eternal."
                                                               Popol Vuh, Mayan text

Years later, Mariela recalled in fuzzy scraps of memories what had happened that day in the market, the day she lost her mama. She waited hours for her to return, watching as the wind swirled trash from the busy day around her. She wiped at tears that blurred her vision, not daring to move away from the place on the pavement her mama had claimed as theirs. She watched anxiously as women in similar huipils with long, black hair darted back and forth as the marketplace prepared to close for the day. She pushed away frightening thoughts, repeating to herself, "My mama will come back; she would never leave me." She tucked a small wad of money into the waistband of her traje, careful to conceal it. Finally, when she could sit still no longer, she walked away from their blanket, carrying the tattered basket they used to hold tamales, and wandered to nearby stalls, expecting to see her mama around the next corner. Fear was gripping her as the light of the day slanted away. She wandered back and forth, eyes desperate and searching for her mama; then she turned back to take her place on the blanket as her mama had instructed. "She will come back soon," she cried as she soothed herself.

A nicely dressed Latina who looked out of place in this part of the market had been standing on the pavement near her, making small conversation in simple Spanish, watching with interest when

Mariela wandered away, then returned.

"Hello, sweetheart, where is your mama? She hasn't returned yet? I can watch you until she returns. The marketplace is not a safe place for a young girl to be alone," she added. Mariela was relieved to have an adult standing by, a woman with a smiling, friendly face who was taking charge.

After a while, the woman said, "Look, maybe your mama had a problem and could not come back. I can take you to my house where I can feed you dinner. I have a room you can sleep in and toys for you to play with while we wait for your mama." It seemed too good to be true. The city woman's kindness was unexpected. She took the woman's soft hand and went with her, assured by the woman's gentle touch and soothing voice.

"How will my mama know where I am?" Mariela asked shyly as they walked.

"Oh, don't worry. I told the nice man who runs the market that you came home with me, and he will tell your mama when she asks where you are. That's the way it's done. Then, she will come for you, maybe tomorrow morning after you've had a nice breakfast with me." The gentle reasoning of this fresh-smelling, kind woman who talked of good food made Mariela feel warm and giddy inside.

The woman's apartment was bright and clean and stocked with food. Mariela was gently tucked in on the living room couch and covered with a soft blanket. The comforts of this new place made her miss her mama less, but still she asked the next morning after a deep sleep, "When is my mama coming?" In truth, she would have been happy to stay with the sweet lady a while. It had been so long since her mama had looked at her with loving eyes, since her mama had talked to her or seemed pleased with her. She felt guilty for not missing her mama more but was reassured that it was just a matter of time before her mama would come.

But her mama didn't come that day or the next or the next. Weeks went by, and still her mama didn't come.

"I'm your mama now, angel. Don't worry, you will be happy here with me. You are already gaining weight and looking so healthy with all the good food," Mariela was told. Mariela was thankful for her full belly, her warm bed, and the toys scattered around. She stopped counting the days since her mama had disappeared from the marketplace. She missed her mama and couldn't understand why it was taking her so long to come back, but she was safe with this woman who now called herself mama. Mariela had become accustomed to looking to other village women for care due to her mama's indifference, so this didn't seem much different. The new mama's life was a puzzle; why didn't she work? How did she make money for all the food she bought? Where was the rest of her family? It was all a mystery, but Mariela's short life had been full of things she didn't understand and couldn't predict, so she didn't give much more thought to those questions.

"I bet you are close to six years old, but you are very small for your age, the size of a four-year-old. That is wonderful," the mama said as she handed Mariela a plate brimming with beans with the squeaky cheese she loved on top. Mariela beamed. She had made this mama proud. One morning as she snuggled on the couch listening to the caged parakeet chirp happily next to her, she overheard her new mama talking on the phone.

"She's very sweet, happy, cute, and can easily pass for four. She's already calling me mama. No one has looked for her at the marketplace. She's ours." Her new mama looked around the corner, still on the phone, to check on her. Mariela shut her eyes, pretending to sleep. "After that last one, we'll need to be more careful. There is talk, and people are getting suspicious. Any trouble and I can put her right back where I found her on the pavement in the marketplace and no one will know a thing." Silence, then: "OK, I can keep her until you find a family ready to pay our attorney, hopefully in the next few weeks. I've already had her four weeks. I have other things to do."

They were talking about her, that much she knew, but she

couldn't understand how her mama and this new lady who called herself mama were connected. Did her mama give her to this lady? This new one was sweeter and took better care of her, gave her more food, but she missed the smell and comfort of the mama she had known her whole life. Having both of them was good, but then she remembered that she didn't have her real mama anymore. She was gone and hadn't returned. She would have to cling to this new one, so she didn't lose her too.

The apartment became familiar. She never left the small space, the parakeet her only companion other than the new mama, who fed her regularly and said nice things to her occasionally, turning her mouth upward into a smile then quickly down as she turned away and busied herself elsewhere.

She was given a few toys to entertain herself on the floor. Mariela wished for a playmate or someone to keep her company, but she was warm and safe and figured that was enough until things changed, which she assumed they would. One morning after she had been fed a filling breakfast of tortillas and beans and then sat alone on the floor talking to an old doll that she had found in the apartment, there was a hard, angry knock at the door. Her new mama rushed to the door, opened it a crack, and a man pushed past her, talking and giving orders as he did; then he looked at Mariela on the floor.

"We can't risk it. There have been complaints of kids going missing. Someone told them about the different kids we've had here, and they could come looking." The man snarled his displeasure.

"Are you sure? She's a sweet thing, eager to please. She would bring a lot of dollars."

"We need to move, set up another apartment away from here. And we need to get rid of this one."

"Shhhh. No need to frighten her. I'll take care of it," said the mama.

"Yes, quickly. We can't wait until someone comes snooping around." Within an hour, Mariela was leaving the apartment for the first time since arriving. Her mama looked nervous and kept telling her to hurry.

"Where are we going?" Mariela asked, sensing her life was taking a dangerous turn. "We're going to the market to buy a few things."

Fearful that this mama could leave her, Mariela looked up at her and flashed a smile. "I can help you shop and carry your things," she said in a desperate attempt to be useful and wanted. When they got to the market near the place where she and her real mama had sat selling tamales, the new mama looked around nervously.

"I need to go into the market to buy a few things. You wait here like a good girl, and I will bring you a treat. Here, hold this bag for me, and I'll be back very soon."

Mariela knew what would happen next. She was being left again, she thought, just like her real mama had left her. Terror washed through her small body. Mariela wanted to chase after the woman but saw her running through the market and realized she would not be able to catch her. So, she stood, then finally sat on the curb, waiting for something to make sense. *What did I do? What's wrong with me?* she wondered as tears filled her eyes.

The sky darkened, and vendors hauled their wares away on their backs. Gangs of dogs roamed excitedly, looking for scraps left by vendors. Then men and woman with desperate, hungry looks walked through the littered streets looking for anything salvageable. Finally, a policeman did a final round through the emptied marketplace and saw the small girl sitting alone and crying.

Chapter 7

Charlotte

"The years teach much which the days never know."
Ralph Waldo Emerson

Back in Oregon after our trip to Guatemala to meet Mariela, my anxiety and doubt dissipated. I calmed myself about my initial reaction to her, which I considered perfectly normal given the gravity of our decision and all the unknowns. Our family talked excitedly about the love and care we would give her when she at last joined us. My attitude changed from trepidation to a sense that Mariela was indeed perfect for our family. For our next trip, Jill wanted to go with me so she could experience Guatemala, meet her new sister, and welcome her to our family. Chris couldn't miss any more work, and missing high school wasn't easy for Chad, so Jill and I made plans to travel, excited about the adventure we'd experience together. Chris and Chad waited at home for the three of us to return.

During the wait for our return, Mariela was transferred to a temporary children's shelter in the capital. This spared us another grueling trip to the highlands where we had first met her, and we only had to take a taxi from our hotel to the shelter. Jill and I arrived too late to go to the shelter that evening, so we slept fitfully and woke up early, forced ourselves to eat a small breakfast, and hailed a taxi to the address written on a piece of paper I had carefully tucked into my passport. The building where the taxi stopped was a massive crumbling structure with bars on the windows. I checked our directions, wondering if we had arrived at the wrong place. We couldn't imagine children living in this derelict building. The grounds were littered and overgrown. A rope swung from a large tree, the only sign of something meant for children.

"This place looks awful. Is this where she lives?" asked Jill incredulously.

"Yes, temporarily. But to be honest, it doesn't look much worse than the place where she had been living in Quetzaltenango, about five hours from here." We entered the compound, and I showed some paperwork to a distracted worker who greeted us and pointed us to a large courtyard where kids played, their gleeful sounds filling the scruffy space.

We stood at the courtyard entrance and watched as twenty or more youngsters chased each other with an old tire spiraling in front of them. I recognized her immediately and pointed her out to Jill, who stood nervously beside me. Neither of us made a move as we observed the girl we would claim in moments. I held Jill's hand, willing time to stop. Jill would in an instant become a big sister to the girl in front of us. I turned to say this to her, but Mariela, running from another child, looked toward the door and saw us. An awkward grin slowly spread across her face as she walked haltingly toward us. Jill, feeling no hesitancy, moved quickly toward her. The two girls greeted each other, embraced, and beamed. Then Mariela turned toward me, and her face transformed. Her shy smile seemed to communicate a yearning to be worthy enough for a mother's love. I wrapped my arms around her small body and held her, then rocked back and forth with her, feeling tender and protective, with a new confidence about my ability to love her.

It had been a good idea to bring Jill. Mariela was softer and easier with her and seemed comfortable with a new sister who was only a few years older. She took Jill by the hand and walked her through the orphanage, shouting to anyone who would listen that this was her new gringa sister. Jill greeted the other children shyly in Spanish, having learned some phrases for the occasion.

The two girls remained inseparable throughout our five-day stay in Guatemala. Mariela remained tentative with me. I'd catch her looking intently at me when I talked, perhaps trying to decide if I was a mother who could be trusted. When I caught her eye, she'd flash a shy smile, then turn quickly away. I reassured Jill: "She will come around. For now, I'm happy that you're here and she is comfortable with you."

"She's so cute. I love being with her," said Jill in her typical caring way. I understood that with patience, Mariela's loving bond with me would grow. I had read that caring for another person plants the first seeds of love, and I was already feeling some expanse in my heart as I watched her. I was confident in my ability to love and attach to her.

Mariela was legally released to leave her country, but before leaving, I wanted her to see more of Guatemala. Setting off as tourists, the three of us went to Lake Atitlan, Guatemala's crown jewel, a large expanse of shimmering water circled by volcanos and villages. We walked on well-worn footpaths through the small Mayan villages. Locals avoided looking at us as we passed but stopped their work when we had gone by to stare at two gringas with one of their children. I imagined what they might be thinking: perhaps gratitude for adopting one of their orphans or, and this I felt more likely, resentment at our ease in acquiring one of their children and returning to our comfortable lives with her. I noticed Mariela looking intently at each village woman we passed. *It's almost as if she's looking for someone,* I thought. *Is she still looking for her mom?*

I searched Mariela's face for reactions as we observed her people, but she averted her own gaze, her feelings impossible to read, a reminder that I had no window into her inner life. I put an arm around her shoulders as we walked and smiled at her lovingly when I could get her to look at me. I felt the first feelings of attachment, an intense desire to know her, a commitment to her well-being, an urge to care for her. The three of us held hands, and I felt the first stirrings of love.

Later that day as the three of us played in the lake, I swam toward her in a teasing attempt to catch her; she allowed herself to be caught, jumped into my arms, wrapped her arms around me, nestled her head in my neck, and allowed me to hold her like a baby in the lapping lake water. Skin to skin, and heart to heart, new mother and child, I felt my heart further expand. I vowed at that moment, *I will love this child with all my heart and make her part of our family forever.* Then she wiggled out of my arms and swam to Jill, smiling broadly when she looked back. I was bursting with something that felt like love. Adopting her had been a good decision, and everything was going to be OK, and I breathed the mountain air with joy.

At a restaurant later in the day, Mariela stuffed herself on the delicious food.. "Que delicioso," she said, grinning at both of us with her full mouth. "We won't have to worry about her being a picky eater," I joked with Jill. "No kidding, this girl can eat," Jill said as she cast a smile at her new sister. At the hotel, Mariela basked in the comforts of soft sheets and marveled at a television show. Accustomed to cold showers, she shrieked at the first splash of warm shower water and then giggled with satisfaction.

When we were buckled in on the plane and ready to leave Guatemala, I felt a need to draw Mariela's attention to the significant moment. "We're leaving your country now, but we'll come back to visit someday," I said in rudimentary Spanish. Mariela stared out the window; there were no tears and no show of emotion as the plane took off, leaving her country below beyond the clouds.

The two girls entertained themselves playing tic-tac-toe, drawing pictures, and laughing as they enjoyed soft drinks and pretzels. I looked out the window and thought of Mariela's mother. *What had become of her? Could she still be alive, and if so, did she sense her daughter was moving out of her orbit?* My eyes filled with tears as I thought of the likelihood that mother and child would never know what happened to each other. I felt the terrible loss that our adoption, full of promise for us, was inflicting on Mariela and her lost mother.

I was taking Mariela forever away from the possibility of reuniting. *I will make up for this loss,* I told myself as I reached for Mariela's hand and held it. She held mine back and smiled up at me. The doubt, so prominent when I first met her, had dissolved.

The three of us leaned on each other, and the girls dozed. We had awakened early to catch the plane, but my rattled nerves and excitement of what was to come kept me wide awake. Occasionally I looked over to Mariela, whose head rested on Jill. It was difficult for me to believe that this girl about whom I had fantasized for so many months was sitting beside me. When she saw me looking at her, she immediately transformed her face to a wide smile as if on demand. While her smile pleased me, I also couldn't help thinking it was a thinnest of veneers. It would be wonderful to fully discover who she was in the months to come. For the remainder of the trip to Portland, I touched her at every opportunity in my attempt to convey love and kindness. She looked at me with her bright, practiced smile.

Family and friends waved frantically at the airport as we approached them. We felt like celebrities as our friends assailed us with cameras to capture the moment. Mariela seemed stunned by all the attention but smiled and waved. She recognized Chris and went to him, then turned to Chad and put out her arms to hug him. Excited friends asked us to pose for more photos, so we threw our arms around each other with Mariela, the star of the show, in the middle of us. Chris and I gave each other reassuring glances. Our new family of five left the airport holding hands and excited for what was to come.

"How'd she do on the way here?" Chris whispered in the front seat of the car. "Does she seem OK?"

"Yes, she's doing great." I smiled and reached for his hand.

Mariela's face couldn't hide her surprise when she saw our home, a well-kept, two-story house in a leafy, attractive neighborhood. She had only lived in a village of huts in the highlands, then in a crowded, dilapidated orphanage. How could she imagine the kind of house where she'd be living?

"It's so big," she declared as she stood at the doorway. Chad and Jill walked her from room to room while we trailed along explaining things in Spanish, trying to see our home through her eyes. We were not wealthy, but our home must have appeared opulent. I stopped our tour to get down on my knees and tell her that we were so happy she would be in our family, in our home.

"I think she is overwhelmed. We've got lots of time. Let's take this slowly," I said to my family, feeling protective when I noticed her exhausted expression.

Mariela's early weeks with us were thrilling for all of us. She was an enthusiastic recipient who delighted us with her gutsiness and eagerness for new experiences. "Let's make a list of all the first things she's done since arriving," suggested Chad one night while we enjoyed pizza, watching Mariela swoon as she devoured it. We tallied up all her firsts and marveled at the long list: first pizza, first movie, first phone call, first card game, first swimming pool, first camping trip, first trip to a big grocery store...

"First playground," Jill chimed in. The list was long, and so was our passion for showing her the life that was now hers.

The bedroom we had decorated for her went unused for more than a month. She liked to sit in it and admire the sunny yellow walls, but when nighttime came, she was clear about wanting to sleep in Jill's room. We moved a large mattress into Jill's room and put Jill's twin mattress on the floor next to it, so the girls could sleep close to each other. "She can sleep in my room as long as she wants. It's like having a constant sleepover." Mariela had never slept alone and wasn't ready to start. She was an enjoyable novelty in our family, and we showered her with attention and love.

"I have fallen in love with her, without a doubt," I said to my brother John after he called from New Mexico to see how we were doing and asked, always pragmatic, "Do you think it's possible to love an adopted child like your own? I'm just curious." He added, "It seems biology plays a huge part in a parents' bond to their children." Always the scientist, he was looking to support his hypothesis. I wasn't put off by his questions or defensive. I was more thrilled to report that I had no doubts about my love, despite my hesitation when I first met her in Guatemala. Since bringing her home and folding her into our family, the love had blossomed and deepened. I was her mother, and she was my daughter, and I was entirely committed to her. We all were. "It's much, much more than biology" was my final answer.

On her first Christmas with us, months after she arrived, we made tamales, a Guatemalan tradition she was enthusiastic about initially. "I bet you're going to love these," said Jill, who had just helped me remove them from the steamer. Both girls had helped pat the masa dough into the corn husks. As soon as Mariela saw the finished product, she burst into tears and ran out of the room.

"What happened?" said Jill, confused at the response.

"We can't know some of the things she's been through, but we'll learn over time and can help her talk about it," I said. In the early weeks and months, she responded to many things in ways that were puzzling, but I imagined her story would slowly unfold with our encouragement and love. When asked about her Christmases in Guatemala or other events of her life there, she was withdrawn, unwilling to say much, especially when all of us were around. But at night when I tucked her into bed and sat with her, she often shared memories from her early life. She called it "our special time," and it was during these quiet passages from daytime to sleep that my bond with her grew and strengthened. I'd softly rub her back, hum, and tell simple stories in Spanish/English.

"I hate Guatemala. I love here," she said as she hugged me and said goodnight.

I had doubted that she was seven from the day I met her. When we learned that she had been through three grades in Guatemala, knew how to read, and had permanent teeth where loose teeth should have been, we knew she was older than her stated age. "Why would they lie to us about her age?" I asked Chris one evening. "We would have adopted her anyway, and it puts everything they told us in question."

"Their only motivation is to find families for the kids, and I guess they assume that a few lies to benefit the kids can't hurt," he responded.

"If she's actually nine, that's fewer years we have to bond before she hits adolescence," I said, giving voice to my fear that the years to solidly bond were passing too quickly.

"We'll know more after she sees a doctor and dentist," said Chris.

"The good news is that she is amazingly healthy and robust," our family doctor announced, "but the bad news is I have reason to believe she is several years older than seven. She's very short for her age, but she is Mayan, you say, so that's not surprising."

Our dentist had similar findings: "All her permanent teeth are in except her molars, putting her at nine or even ten. But her teeth are remarkably free of decay. It is clear she has eaten a simple diet without much processed food or sugar. Luckily for you, she doesn't need anything but a very thorough cleaning," he added with a smile.

We had started her in third grade in our mostly white neighborhood school where she was initially a popular novelty. She learned English rapidly, and her math skills, acquired in school in Guatemala, put her on par with schoolmates. She was accepted in the early weeks by peers because she was gutsy and smart, and she excelled in every physical endeavor. Her time on the streets and years of enduring orphanage life had made her a tough survivor, and her aggression singled her out among third-grade girls.

She was never far from my side in the early months; I spoke to her constantly in soothing tones of rudimentary Spanish interspersed with English words and pantomime. "Look at this—I've labeled everything for you in English," I said as I pointed to the table, chair, and lamp with stickers on them. She smiled and said the words out loud. Her reading skills in Spanish were good, but she had some difficulty sounding out English words. One of us was always on hand to help her. Everything was done in an effort to comfort, teach, and show her she was loved. Her face lit up quickly with a broad and beaming smile in those early months. She was eager to please, and I felt proud that we were easing her so lovingly into our family life. Those initial fears that it was not a "fit" moved far to the background and then disappeared altogether. At bedtime, I continued the routine of rubbing her back while singing simple songs of love and belonging and listening to her tell stories of her life.

"Do you want a story?" she asked me one night, turning the tables on my frequent question to her.

"Of course, yes, you tell me a story." Her English had become better than my Spanish, so we spoke in English. She wanted to tell me about her life in the orphanage.

"I cried so much but only at night when no one could hear me. I was lonely. I hated the orphanage and wanted my mama to come. But she never came."

I could see her eyes glisten with tears in the dark. I had assumed wrongly that she had adjusted well and been more or less content to live in the company of other children, cared for by a few familiar adults. "Life in the orphanage was hard," I ventured. I stroked her hair and didn't rush her.

"Kids did bad things to each other when the adults weren't looking. Boys hurt girls," she said, but when asked if that happened to her, she looked away and changed the subject. I would never know for sure and assumed her shame was too great for her to disclose abuse. Despite her nondisclosure, I assured her, with her wide-eyed attention, that it was never the fault of the younger child when such a thing happened.

Each night she revealed another part of herself, her losses, the confusion, and the fears always present in her life. Then one night as I sat on the edge of her bed anxious to say goodnight so I could have some quiet time for myself, she brought up her mama. I waited anxiously to see what she would say about the ghost mother she never spoke of who seemed always lurking in our midst.

"I don't know why she left me," she started. "She was sad all the time; then she got mad at me. I remember when she left me like a piece of trash on the street and never came back," she said with her voice trembling.

"You remember the day she left, sweetie?"

"Of course I do. I will never forget it," she said gravely. "I sat in the marketplace until it was dark, waiting for her and crying; then the police came and took me to an orphanage. I was little. I can't remember everything. It was the last time I saw her." Her voice trailed off. Her face was a stricken mask. Her small body was rigid.

"Maybe she meant to come back but couldn't." I tried to insert a new story, wanting to plant the seed of a narrative that something outside her mother's will prevented her from returning. She scoffed and looked away. She wasn't open to a different story. I began to understand that the story she had always told herself was etched into her being.

Another night as I sat with her, she said, "I wasn't worth it for her to stay. She didn't want me. She didn't care what happened to me. She left me on the streets and walked away. Something was wrong with me." Her heartbreaking conclusions spoke of defectiveness and being unlovable; all assumptions about herself were negative. My heart ached for her, and in the dark, my eyes brimmed with tears. Then her hurt transformed into anger before my eyes, her face hardened, and her breath quickened. Her injuries were gaping wounds that bled in these late-night mother-daughter exchanges. I expected tears to follow, but instead there was angry resolve. "I don't want to talk about her anymore. I hate her." The memories were sharp and jagged, opening wounds. She didn't reach to me for comfort at these times.

When I tried to talk about what she had revealed in the light of the following day, she dismissed me quickly. "Oh, forget it. I was acting like a sad little kid. I'm over it." I knew she wasn't over it, and all I could do was wait for her to open up again. I was poised to offer my love and reassurance when she did, but it seemed the anger she felt at her mother for leaving was now regularly offloaded onto me. The mother who had abandoned her, whatever the reason, wasn't available to be the recipient of her wrath, but I was. I understood this dynamic. I accepted her anger toward me as part of her healing process. *Bring it on,* I thought, *let your anger out so you can let the love in.* It occurred to me that I had also been the recipient of my mother's unresolved hurt and anger at being left by her mother. Both my mother and my daughter displaced their anger toward their mothers onto the willing recipient in their lives, me.

Chapter 8

Mariela

"Open your hands if you want to be held."
Rumi

Mariela woke to the drone of English coming from the kitchen and saw the light peeking through her flowered curtains, exposing the pale yellow of her bedroom decorated by parents who said they loved her. The books that lined her desk, the drawers filled with clothes, the puzzles, dolls, her own chalkboard, all of it amazed her. She remembered the rumors of orphans talking of just such things, but she hadn't believed it was possible. Listening to the rain gently fall outside, she pulled the covers over herself to retreat from all of it.

The first months with the American family were a blur of confusion and endless activity. She was learning English quickly and was proud of that, but listening to it all the time exhausted her. She often thought that life in the orphanage was easier, or at least more predictable. In that awful place she had called home, she knew what was expected of her. Then she remembered the long days of hard work, the numbing routine and deprivation, being part of the noisy crowd of orphans without anyone who really cared just for her. "I hated it there. No, I loved it there and hate it here. Shit!" she whispered under the covers, proud that she had uttered her first English cuss word. "I hate it both places and don't belong anywhere." Her thoughts left her reeling with confusion and sadness, and she had only been awake ten minutes.

She was relieved it was Saturday, when there would be no long, noisy school halls to navigate, no chaotic cafeteria where she'd sit shyly among the white girls who hammered her with questions and confused her with their giggling. And she wouldn't have to pretend on the playground that she knew the rules of the boisterous games her classmates played. She was hobbled by all she didn't know but intent on hiding her ignorance. It was more relaxing at home, but even there she was on guard, trying to please the family who had adopted her, always feeling the outsider, not knowing how to fit in.

Since arriving in the US, everyone noticed her, asked her questions, and watched her every move. Exhausted by performing, she doubted she could keep up the sweet-girl act for long. She wanted to scream at them in Spanish, her second language, or in Quiche, her first, and tell them she wasn't stupid, she had survived without them, had done many things in her life, and they were not in charge of her. But a familiar pang signaled the awful truth that she needed them and wouldn't survive in this new strange, cold country without them. She was a lost girl, left by her mother, picked up by strangers and given to the Americans and at their mercy. She hated that helpless feeling. It reminded her of life on the streets with her real mother and her early days in the orphanage when she was always scared, never knowing what might happen next.

She heard her new mom, Charlotte, calling her, "Mariela, time to get up. We're having pancakes this morning." Soon one of them would come knocking at her door, smiling, encouraging her, trying to prove something—what, she was never sure. She would have to join them, laughing together at things she couldn't understand. Maybe they were laughing at her. She pulled the covers over her head and remembered praying, head covered in her orphanage bunk, that a family would adopt her. When she learned she had been chosen by the Norte Americanos, her teacher had told her how lucky she was. But it didn't feel lucky to try to fit herself into this family of lookalikes who belonged to each other. Sometimes she hated all of them for what she could never have.

"They can dump me anytime," she fumed, struggling to understand what she meant to them and why they wanted her when the truth was simple, that she needed them more than they needed her. Her own mama walked away from her, leaving her with the same tormenting question, "What is wrong with me?" that she whispered to herself now. Then she thought of herself, sitting with her Mayan mama on the streets, both of them cold and hungry, kicking at stray dogs who sniffed their meager belongings. Other mothers stayed with their children; hers didn't. The conclusion was obvious: she was unlovable and defective and unable to keep a mother's love. *When will this new mom get tired of me?* she wondered.

"Come join us, sweetie—we're waiting for you. How'd you sleep? Are you hungry, sleepyhead?" her new mom called.

"OK, I come in a minute." She tried to sound agreeable but groaned and delayed another minute, then threw off the flowered spread. She dressed in an outfit pulled from her crammed dresser and remembered the rags she had worn not long ago.

She looked in the mirror and saw her dark skin and straight, black hair, her slanting eyes, and wondered how they could love her. "You are so ugly," she mouthed to her image. Jill would be sitting at the breakfast table with her styled, curly hair, her sparkling blue eyes, and her creamy skin, a nice sister who was a constant reminder of everything she could never be.

She walked slowly down the carpeted hallway toward the family who had wanted her enough to pay lots of money for her, but she had nothing to give them, so it didn't make sense. What was in it for them? She knew from her years on the streets and in the orphanage that life was about exchanges, and having nothing to offer meant having no value. In the orphanage, many girls had what boys wanted: a body that could be touched, fondled, or more. For this, the girls got bigger meal portions or even money and felt special for a while.

When older boys had tried to have sex with Mariela, she thought she had fought them off and screamed. There were a few muddled memories that remained blurry and frightening. She was no longer sure what happened; her memories were locked away, and she wanted to keep it that way. The shame and disgust she felt were proof of her defectiveness.

She was powerless, exposed, and dependent on this family whose motives she didn't trust. Chad and Jill trusted their parents, knew they were loved and had always belonged. Mariela knew they expected her cooperation and love, but she wasn't willing to give it so easily or maybe at all. The only solution was to manage them so they would take care of her, but trusting was out of the question.

She wasn't sure where she would go now if things fell apart. Guatemala was far away, and official adoption papers were signed. She would have to make it work. Obtaining the mom's love seemed essential, as she seemed the most invested, demonstrated by her devotion to caring for all of them with her easy affection. Mariela harbored deep suspicions of things she couldn't readily figure out for herself. Trusting anyone was a recipe for being controlled, manipulated, and discarded—she did know that. She walked into the kitchen to join the family with a sense that it was only a matter of time before they would betray and leave her. No one had ever stayed with her, and luck had never been on her side. She put on a practiced smile and sat down with the waiting family to eat her pancakes.

Occasionally, the family got impatient or frustrated with her when she pushed them too far. She could see them trying to clamp down on their rising irritation, struggling to remain calm and caring in the face of her belligerence. Better to find out sooner than later that their supposed love was conditional. *They can only pretend for so long that they care about me, and then it will all fall apart,* she reasoned. She had smiled to herself recently after being asked to leave the table when she cussed out the dad with impressive bad language she had learned at school, feeling a small thrill at getting the rejection she expected.

There had been an incident at school the week before that still stung. She sat in her class surrounded by her classmates who half listened but understood everything, while she strained to understand enough of the rapid-fire English of her teacher to make sense of what she was saying. She looked around the classroom at the pale skin and various colors of hair her classmates had and felt the pang of the unattainable. She could never have what they had no matter how hard she tried. Then, she stiffened when she heard the assignment.

"Students, go home and pick any picture you want from when you were a baby or toddler and bring it in tomorrow. This is an important part of the project we will be working on." While the other students giggled about which picture to choose from family albums, her clammy hands clutched her desk as shame enveloped her. She had no pictures of her first nine years of life. The adoptive family had filled a photo book of her already, but before coming to the US, there was nothing. Her life in Guatemala with her first mama, her real mother, didn't exist except in her blurring memories. There were no witnesses to her early life, and this assignment was another bitter reminder of how different she was, how defective and lacking.

She rode the bus home that day and avoided looking at anyone, wiping at her tears with her sleeve, angry at the stupid neighborhood full of people who belonged, hating her teacher for making her feel the deep well of shame. Her mom greeted her at the door with a big smile, and Mariela lashed out with anger. "I hate you. I hate my school. I hate this whole place, and I wish I never came here!"

"What happened? Tell me. I'm here for you. Talk to me, sweetie," Charlotte pleaded.

"I don't have even one picture of me as a baby or little kid. My real mama didn't leave me with anything." She stomped past Charlotte, who had reached to comfort her. She wouldn't understand for many years that poor Mayan mothers didn't have photos of their children. She ran to her room and slammed the door. The last thing she needed was this mom trying to act like she understood when she didn't. The following day, she refused to go to school. She couldn't face all those kids showing their photos and laughing with each other. Charlotte had allowed her to stay home and seemed uncertain about how to make the situation less painful. Mariela was grateful that she could miss school. But it didn't change anything. She would go back to school the next day and the days after that and sit among kids who knew who they were, and she never would.

Charlotte signed her up to play soccer, and she quickly became a star on her team. On the soccer field one rain-soaked fall day, she scored a third time after aggressively controlling the ball and charging toward the goal, leaving defenders in her wake. Parents on the sidelines came out from under umbrellas and applauded, and teammates cheered. At times like this, she beamed proudly and smiled at her teammates, happy to belong to a team. But the feeling only lasted as long as the game.

"Where did you learn to play like that? I wish my daughter was half as aggressive on the field," an enthusiastic father teased her after the game.

She grinned but looked away, unable to say she had learned on the streets and in the orphanage to be aggressive, to kick and fight like her life depended on it. Her hard-hitting forcefulness was born of necessity. There had been no one else to fight for her.

Whatever positive emotions she felt, the heaviness of loss and hurt tethered her and pulled her back into a cloud of shame. It loomed around her and with little warning transformed to rage. She was self-conscious about her looks and suspicious of others' positive comments. She pretended not to care what others thought, and acted tough and aloof, which left potential friends wary of her. She was careful to conceal her anger in the first year, fearful it would be her undoing in her family and at school. As she felt safer, she allowed her fury fuller expression, which should have been a predictor of much stronger storms to come.

She quickly learned to manage what others thought of her, trying on different responses to questions. A popular blond classmate approached her on the playground one day. "Hey, where are you from? You're adopted, huh?"

"I'm from Hawaii," she said. It rolled easily off her tongue. She wouldn't risk saying Guatemala, a poor country that she assumed her classmates wouldn't know.

"Wow, cool, do you surf?"

"Yeah, I used to surf all the time."

"What happened to your parents?"

"They died in Hawaii, so I came here to live with a new family." She was in charge of her own history and could say what she wanted.

When her parents weren't around, she snooped in their bedroom, looking for clues of something—she wasn't sure what. She opened drawers, looked through all their clothes, opened the medicine cabinet. She stared at the photo of two old people on her mom's dresser. The two people in the photo, her mom's parents, were coming to visit, and she had no idea what to expect from them. The resemblance between her mom and this old woman was obvious, and it amazed her. *Do I look like my mama?* She wondered as she flopped on her parents' huge bed, enjoying the luxury and privacy, and allowed her mind to wander. *I can't remember you—what did you look like?* She squinted, trying to bring into focus her Mayan mama, but the image blurred. Concentrating, she focused on what she remembered, but her mama's back walking quickly away was all she could conjure. Her vanished mama.

She pushed away this anguished thought and continued to study her parents' bedroom: the sturdy wooden furniture, the soft pillows and spread, the lamps. She realized that, as strange as it was, this place was becoming familiar. Her life in Guatemala seemed long ago, fading and foreign. "Who was I on the streets in Guatemala, or among all those kids in the orphanage?" she wondered. That life felt far behind her; this life was not yet hers to inhabit.

She gazed at the photos again. This couple would be coming from Arizona in the summer to stay for many weeks. She had never met them but listened carefully when the family talked about them. Grandparents...what did that mean? Could they tell her what to do? Would they like her? Was there something in it for her to welcome these two old people? She straightened the bedspread and left the bedroom to find Jill.

"What are Mom's parents like? Are they nice, and will they buy us things?" she asked.

"They are both nice, and sometimes they buy us things, but not that much, really." We usually do fun stuff when they come, and Grandma tells funny stories. Grandpa always helps with projects. You'll like them, don't worry," Jill said, hardly looking up from her homework.

Then, school was over for the year, and the pace of the days slowed. There were no long homework sessions at the kitchen table on rainy evenings or during early mornings before hurrying to get to school on time. She was relieved when the cold rain finally stopped and she wasn't forced to wear rain gear or heavy coats. The long, warm days going barefoot with windows flung open reminded her of Guatemala.

On the summer day when the grandparents were due to arrive, her mom left instructions to keep the house clean in her absence. She was doing last-minute grocery shopping. "They will be here by six this evening, and I need all of your help to get ready." Charlotte said with panic in her voice that Mariela didn't understand. She opened the refrigerator and reached for a piece of leftover pizza. Her mom would be home soon, but until she arrived, she'd do as she pleased. Chad and Jill wouldn't bother her; they were doing their own thing in other parts of the house. She sat on the couch, turned on the TV, and savored the chewy, cheesy pizza, food she now adored, food that hadn't existed for her less than a year ago.

The grandparents beeped their horn many times as they pulled into the driveway on the crisp-blue-sky day, an hour before they were expected. Everyone in the family stopped what they were doing and ran outside to meet them. Mariela observed as they greeted and stiffly hugged each other. There were no kisses on cheeks as she had seen families in Guatemala do. The grandma and grandpa turned to her.

"You look older than I imagined," said the grandma, looking her up and down. "But still, you are very short, which I guess is not uncommon." Grandma was saggy and gray-haired and said whatever was on her mind. Grandpa, a large, bald man, towered over all of them but was quiet with kind eyes.

Mariela watched as her mom tensed. "Let's watch the comments, Mom," Charlotte said.

"Now don't be all sensitive the minute we get here." Grandma walked into the house and immediately announced how exhausted and hungry she was. Dinner was put on the table in a flurry of activity as Grandma kept talking.

Mariela hadn't seen her mom like this before, quiet but obviously uneasy, trying hard to look like everything was OK. It was strange to see the two of them together, mother and daughter, and they felt heavy together. To Mariela, Grandma was bold and funny and kept things stirred up around the house. In some ways, she realized, it was good to have Grandma around to be the outsider, the focus of attention.

One night Mom and Dad announced they were going out and leaving Grandma and Grandpa in charge. Chad got on the phone immediately with his girlfriend; Jill made herself comfortable reading a book. Grandma, seeing that they would be alone with Mariela, started right in on asking questions. "So, are you glad this family adopted you?" While Mariela considered how to answer this question, Grandma answered for herself, "You should be. You are one lucky girl. They took you out of an orphanage and are giving you a good life in the greatest country. You should be very appreciative, and I hope you are."

"I guess so." The anger was starting to rise, and she felt trapped.

"You guess so—what do you mean?"

"I don't know." She fumbled with her shoestrings and looked away, not knowing what to say. The word *lucky* left a bad taste in her mouth. Finally, she said she was tired and went to her bedroom. She flopped on the bed, fuming. How dumb to tell her she was lucky. Was it lucky to have your real mom dump you on the streets of Guatemala City and never come back? Was it lucky to leave your country and then be surrounded by people who expected you to do things their way? Was it lucky to live in a family where no one looked like you? Was it lucky to have a brother and sister who made good grades, had friends, were happy and friendly, and were loved by two parents they looked like? They were a constant reminder of what she lacked, and there was no way to feel lucky about that.

She started to cry, thinking of all the people who had told her how fortunate she was, how blessed, how special that she had been chosen. She was sick of all of it and never wanted to hear that lie again. She was a discarded kid who had belonged to a poor Mayan woman who had nothing. They had lived on the streets, and maybe her mother died on the streets. She only knew that her mama never came back for her. The anger built as these thoughts raced through her mind. She took a pencil and poked at her skin. She didn't care. She wasn't worth anything to anybody. Miserable and alone, she needed to be held and comforted, but she had no one, she told herself. No one had ever been there for her, and they never would be. "I don't need them. I hate them all." She heard Grandma talking to Jill in hushed tones. *Jill has everyone. I have no one.* She took the pencil and slashed dark lines through a picture of the family.

The following morning, Grandma cornered her and said right in front of Mom, "I think I hurt Mariela's feelings last night when I told her she should be appreciative of all the things you do for her. She got mad and stomped off." Mariela wasn't used to the family saying things like this right up front. Grandma wasn't scared of any of them.

Her mom seemed to consider what to say for a moment, then said quietly, "It's better if you don't interfere, Mom."

Then Grandma looked straight at Mariela. "You're not the only one who's had a rough time of it, child. I went to an orphanage myself when I was twelve, and that was no picnic."

"You were in an orphanage?" Mariela turned toward her.

"Yes, I was. My dad died, and my mom got all depressed having seven kids and no way to feed us. She gave the oldest four of us to a children's home—that's what they called it. That's all I'm going to say. Just don't you be thinking you're the only one who's had it tough. And be thankful that this family wants you, ya hear?"

Mariela turned and left, not angry exactly, although she had every right to be, but more curious about what she had just heard. Her mom was raised by this woman, an orphan like herself, and her mom had adopted her, an orphan. And her mom had a difficult time with both of them. There was the slightest feeling of solidarity with Grandma. She was a tough and angry survivor too, not to be controlled, not to be messed with. Maybe she and Grandma could understand each other, have an alliance that would leave Charlotte baffled on the sidelines.

Chapter 9

Charlotte

> "Maybe you are searching among the branches
> for what only appears in the roots."
> Rumi

Mariela demonstrated her anger and fierce need to control situations on a regular basis within a year. We were shocked to hear that, after being in school in the US less than a year, she forcefully pulled an older boy out of his seat on the school bus and hit his head against the bus window when he made a racial slur against her. She didn't know what the slur meant but knew it was bad by the reaction of the kids on the bus. Her reputation at school as a tough girl was solidified by this much-discussed event.

We had willingly embraced a child of color into our family and failed to recognize what this would mean for her in a predominantly white school and neighborhood. We underestimated her difficulty fitting in and her hostile responses when she felt the sting of not belonging. We were proud of her for standing up for herself but didn't support her doing so with violence. For the first time, I realized that "color-blind," considered a good and achievable trait by progressive people at the time, also meant that well-meaning white people were naïvely ignorant of what people of color had to deal with because they never had to deal with it themselves. She would be on the front lines while we sat on the sidelines of her ongoing struggle. We'd support her but remain ignorant of her experience. And her aggressive, understandable, fury made me worry about her safety.

Once when playing soccer, an opponent tripped her while taking the ball away; it was part of the game but misunderstood as an attack. She pushed the girl to the ground and proceeded to jump on top of her. The parent spectators were horrified as she pummeled the shocked girl. After being pulled off, Mariela sat indignant on the sidelines. "She thinks she can kick me just because I came from an orphanage and my skin is darker than hers. I showed her she can't mess with me," she fumed. Her talent and aggression in sports both thrilled and frustrated her coaches, who wondered if they would be able to redirect her energy. Coaches asked for our help. They wanted her to develop anger control so she could benefit from being successful on a sports team. We agreed that it was a great idea, but a frightening realization that we had limited ability to control her was taking hold.

A well-respected child psychologist friend and colleague was eager to help our family understand, as best he could, what Mariela needed to help her heal.

"How about therapy to help her deal with the abandonment and her story of being unlovable?" I asked one day as we drank tea together in the staff room of our clinic.

"Your family, my dear, is providing the therapy she needs now. Your love and acceptance, listening and soothing is the best thing for her. Therapy will come later, when she's an adolescent and the shit really hits the fan." He laughed. I didn't smile. "What?" he said. "Don't be surprised. All adolescents become unstable for a while. Adopted ones just unravel more." When my face revealed my anxiety, he reassured me with a generous grin. "You'll all be OK. Don't look so grim. You'll get through this. Just keep letting her know she's loved and listen, listen, listen."

One night not long after that conversation, as I tucked her into bed, our continuing evening ritual, Mariela said, "Do you want to hear something really bad?"

"Of course, I do, if you want to tell me." I held my breath in anticipation.

"I saw the soldiers do bad things to my mother. They lay on her and made her cry. I wanted to kill those soldiers."

"Oh, your poor mommy," I began.

"But she didn't have to leave me."

"Maybe your mommy only left you because she didn't know what else to do."

"You don't know that. You don't know anything." A wall went up. I had pushed too hard, commented on what she told me, and offered her another way to look at it. I was an experienced mom and a therapist, and I couldn't seem to get it right for her. My earnest attempts fell short again.

I was desperate to infuse her heart with love and heal the wounds of her abandonment and was always on the lookout for opportunities. I wanted to envelop her in a protective cocoon. If she would allow enough love and goodness in, I trusted the damage of her early years would be repaired.

My passion to heal Mariela gave my life a new direction, and less satisfying endeavors faded into the background as I focused on her. "It's the most important thing I've ever done," I told friends. The doubt I had initially felt about her had transformed into an intense bond and commitment that was razor sharp. I likened Mariela to an empty vessel who would receive our love until it filled and expanded her heart.

I was a devoted mother to my two older children, having unconditionally loved them since the day they were born. I had never questioned that love. I didn't question my love for Mariela either, but my determination to help her heal came from an intense desire to get it right for her, so she could open her heart to herself and to those of us who loved her. I cherished the times when I felt she was opening to the love. I soared with enthusiasm, but when my attempts were met with anger or withdrawal, as they often were, I felt sad and defeated.

"She's like a surly, ill-tempered teenager, and she's only ten or maybe eleven," I lamented to Ann, a single friend with no children who had considered adopting until she was dissuaded by stories of heartache caused by adolescent adoptees. "The difficult thing is trying to make up for lost time, like a race against the clock to get enough bonding before she pulls away as any normal teenager will do," I said.

"Makes me happy with my decision not to adopt," Ann said with a look of resignation. I saw Ann's conclusion as a challenge. I believed with all my heart that love would heal, and I was willing to invest whatever it took.

I became the object of Mariela's intense focus, and Chris, Chad, and Jill were often ignored or seen as a threat to our bond. She shadowed me relentlessly and needed endless reassurance. "Do you still love me?" was her constant query. In the early months, this was endearing, but her need for reassurance didn't ease off, and I started to feel drained by her continual need for it. I began to suspect that my outpouring of love and reassurance was trying to fill a vessel that had a hole in the bottom. Nothing seemed to be enough; she was never satisfied. As soon as she got what she wanted, she invariably wanted more of it, whether it was attention, food, or belongings. "She's insatiable," I'd mumble to myself as I tried to please and comfort her. I wanted so badly to stitch her wounds so her heart could repair and open to us, but I felt completely ineffective in my attempts.

Her initial enthusiasm for Chad and Jill had waned. She enjoyed their attention but also resented them, envious of their position as biological children. "You love them more than me. Don't pretend you don't. They look like you; I don't!" she screamed in heavily accented English as she stomped out of the room one evening. Trying to reassure her did no good. At times like these, my thoughts went to the darling, smiling girl in the orphanage who had begged us to take her. It reminded me of fantasizing of the lover not chosen when the going got tough with the chosen one. I banished those thoughts quickly.

Mariela frequently maneuvered to put herself between me and

her brother or sister and did things to manipulate my attention away from them. Happiest when she was wrapped around me tightly, restricting any movement away from her, she'd sit on my lap with her face close to mine until I needed to get some space to breathe and would gently move her. Interpreted as rejection, she would walk away angry and hurt and slam her bedroom door minutes after she had been embracing me with warmth. Anything interpreted as rejection was fodder for her strongly held belief that she was defective. Jill was affectionate by nature, and when I spontaneously hugged her or tucked her into bed at night, Mariela pouted and hissed under her breath. Frustrated by her response, I did my best to convince her that there was plenty of love to go around. I was beginning to wonder if no matter what I said and did, even with the utmost conviction, wouldn't ever move her away from the "truth" of her early experiences.

Jill, who had changed positions from youngest to middle child and was always a peacemaker, offered, "Mom, if she is going to get all mad, you don't need to tuck me in. It's OK—she needs you more..." I was uneasy with this capitulation to Mariela's acting out but reasoned that catering to her demands was temporary until she started to feel more secure in our family. Years later, Jill would tell me through tears how she had resented putting her own needs aside, how she resented Mariela for being so demanding. I had depended on Jill's good nature and willingness to subsume her own needs so I could try to increase Mariela's security.

She had been with us just over a year when the proverbial honeymoon, which had been brief and stormy, ended like a car screeching into a collision. One Saturday morning as we all did chores before heading out to watch Chad's soccer game, I asked Mariela to participate by emptying the household trash cans into the big one outside. She looked at me defiantly. "No, I'm not here to work for your family," she snarled.

Her resistance and opposition were starting to fully occupy the family landscape. I explained calmly that we were all family and all of us contributed, pointing out that Chad and Jill were busy doing their chores also, but she remained hostile and didn't budge. Handing her a garbage bag, I urged, "Here, take this outside to empty it, please." She let it drop, and the rubbish spilled down the stairs, leaving an ugly trail. She smirked. I tried to calm myself. "Let's pick up this mess so you can take it outside." My frustration mounted, but I was determined to avoid showing her my anger. She refused, so I picked it up myself, muttering as I did but determined to avoid power struggles I couldn't win.

After many such confrontations, I decreased my requests of her. It wasn't long before all the interactions in our family changed, as we were all increasingly controlled by Mariela's anger and opposition. Even Chad and Jill avoided challenging her and feared an eruption of anger. We were afraid to punish her for noncompliance, believing it could undermine her sense of safety and security with us. I thought that she was manipulating us by her hostile tantrums, pouting, and frequent outbursts, but I couldn't be sure and decided to err on the side of providing continued support and love, with some limits on behavior that was clearly out of line. Believing that she could be healed by understanding and devotion, I practiced more patience than was normal for me and encouraged my family to hang in there during this difficult time.

Believing Mariela would benefit from spending time with a child of similar background, I contacted our adoption agency, and they provided the contact information for a girl who had been in the same orphanage as Mariela. She had been adopted about six months after Mariela by a single mom living only an hour away. I called the mom, Diane, and suggested we get the two girls together.

"That would be great. It might help normalize their experiences," said Diane, who was friendly and open. "Yes, it would be great if they could develop a long-lasting friendship since they share a similar early-life experience," I added. Diane and I enthusiastically set a date, feeling hopeful about the connection the girls would make.

Mariela seemed mildly excited to see Marta but expressed some reservations. "I knew her, but she wasn't my friend, and I didn't play with her much. She wasn't very smart. Just because we were both orphans doesn't mean we liked each other," she said. I had imagined they would talk about shared experiences in Guatemala, share their stories of adjustment, and maybe develop a friendship that Diane and I would be thrilled to support. Diane and I sat in the living room drinking coffee and talking while the two girls sat on swings in our yard.

"Do you ever regret adopting?" Diane asked me after we had talked thirty minutes or so about the challenges we had faced. Could I be honest with her? I did have regrets when I was at my wits' end and felt disheartening frustration. Typically, after feeling this regret, I'd feel guilty and wonder about my misgivings. It didn't seem right. I loved her, and that love was unconditional, wasn't it?

"No, I don't have regrets," I heard myself say, knowing it wasn't the whole truth. "It hasn't been easy, but we have all learned so much about love. Worthwhile endeavors are often difficult," I added in the same breath. "How about you?" I ventured.

"Well, sometimes I'm not sure taking these kids out of their country is a good thing. I wonder if giving the money to an orphanage to improve care there would be a better thing. Of course, they live on the streets after they turn fourteen, I hear. Not to mention that corrupt government would no doubt pocket the money." She took a sip of her coffee and added, "I'm not sure I'd do it again, although I do love Marta. I only see struggles ahead, no clear sailing." Diane looked me in the eyes, waiting.

That level of honesty was both liberating and unnerving. I hadn't dared voice my ambivalence and confusion about adopting Mariela. I wondered often about the arrogance and idealism that had motivated me, or anyone, to pluck a child out of her country, knowing so little of her prior life and culture, with the expectation that in the rich soil of our family, she would grow and flourish. I was no longer sure we had done a good thing, certainly not for our family's ease but perhaps not even for Mariela.

"No, honestly, I'm not so sure it is best for anyone," I said, disclosing this well-guarded feeling. "It's been much more difficult than I ever imagined." Then I back-paddled quickly, "But we all love her and have a hard time imagining life without her. Things worth doing are not always easy." I smiled, aware I was repeating myself. "We're devoted to her and will make it work," I added hastily. Was I trying to convince Diane or myself?

"Do you know what happened to her family?" Diane asked.

"No, not really. And I suspect what we were told was all fabricated. Mariela says her mother left her at a marketplace. She remembers seeing her walk away."

"How tragic," said Diane. "Marta was left at the orphanage by an aunt who said she couldn't keep her any longer."

"These girls have lost so much," I said.

"And now they have a chance at a new life here."

"When you bond with a child, you're willing to do whatever it takes to help them."

"It's a good thing. It helps when the going gets tough," Diane said just as the girls came inside and the most honest discussion I had dared to have ended.

After Diane and Marta left that day, I sat for a long time considering what I had said to Diane. I desperately wanted to make things right for Mariela. I loved her, we all did, but I couldn't seem to convince her of that. Her mama had left or lost her on the streets, and she had been swept up and put in an overcrowded orphanage. What had possessed me to think I could swoop in, rescue her from her fate as an orphaned child in war-torn Guatemala, and turn her story around, make it right for her?

Chapter 10

Charlotte

"Grace comes to forgive and then forgive again."
Rumi

"That little shit doesn't know how good she has it," said an opinionated coworker in an awkward attempt to be supportive when I rushed in late to work and shared that an argument with Mariela had held me up. It was pouring rain and cold outside, but she had refused to wear a coat, throwing it at me as I handed it to her. I had relented after she screamed that I couldn't tell her what to wear.

"Does she have any idea what a nice life you've given her?" another coworker added.

Their attempts at support weren't helpful. Their comments left me feeling justified in my anger and frustration but just as quickly feeling guilt for judging my orphaned child for her aggressive behaviors, blaming myself for expecting too much from her.

Sometimes things got easier for days at a time, and I'd reel with hope. "Come for dinner, Mariela—we are all at the table," I'd say, and we'd all tense, ready for a snarl from her bedroom.

"I'm coming…" she'd answer, sounding pleasant. Tentative smiles and raised eyebrows showed our relief. She could be funny and engaging, and at those times, we'd laugh with her, delighted at her quick humor. "I run faster than any girl on my track team. I ran from mean kids in the orphanage; that's where I got my training," she'd banter.

We laughed with her and enjoyed the shared moment of openness. Shifting sands of emotion defined our life with Mariela.

During the following year, things shifted more toward the harder. There were unreasonable demands followed by loud tantrums, then at times complete inexplicable meltdowns that left us bewildered and exhausted. Family vacations were nightmares. "How is it possible for one child to completely spoil the fun? We simply can't let her take over. We must be strong and loving at the same time and show her we can have a good time no matter what she does," I proclaimed to Chris before a five-day camping trip.

My resolve was abandoned a few days later when she sat down on a hiking trail, refusing to go farther. "I hate walking in the woods. I'm finished, and you can't make me walk more!" she screamed. The rest of the family walked on, and I stayed behind with her as the voices of my family trailed off into the distance. I tried to figure out how to stay calm, set some limits, and convince her that there was something in it for her to cooperate. We had learned by then that putting a gentle hand on her to direct her caused severe reactivity. She kicked and screamed and resisted like her life depended upon her staying in control. My confidence about parenting her had diminished; I felt controlled by and held hostage to her hostility. Demonstrating love and support when I felt like screaming was often difficult to pull off. The friend who had told me that our family was the "therapy" she needed didn't know how much energy it took to get through each day. It wasn't easy to understand or meet her complex needs. Taking care of my own needs while providing a therapeutic environment for her often felt like too much of a challenge. But I still firmly believed that once through the "adjusting phase," then the "testing phase," she would settle into a better place where she understood she was loved and trust our good intentions. We tried family therapy for several months, but it became clear that the therapist was at a loss to help us navigate the fine balance of providing a secure environment and demonstrating unconditional love while setting necessary limits.

The therapist said, "It is very difficult to change the dynamics when Mariela is completely unmotivated to do so. She doesn't seem to be bonded enough to care what happens. I'm not sure she has found a real sense of belonging in your home." This statement, meant to be an observation, delivered a punch of harsh reality I was unprepared to hear.

"I wonder why I did this to our lives," I finally confessed to Barb, my friend who had endless patience and interest listening to how things were going with Mariela. "Things were so easy before her..." I confided but added a weak laugh to lessen the impact of what I was saying. "I knew adopting her would be a challenge, but I never expected it to be this hard. Climbing Mt. Everest would have been easier, and I would have gotten a lot more accolades," I said.

"Don't beat yourself up. You've got a good heart, and you gave a kid a chance. You don't have control over what she is able to do with that chance," she said with empathy. "Do what you can until she turns eighteen. If things don't turn out like you hope, she'll be an adult, and everyone can move on." Hearing it like that, it seemed like a matter of holding on and doing my best until I let her go. The idea was as unappealing as it was unthinkable. I wasn't good at letting go of things that didn't work well; I only knew how to dig in and try harder. Giving up on my fantasized adoption story of rescue and healing seemed as unattainable as swimming the English Channel.

My hope was that she would heal with enough love and support, and my work was to find the keys to unlock and heal her heart. Years later, I would recognize that this pattern of thinking was similar to the ones I had with my mother and with Chris. I felt responsible for taking emotional care and winning the love of impossible people in order to bind them to me, motivated by my own sense of inadequacy. Being a caregiver fit like a well-warn glove. It was what I had been doing since childhood.

Once when feeling desperate for support, I called Janice at the adoption agency. We had attended a three-session class while we were waiting to adopt Mariela, but the information hadn't seemed as relevant as it did now. She reassured me. "She's well out of the honeymoon phase that most older adoptees go through and into testing you to be sure you are really there for her. Hang in there with her; she expects you to abandon her like her mother did. These older children aren't easy, but all they really need is love and commitment." It helped to hear again that we needed to stand firm in our commitment and love and show her we were with her for the long haul no matter what. I encouraged the family with new resolve. "We have to demonstrate that we love her and are here for her; come hell or high water, we'll never leave her. Then, she'll learn to trust us, and things will settle down." I looked around the room at my husband, son, and daughter and saw their skeptical nods of half-hearted agreement.

Mariela's angry lashing out, which I saw as a misguided plea for reassurance, got more sophisticated as her English improved.

"You've never loved me—it's all an act."

"I hate all of you!"

"You're not my real family."

"I never asked to be part of this family."

As I groveled to assure her of our devotion, she remained unfaltering in her story of rejection. It helped to imagine myself, as Susan, a good therapist friend, suggested, as a grounded and steady oak tree receiving the battering winds of her rage that had never been expressed to her biological mother.

Susan continued, "You adopted a child who is already who she is and who she will become. It's really more like a marriage; you can do very little to change her, and trying so hard is exhausting you." She looked at me with caring concern. I didn't doubt that what she said was true, but I wasn't ready to give up trying. I thought of myself at the wheel of a big ship struggling with all my might to change the course. Mariela was still a child amenable to change if I was willing to stay at the wheel, I thought.

Often at night when the house was quiet, I'd fitfully replay scenarios I'd had with her, judging myself for mishandling situations, imagining there was a way to instill trust and cooperation if only I could find the puzzle piece. I vowed to do better.

Then, unpredictably, she'd delight all of us with a funny antic or good-natured cooperation. She'd come home from school in a great mood and wrap her arms around my waist, telling me how much she loved me. She would romp with delight with our terrier or amaze us with all that she had learned in such a short time. She would shoot baskets with Chad or challenge Jill to a game of badminton. Or she'd cry and be vulnerable and tell me how much she missed her friends from the orphanage. My heart expanded with hope. But those easy and enjoyable times didn't last long, and when she fell back into hostile acting out and hateful rages, my distress intensified.

With friends, I frequently launched into a litany of frustrations or small triumphs about Mariela, not sensing that they were tired of hearing about the Mayan girl who had taken over my life. One suggested that she may never trust or attach and that I needed to prepare myself for that. Acceptance of this was unimaginable; it would have been like walking away from a nearly built home I had dreamed of and designed. I could not accept that there were limitations to what love and determination could change and was not ready to discard this well-worn strategy that was fundamental to who I was.

Chad and Jill continued to do well in school, on sports teams, and with friends, but they were often tense at home as they worried about the next tirade that would send our once-tranquil home into turmoil. It couldn't have been easy for Mariela to witness her siblings excel while she struggled with demons none of us could see. I didn't compare Chad's or Jill's accomplishments or behavior to hers and never set my biological kids as a standard for her to attain. But I misjudged how much she measured herself against them and always felt deficient. She was short, only 4'11", and would never grow taller, had dark skin, spoke with an accent, and didn't have the solid footing and sense of belonging that Chad and Jill took for granted as our biological children.

"You want me to be just like them, but I don't want to be like them, and I never will!" she yelled. I told her simply that she was valued and loved for who she was, and I naïvely assumed at some point she would believe that. But she couldn't absorb these sentiments or believe she was worthy of them. She brimmed with self-loathing, and the negative voices in her head, whose strength and tenacity I underestimated, were much stronger than the positive ones I was determined to impart. The discord inherent in our family dynamics, which included Mariela's sense that she would never be enough, brewed below the surface.

"I thought she was healing, that we had unlocked the secret to bonding her to us, to trusting our love," I cried after the kids were in bed while debriefing a tough interaction with Chris.

"Two steps forward, two steps back," he responded dispassionately, which was his way of dealing with the ups and downs of our life with Mariela. The full emotional weight of our relationship with Mariela was beginning to fall on my shoulders. Chris frequently took her to sports practices and helped her with math homework but did so in an impassive manner, perhaps to balance my intense focus, I reasoned.

My unconscious hope that adopting Mariela could strengthen our marriage was misguided, and the reality that our already disconnecting marriage was being further frayed by regular upheavals could not be denied. My attempts to reach out to Chris for support and solidarity were met with stony silence. It was clear that he found our marriage a difficult burden and no longer fun. He increasingly buried himself in work and recreation with Chad and Jill. He didn't remind me that I was the one who had wanted to adopt Mariela so desperately. He didn't have to. I had plenty of self-imposed guilt about throwing our family into chaos.

I soon became painfully aware that instead of bringing us closer, parenting Mariela left Chris and me feeling incompetent, confused, and increasingly unable to reach to each other for solace. Our emotional styles were different, and our marriage wasn't strong enough to withstand the frequent storms. I needed to process our frustrations, and Chris tended to stew silently. We lacked the resources to recover together from the upheaval. I felt more and more alone, and my emotional resources were fully taxed from parenting Mariela and two teenagers. I worried about our growing estrangement but didn't know how to build a bridge to Chris and had begun to doubt if I had the energy and desire to do the work. Our marriage had been through ups and downs over the years, but a part of me believed we had enough history and fortitude to work through hard times. Like many women, I had been the glue, the caregiver, the relationship sustainer. Subjugating my own needs for the welfare of others didn't bring me the fulfillment it once had, but it did provide a secure niche that I had been raised to believe was my role.

"Let's talk about our marriage and what we can do to strengthen it." I attempted to start a conversation again one evening that I hoped might begin to shift things. I was tired of living by the same rules and was asking for change. It would be better for both of us if he could engage more, express his feelings, and open up to me, I reasoned.

"Please, I'm exhausted, and this kind of talk gets us nowhere," Chris said while getting ready to stand up from where he had been sitting.

"It may get us nowhere, but our marriage is going downhill fast, and I can't rescue it alone." I could feel the pressure in my voice building, trying to get his attention, shake him up, make him see how unhappy I was.

"Charlotte, I've asked you to give me some space. I don't know what to do to make you happy," Chris said, his voice diminished, almost begging me to back off.

"I just want to be able to work on things together, to talk and share what we're feeling." The tears were welling in my eyes, and now I was begging.

Years later I would see the folly of these conversations. I was asking for something that he had no idea how to give, and I felt hurt and offended that he wouldn't give me what I needed. Chris was happy enough with the status quo of our marriage, and my newly expressed discontent was frightening and frustrating. We had reached an impasse.

Mariela had been in our family a little more than three tough years when I told Chris I couldn't coax or cajole him anymore; I needed his full participation with her and in our marriage. I had outgrown my focus on Chris's needs at the expense of my own and had begun to feel my own strength and my unmet needs. I wanted to discard the restrictions I had placed on myself and grow intentionally in a new direction. Our already fragile bond was further stressed. The tie that bound us together for twenty years loosened and frayed when I turned inward. Laughter became less common, I turned more often to women friends for comfort and support, and he began to work late and stay away from home. One Saturday morning while changing our bed sheets together, he commented, "We've been doing this so many years. I wonder how many more…?" His voice trailed off.

"What are you saying?" I stopped struggling with the sheets and asked.

"Nothing really," he answered under his breath. I continued with the sheets but felt a blow to my stomach. A veil of denial lifted, and I saw the truth. Our marriage was perhaps beyond repair. Neither of us was happy. We looked at each other across the bed for a moment, then turned away, both sealing our pain within and saying nothing. I could never say for sure when the marriage became so distant, so difficult, so charged with despair, but attempts at resuscitation were futile, and we both knew it.

He had found escape elsewhere, with a younger woman at his office. Months earlier, when he announced his intention to go night skiing one night a week, I agreed to his plan, thinking the respite from family tension would be good. Then one evening, I awoke at midnight and discovered he still wasn't home. I sat on our couch, hugged my knees to my chest by the light of a table lamp and waited in the early-morning hours until he arrived, alcohol on his breath and sheepish. I knew the ski slope had closed many hours earlier. My final trance of denial lifted.

Stunned to learn that he had been seeing another woman for months, I sat in disbelief. Heartbroken and angry, I felt stupid for trusting him. Clobbered with the sobering realization that love and care of another offered no assurances of their fidelity, I was furious. Attempts to reconcile and forgive, done in whispers when our children weren't within earshot, were pointless. There was too much bitterness, anger, and distrust. He continued to stay involved with the other woman, and I was unwilling to wait it out. After several months of upheaval, Chris packed his things while the kids and I watched. Back and forth from the house, he carried his things, quickly, silently, shamefully, until on the final trip, he simply turned with a guilty small wave. We stood for a while until I broke the silence. "We'll get through this, you guys. You are loved; this has nothing to do with you. We both love you and always will," I managed to say and then suggested we rent a movie.

It was useless. We didn't know what else to do, but none of us could watch the movie. The kids gradually left the room, and I was alone. My husband of twenty-one years, my high school sweetheart, the father of my kids, had just left, and I wanted to hurt him, beg him to come back, kick him, and tell him we needed him. I was a mess and had no idea how to heal our fractured family or myself.

Chad, a freshman in college, believed he could mediate a reconciliation between us. He made some attempts, and we loved him for it, but by then, to be honest, I had taken my cards off the table. Jill, a high-achieving sophomore in high school, studied harder and ran faster on her track team to keep from feeling anything. She and her dad had been very close, and his leaving had unsettled her at a time when she needed grounding. I knew she was grieving and in turmoil, but my attempts to comfort her and suggest she talk to a counselor were met with walled-off silence, another reminder of how little control I had not just with Mariela and Chris but with all the loved ones in my life.

Mariela's reaction to the only father she knew leaving the family was "Good riddance, who needs him?" But I knew this was her defense against another abandonment. Mariela's relationship with Chris was less intense than with me. They were less reactive to each other and much less involved emotionally, but they had shared tender moments playing basketball, board games, and reading together. Our ruptured family couldn't have been easy for her, but her defensive attitude made it easy to overlook her loss, and at the time, I was often too distraught to focus on it. In guilt-ridden moments, I admonished myself for bringing Mariela into a troubled family that I should have predicted would fall apart, leaving her cleaved again. Or my perspective shifted, and I imagined our marriage surviving had I not been obsessed with the ill-advised idea to adopt an older child. Either way, during my worst times, I shouldered total responsibility for failure.

One evening when I told her she had to do homework and couldn't watch TV, she lashed out. "I can see why he left you." I tried to ignore her wrath, but in my tenuous state, it was a stab to my heart. At those times, I reeled with uncertainty about raising her on my own. Chris assumed the kids would stay with me; he had moved in with his girlfriend. He wanted to see them, but it would be months before they were willing. I would have welcomed a break from Mariela but didn't want to destabilize her by making her see him until she was ready. At times when I was bolstered by friends, my perspective allowed a kinder and fuller picture of the end of my marriage as not so much a failure but a change that allowed me to grow. But in those days, I couldn't hold on to that perspective for very long, and soon I'd be back in an ugly stew of self-recrimination, anger, and fear about the future.

I was a frightened, lonely, divorced mom with an adolescent spiraling out of control. Mariela taxed my limited energy with her nasty attitude and accusations that seemed undeserved. "I think Mariela did you guys in. She is such an emotional drain," said Kathy one day as we hiked in the gorge. She was a dear friend I had known for fifteen years; we often shared outdoor adventures together, and both of us were recently divorced. My former marriage, a frequent topic of conversation with Kathy, wasn't helped by the constant blistering winds that Mariela's budding adolescence delivered, and most of my closest friends who knew me before Mariela came into my life assumed she was the culprit of my marital demise. I knew she was not to blame for a marriage that perhaps wasn't meant to last even the two decades it had.

I had been warned by a therapist that adopted kids often become completely destabilized in adolescence, and I had tried to fortify myself for this stage. The divorce left me less able to cope and Mariela fully armored and ready for battle against my depleted defenses. What I had hoped were transitory problems, adjustments to the divorce and to adolescence, I began to suspect were personality traits, honed by life experiences and less amenable to change.

"Mariela, I care about you, and I can't let you leave the house at night," I said as she got ready to leave through the back door at nine on a school night to meet friends. "You're still young, and it's my job to set limits, so you will be safe. Let's talk about what you want to do this weekend and try to reach a compromise," I heard myself pleading.

"Don't try to act like you care. You just want to control me, but you can't!" She stormed toward her room. I had won this one battle, but I knew there would be more to come, and I began to suspect that she was right. I wouldn't be able to control her. We lacked the glue that binds child to parent and helps the child trust that the parent is acting with love on their behalf. The more I tried to persuade and influence her, the greater contempt she had. Exposing my vulnerability to win her cooperation backfired, and her hostility increased.

With so few years in the family before sliding into adolescence, Mariela wrenched away from our fractured family with speed and ferocity by thirteen. She was determined to do what she wanted without my interference, and she became good at covering her tracks. She easily outmaneuvered me, and when I caught her doing what I had forbidden, her pleas were calculated to wear me down, which she often did.

Mariela's eighth-grade teacher with whom I had shared her history called me one day. "She seems distressed and short-tempered. She's picking fights and cussing, and her grades are declining. She's a smart girl, but her behavior will continue to cause her problems. I know she's been through a lot, but we need to get her back on track," she said, looking to me for help. Over the years, I often heard from teachers that she was very smart. She learned quickly and had always done well in school. Then, she stopped trying to do well and seemed determined to fail.

"My husband and I just divorced, and I plan to get her into counseling to deal with it," I said. The truth was she had refused to go to counseling, but I wasn't done trying.

"That can't be easy for her considering all the losses she has had in her life. No wonder she's having a tough time." She hadn't meant to slam me with guilt, but there it was. I had failed Mariela by not keeping my marriage together. I hated Chris for not being there to shoulder this shame with me.

Balancing my full-time work at a mental health clinic with parenting left me too exhausted to do either of them wholeheartedly; I was nagged by a sense of incompetence on all fronts. I was alone for the first time since I married at twenty, and it was a rude awakening how dependent I had been on Chris. During the first winter I was single, a large branch crashed onto our roof during an ice storm and came tearing through the ceiling of our living room, a terrifying experience that left me shaken and weeping.

Within months of Chris moving out, I had jumped into the dating scene to try to distract myself and prove I was still desirable. Chris's affair had messed with my confidence. Part of me knew I'd be better off focusing on the feelings stirred up by being alone, but my desire to bury feelings felt urgent. My friends commented on my frantic social schedule. "You need to get to know yourself, Charlotte. Go deep into your core and see who is there," said my therapist friend and coworker who had done a lot of work on himself since his divorce. "You stay so busy and distracted, and it seems like it's an attempt to keep from feeling something you absolutely need to feel." I couldn't deny that I was exhausted and no closer to feeling a connection with myself.

Months later, I found a therapist who helped me slow down and look closer at myself, exploring my tendency to take on emotionally distant and impossibly unattached people in an attempt to right the pain of my childhood with my narcissist mother. My misguided attempts to prove myself lovable left me searching outside myself for validation and self-worth. This wasn't a completely new insight, but the pattern revealed itself as if I was waking from a dream. I was vulnerable and open. For the first time, I felt the pit of loneliness and unmet need for affection from my mother and father, neither of them able to show or express love. I felt the yearning for connection and acceptance that I worked hard to earn, and I allowed myself to weep and feel compassion for myself.

My therapist, a kind man with a wicked sense of humor and razor-sharp intuition, set me on a healing path that I would follow for years to come. He wisely counseled that insight, behavior change, and practice would help me avoid falling into painful patterns that weren't helpful. I was determined to work hard to release the grip of past compulsions. The vacillation between anger and righteous indignation and sadness and self-doubt at last slowed, and I found a more grounded middle space. I learned to tolerate painful feelings and confusion, how to soothe myself and not further shame myself by harsh self-judgments. This acquisition of skill didn't translate to inner transformation, as I hoped, however. That would take years.

Chris had moved on quickly but not with the woman with whom he had the affair. That relationship ended within months after their tryst delivered the final blow to our ailing marriage. He got involved and later married a younger woman with two children and was in the thick of helping her raise them, leaving me with the sole responsibility of a college student and two adolescents, one distressed by our divorce and the other one gone off the rails and needing therapy but refusing it.

The miserable feelings fomented by Chris's affair and his rapid departure from our marriage didn't heal quickly or easily, but I became less reactive and more able to see the dynamic leading to our demise more clearly. I often felt bitter toward him despite my best efforts, but I worked hard to keep my reactions neutral in front of our kids. I wasn't always successful. When I was alone, I sometimes dissolved into waves of bitterness and hurt and it took hours to regain my equilibrium. It was a jagged process..

Over time, I pulled myself together more quickly, and I actually started to feel the beginnings of the neutrality toward Chris that I had become so accustomed to faking. I began to understand that our divorce was positive and even inevitable. We had been trapped by an unconscious dynamic that didn't provide fertile soil for growth, and his leaving with someone else, while hurtful, freed us from a painful pattern.

As Mariela moved further into adolescence, she rarely missed an opportunity to challenge me, and after Chris left, her aggression intensified. She opposed all my attempts to set limits and control her. I was no match for her strong will by myself. I had complained that Chris was not involved enough when we were married, but when we were together, I knew he had my back, at least. I counted on him to listen to my frustrations and support my efforts. After he left, I felt alone on a wrecked ship and scared about what lay ahead in the troubled waters. The life raft I wanted to be for my kids was unsteady, and I wasn't sure I could keep us afloat.

The hours of listening to Mariela as she talked openly about her mother and her years in the orphanage had sealed the loving bond I had with her, but those days came to an end. She shut down and walled off her early childhood years and would no longer talk about them. All the doors to her heart banged shut in adolescence, and there was no more prying the door open. It was bolted. My therapist shared his belief that I was a safe receptacle for the anger she hadn't expressed toward her mother for abandoning her. "You just have to let her emote and express her anger. Work on being nonreactive. She's a hurting adolescent who doesn't know where she belongs. There is a river of sorrow behind her rage," he wisely stated, and I shifted to empathy for her.

Stiffening my back, I faced her onslaught of anger, telling myself I needed to withstand her blustering storms. But I often felt sorry for myself. I didn't deserve her anger and had done nothing to hurt her, I'd say to myself, regretting the day I walked into the orphanage to claim her. "This is harder than I ever imagined. I'm so ready to be done with her," I cried. Later, when I regained my perspective and internal strength, I reminded myself of her instability and sadness, and my empathy would help loving feelings surface again.

"Shit, there is no place to be with this. No easy answers, nothing I can do but wait out her adolescent turmoil," I said to my friend Barbara as we walked together at lunch break from work. "Kids mature and get out of these miserable adolescent stages. I just have to hang in there and love her." Barbara had heard it all before and was always a good listener, but I knew I must be trying her patience with my endless talk of Mariela. Before walking back into the mental health clinic where I put in forty hours a week trying to help others adjust to a multitude of internal and external stressors, I tried to lighten the talk and gather my resources.

"So, do you have any fun plans for the weekend?" I asked Barbara.

"Yes, Dave and I are off to the beach. How about you?"

"Um, not sure yet, but we'll think of something," I said, knowing that whatever I did with Jill and Mariela, it would involve managing my feelings, an exhausting task.

Back in the clinic, I took a few minutes to ready myself to face a group of young mothers who were experiencing depression and anxiety. They filed into the room, happy to be there for the support, skills, and friendship the group offered. Within minutes, I put aside my raw feelings and focused on the young women who had been brave enough to walk through the door to tell their stories to each other. The group ended, and they walked out looking lighter and a bit more hopeful, bolstered from the support. I was envious. I needed a support group, a place to connect with others who struggled when there were no easy answers. I wanted to be understood and comforted by others who had dealt with similar life experiences.

When I talked to the social worker at the adoption agency, I had asked her if she knew of resources for adoptive parents.

"No, we don't know of anything, but it's a great idea. Perhaps you would be the perfect person to start a support group and get the support you need also?" she suggested in an enthusiastic tone that I found maddening. *Does she have any idea how strapped I am for time or energy? Evidently not,* I said to myself, feeling resentment at the agency that had facilitated the adoption, then left me to figure things out.

My therapist was a lifeline of support, but a group of supportive women stuck in compulsive patterns trying to take care of others would have been helpful. I had attended an Al-Anon support group at a friend's urging, but it didn't seem like a fit. Besides, I told myself, much of what I heard was old news. While sitting in the Al-Anon groups, which were primarily attended by partners of substance abusers, I focused on the ways I was different from the other women. They stayed in destructive relationships, I said, while I made a commitment to a child, an orphaned child, whom I could not abandon. I already knew I couldn't change Mariela; I already understood my self-esteem was tied to helping others; and I realized my mother's narcissism kept me hungry for approval and acceptance. Later, I would more fully understand that knowing the origins of the problem and having the skills to change behavior did little to emotionally or spiritually change my relationship to myself. That would take a lot more practice. Al-Anon could have helped me change my relationship with myself, but I wasn't ready for that.

If only I could find a skillful therapist for Mariela who would help her heal from her childhood losses, I reasoned, then Mariela's problems would move off the center stage of my life. I couldn't change that Maria, Mariela's mother, left her on the streets to an unknown fate and never returned, but perhaps a therapist could help her change the story about it, so she could understand that she was not the cause of the abandonment. Several times during the years, she had seen a therapist briefly but had always refused to return after a few sessions. It had seemed counterproductive to force her, but I approached the subject gently again.

"I've heard there is a very nice counselor who helps teenagers and talks about anything they want. Maybe it would be good for you to talk to her about your life. What do you think?" I had already made an appointment and now had to convince her to go. "You might even want to talk to her about your mama, about what happened in Guatemala. It could help you." I gently coaxed.

She scowled. "What do you know? Don't talk to me about my mama. I'm done with her. She left me like a piece of garbage on the street. I don't want to talk about her."

"I don't know what happened with your mom. But I do know that you didn't deserve to be left. She lost you, and we found you. Come here. I'm here for you," I said through tears, holding out my arms to her.

But she stiffened and stayed where she was. Her eyes filled with tears that she quickly wiped away with a sleeve; then she sneered. "I don't want to talk to some stranger. Why don't you go if you want to talk to a counselor?"

Eventually, she agreed to talk to another therapist that a friend recommended, but I never knew if she talked about her first mama, about being abandoned, about all she lost and hadn't found. Again, she refused to see the therapist after a few sessions, saying it made her feel worse.

"I'm sorry, but I can't physically make her come see you. I wish I could, but she's refusing," I said to the therapist upon whom I had put my hopes.

"She will learn to trust and heal through her relationship with you. Hang in there with her. This will get easier, I hope" were her parting words. There it was again. I could heal her with ultra-loving therapeutic mothering skills. It was said to give me hope, but it further locked me into a pattern. Every opening Mariela gave me, I forged ahead with statements meant to convey my love and commitment. My efforts, however, seemed as futile as mine had been at getting my own mother's approval.

While I expended energy trying to understand and comfort her with expectations that my efforts would heal her wounds, my own wounds with my mother festered. My daughter and my mother were a source of grief and frustration and would remain so for years. I likened both of them to a thousand-piece puzzle of clear blue sky that could take years to solve, but I believed it was possible.

Chapter 11

Mariela

"People only see what they are prepared to see."
Ralph Waldo Emerson

Mariela considered her family as she sat outside high in a tree looking at the back of her home. By now, she could better predict the family members, and each presented their own challenge. Her father, Chris, was less willing to bend to her will and often seemed to be off in his own world. Since he left the family, she found him easier to manipulate. He seemed eager for her to like him and didn't enforce the rules like Charlotte insisted on doing. He acted like he cared about her at times, but at other times, hard as she tried, she could not keep his attention.

Her mom was a social worker; she had lots of friends and was always busy doing something. She held the family together. They all looked to her for direction. She was the one in charge but, in a strange way, didn't seem to know it or use the power she had. Getting her attention had been the grand prize, but Mariela was no longer willing to grovel for it as she had in the early days. And Mariela didn't entirely trust it anyway; her mom could be pretending to care about her. Anyone who had so much power over others could simply withdraw their love and leave a vacuum too great to bear. She wasn't ever falling for that again. She had done a good job of pushing her mom away by being rude and uncooperative, just to see what would happen. Her mom stubbornly hung in there with loving reassurance, but her own heart knew the truth. It was just a matter of time.

Chad had surprised her a few times when she threw a fit, hurled something, and stomped off in anger. "Cut that shit out, you little brat," he said to her under his breath, so their mom couldn't hear. She didn't trust him, and it scared her that he stood up to her, unfazed by her anger. He had stopped having anything to do with her, and it was confusing. As much as she told herself she couldn't care less, she wanted his approval. But he had simply turned his attention elsewhere, as if what she did was of little consequence. When he went off to college, she repeated often, "Good riddance," liking the way the big word slid off her tongue.

Jill was the perfect kid, the sweet one, the one who got her feelings hurt but said nothing. She got straight As, rarely got in trouble, and really tried to be good to everyone. She was easy to manipulate, easy to control, and quick to forgive. Most of the time things went well between them, but when Mariela saw Jill and their mom laughing or talking together, it made her blood boil. It was obvious that those two really liked each other, and it was infuriating. *Does she expect me to be perfect, sweet, and smart like Jill? Well, I'm no ass-kisser. Who wants to be like her, a pushover?* Mariela fumed.

She had honed the skill of pretending long before she joined this family. Acting was helpful to win people over, and she knew she was an expert. She could put on charm like an expensive coat, then whip it off when she no longer needed it. Her survival had depended on it. When she met friends of the family, they remarked how friendly and well-mannered she was, and their looks of approval in the face of her deception were a victory. As long as they didn't expect something from her, things went well. But if anyone expected her to cooperate, to think of others, feel compassion, or understand, it felt like they were trying to wrest control away from her for their own purposes.

"Mariela, part of being in a family is sharing and showing concern for others. We're a team and have to help each other," Charlotte said many times. What nonsense that was. She still lived by the rules she had learned in the orphanage: each person for herself. If anyone challenged or disagreed with her, it was an afront that demanded a hostile pushback.

There was always something the family wanted from her: to share, appreciate, give up, give in, open up, or understand. Their demands on her were endless, and they acted like it was the most natural thing for her to acquiesce willingly. But it never felt natural or like a good deal. She was asked to think about others' feelings, but who had ever thought about hers? Since her mama left that awful day in the marketplace, she had played it smart and made sure she didn't care too much about anyone. She would never give like that again, never be tricked and discarded. It wasn't a choice. It was the rule she lived by, as elemental as her own breath.

"I can take care of myself. I don't need anybody else. I only get what I need from them," she repeated until she believed it to be true. It became the rule book carried in her hip pocket.

School was challenging, but in many ways, it was easier than being with the family. Bold and gutsy after years in an orphanage, she was admired for her spunk but held at a distance by peers. There was no holding her back on sports teams. She played like her life depended on it, and she became well-known for her athletic abilities and aggression. She liked to brag to her mother, "Other kids know better than to mess with me." More than once, she had taken on an older kid, leaving them surprised and shaken. She fought with a vengeance and never backed down.

She heard Jill talking to her mom one day. "Everyone talks about her—the girl who fights and pushes and cusses, and she's my little sister. It's so embarrassing."

"I know, sweetie, she's had a tough time of it. We have to be patient with her. Her life hasn't been easy."

Mariela seethed at the thought of the two of them talking about her and pitying her.

As she entered adolescence, her family became more annoying

and her friendships more challenging. There was little diversity in the small town on the outskirts of Portland, and classmates routinely asked questions that wilted her normally bold affect. "What are you, anyway? Mexican, Eskimo, a mixture?" one boy taunted her before she slung insults at him, causing a peel of laughter from onlooking eighth graders. Her mom made sure she had clothes worn by all the middle-schoolers, and she styled her own hair like the other girls, but it was useless. She was dark and different and would never fit in no matter what she did. It was easier to hang out with the kids who had problems in school; they accepted her and encouraged her anger and sarcasm and withdrawal from kids who were doing well. This new group of kids thought she was funny and tough. It felt good to belong to a group, even if they were all considered losers. Sneaking away from home at night, stealing from local stores, skipping school…it was all exciting and put her in good standing with a group of adolescents looking for a thrill and acceptance from each other.

"You have too many rules. You can't control me, so stop trying!" She yelled at her mom on a regular basis before stomping away. "You're jealous of me because I have a life and you don't! Leave me alone!" She sneered. The more evidence she had that she was able to wear her mom down, the more contempt she felt toward her. She was an expert at getting her mom's attention, softening her, getting her sympathy, then maneuvering around her to get what she wanted. Charlotte was an obstacle to be stepped around and dealt with, she boasted to her friends. "My mom is a sucker; she needs me to care about her even though I don't. I just have to act like I do, and she falls for it." She was unsure if this was entirely true about her mom, but it didn't matter, as it was how she felt about most people.

At times, despite her best efforts, a vast emptiness emerged, and she yearned to be held and rocked like a baby. Desperate to fill the hollow, she stood at the edge of belief that her mom could fill the void. But that longing was so terrifying that it was immediately tamped down. The unbearable yearning to be loved and her solidly constructed wall, built with the mortar of shame and loss, were at painful odds with each other. One time after a particularly vicious fight, her mom approached her with swollen, tear-filled eyes expressing her love and commitment and even apologized for the difficulty of their relationship.

Perplexed by her mom's vulnerability and feeling she was being manipulated, Mariela lashed out before a softer sentiment could surface. "Stop trying to act like you care. You're not my real mom. She discarded me on the streets, so why would I trust you?" It was a victory to express hostility rather than weakness.

She stood quietly and listened to her mom's phone conversations one morning and heard her confide to a friend, "I knew she'd have a tough adolescence, but I didn't expect it to be this bad." With a chuckle (that sounded fake to Mariela), she said, "I can hardly wait till she's eighteen and goes off to college…if I survive until then." Mariela felt vindicated; she had always suspected Charlotte wanted her gone.

"She's finally had it with me and is planning to throw me out," she told a group of friends with her own affected laugh. She expected to be discarded, and she told herself she didn't care. She had learned long ago that when you expect bad things to happen, it's not so awful when they do.

She had been shocked when Chris left the family less than four years after she had been adopted. Her suspicions ran deep that she was the cause of his leaving just as she caused her real mama to leave. None of it made sense to her, the way people got bound to each other and cried when things broke apart. Charlotte acted like it was a tragedy for the family. Chad and Jill were terribly upset about their parents splitting up, like they really cared about their dad and needed their parents to be together. What a bunch of spoiled babies who didn't expect bad things to happen and didn't know that people always leave each other. She knew all too well that in the end, everyone leaves, even those people you count on, even those you love. She congratulated herself for being smart enough not to care and tough enough not to be surprised or sad when things didn't work out.

Mariela saw her hardening self-protection as coming into her true self, at last old enough to resist control and defend herself against others. It mystified her that her mom and others could be so naïve and trusting of others, and she felt smug behind her protective wall. When she and Lucy, her new friend, got caught shoplifting a few cheap things from a local store, Mariela was surprised when her mom didn't come to her defense against the authorities who wanted to punish the girls with public service.

"Why are they making such a big deal out of it?" she asked, hoping that her mom would agree and rush to make a phone call to fix things. Mariela was shocked when her mom refused to call juvenile court and instead allowed the consequences, spending five Saturdays in a row picking up trash.

"You say you love me. What kind of love is that?" she screamed, desperate to make her mom feel guilty so she'd get her out of the trash detail. But her mom, who was increasingly difficult to control, refused to get involved. Her mom tried to impose control by grounding her when she stayed out past curfew, but she easily got around that by sneaking out or staying away from home entirely. It was a challenge for her mom to stay one step ahead of her. Once when Charlotte tried to keep her from leaving, she hurled a dish across the room, narrowly missing her. She sometimes surprised herself with her violent reactivity, but she needed to teach Charlotte to back off.

Things were getting ugly and were spiraling quickly. Everywhere she went, there were consequences. She was kicked off sports teams for roughing up an opponent; teachers held her after school; Chad and Jill wanted to avoid conflict with her, so they sidestepped her altogether. She was lonely and sad much of the time and suspected she was terribly flawed, but staying hateful toward others helped her displace the contempt she felt for herself.

She screamed after being told she couldn't go out, "You and your stupid rules! Why did you take me away from the orphanage? I was happier there; you ruined my life!" As she shouted the words, she knew they were wrong. She had felt emptiness and yearning as long as she could remember. She knew it didn't begin with this family, but it was far better to seethe and spew hate toward them than to feel helpless, at the whim of others. Her dream of coming to the US for happiness and belonging had shattered. She suspected nowhere would ever feel like home.

She began to attract the attention of boys by the time she was fourteen, providing an enticing new development. She was exotic looking; flirting was easy, and so was pretending. She dressed and acted in ways that had them at her heels smiling with enthusiasm, and soon she was meeting a bevy of eager boys. She was on the phone constantly and laughed with lightheartedness before turning her anger on her mom, who stood by ready to spoil the fun by telling her to hang up and study.

In the next year, she had numerous boyfriends who were keen to spend time with her. She had begun to skip school and take the bus to a mall in Portland to hang out and flirt with older boys. They were far more interesting than the Oregon City boys. She flirted with a lanky Black boy who immediately fell for her, the short Mayan girl with an attitude. Both were looking for connection and comfort that eluded them at home.

He was seventeen and a smooth talker who told Mariela she was special and beautiful, something she had waited for her whole life. Hearing that she was special from her mom no longer had an impact, but hearing it from him was thrilling. Their pact to meet secretly was enticing, their encounters exciting, and before long, her relationship with Miles was the most important thing in her life. She now had someone in her life who was just hers, and no one could keep them apart. She regularly skipped school, which felt like a waste of time anyway. Teachers failed to call home to report her absences, having given up on trying to rescue her from a downhill slide. Her time with

Miles made her feel alive and unique.

One day, he suggested they go to his apartment when no one was home. She eagerly agreed, and it wasn't long before they were having sex on a regular basis. It felt like the love and bonding she had yearned for, and having a secret lover made her feel like an adult. Her mom had lectured her about the dangers of becoming sexually involved. *But to hell with her,* she thought. *She can't control what I do with my body.* And Miles really loved her, of that she was sure. Needing her family was now a thing of the past. When she was home, she retreated quickly to her bedroom, shut the door, and responded angrily to any interference from her mom.

Even an insistent call to dinner could cause an uproar, and one evening Mariela screamed at her mom from her bedroom, "I hate you, and I wish I could live with Dad. He's not such a pain!"

"OK, I can look into that" was her mom's response that started the ball rolling in that direction. She was surprised her mom agreed so readily; it seemed that her hostility had finally forced her mom to ask Chris for help. Mariela had begun to spend some weekends with Chris and enjoyed the freedom she had in his home. As she packed her last things to go to his house, her mom lectured, "Mariela, please listen to your dad and obey his rules. He and I will be talking about how you are doing. And don't spend too much time with your boyfriend. You're still young and need to focus on school and friends." Her mom helped carry Mariela's things out to Chris's waiting car. She knew she had worn her mother down and that her absence would be a welcome relief. She wanted to leave and yet resented her mom for letting her go. She knew Chris would not keep an eye on her; Miles lived close to him, and she would get to spend more time at his house without interference. "Thanks for giving me a break," she heard her mom say to Chris after Mariela buckled into the seat. "Please keep an eye on her." Mariela gave her a dirty look without saying goodbye.

Several months passed, and the relationship with Miles continued providing both distraction and excitement. Living with Chris was easy. He was busy working and spending time with his girlfriend, who he would soon marry. As long as she did a few chores and dabbled at her homework, he asked few questions. Her mom was always getting in her business; at least he knew to stay out.

Then she realized she hadn't had a period for quite a while. She had not worried much about getting pregnant, thinking it was unlikely, and if it happened, well, it was meant to be. Not sure what she should do, she decided against going to Miles right away. He wouldn't be happy about the news, and at seventeen, he'd be as surprised as she was. When she finally told him weeks later, he was proud and happy. "Wow, we're going to have a kid…cool." His response emboldened her. She was ready to tell her mother and see what happened.

"I need to talk to you a minute," she stated flatly on a weekend visit with her mom, who raised an eyebrow to this unusual request and waited. "You know Miles? Well, we're in love, we're going to stay together, and I'm going to have his baby."

Her mom, not wanting to believe what she thought she heard asked, "And when do you plan to have this baby?"

"Maybe in about seven months or so." The secret was out, and her mom couldn't do a thing about it. She had Miles and didn't need her mom, except to answer a few questions about being pregnant, a fact that upon closer consideration, she wasn't too thrilled about. It had been a shock to find out how easily it happened. But now she would have a baby, someone to love her forever, and she and Miles would have their own family. The idea of getting fat and suffering all the pain she had heard about wasn't appealing, but there were definitely plus sides to it.

Her mom looked shocked, but it hadn't gone as badly as she anticipated. There had been no yelling, no tears, no attempts to take control of the situation. Instead, her mother took her to a counselor who asked her to consider adoption of the baby; then her mom joined forces with the young Black counselor, both of them reminding her that she was only fifteen and that she could get on with her life and give her baby to loving and mature parents who were ready for the responsibility.

"Adoption? Never!" She would not abandon her child. She was keeping her baby, and it was her decision, no one else's.

"Please consider it, Mariela. You are so young. There will be time to have a baby in the future when you are older," her mom begged, not looking hopeful about her ability to influence this decision.

"I've got a baby in me now! And I'm going to have this baby. My life, my decision, so back off!"

Her mom seemed to know there was no use in trying to change her mind.

The pregnancy was miserable. She had flaunted her shapely curves and enjoyed the attention she received from boys, but she lost her waistline, and her belly soon protruded from her small body, making her feel fat and unappealing. She was nauseous and exhausted. Instead of friends envying her status, as she had hoped, they kept their distance like the condition was contagious. She tolerated her mom taking her to appointments but didn't have much to say to the doctor.

"This must be a little scary for you—you're very young," the doctor said, trying to engage and involve her. But she didn't have questions and just wanted to get through it. Women on the streets of Guatemala seemed to do fine without the help of doctors, and she wondered why all the fuss was necessary. People in the US made such a big deal of everything. Soon she'd have a baby who would adore her, need her, and never leave her, and she'd have Miles in her life too. She'd have no need for her family and all their demands ever again. Everyone told her that life was going to get harder when she had a baby, but they were wrong; her life would be better.

"I'm sick of living with people who don't care as much about me as Miles does," she declared to the hip caseworker assigned to work with pregnant teenagers. "My adoptive family has never really accepted or cared about me," she continued. "My mother even tried to talk me into giving up my own baby for adoption," she added. She had decided to share some of her traumatic history and difficult adjustment with the young, sympathetic caseworker, who looked encouraged. The caseworker was new at her job and saw this openness by an aloof teenager as a sign she was good at her job, not suspecting she was being manipulated.

Mariela, only fifteen years old but feeling much older, left the meeting with a list of resources for financial aid, housing, and other assistance, proof that she didn't need to grovel to her mother when it was easier to get what she needed from strangers. She and Miles were making plans to move in together, get on welfare, and have their baby. Both were excited about creating a family of their own and freeing themselves from the families they had already rejected.

Chapter 12

Charlotte

"Be like a tree and let the dead branches drop."
Rumi

I left work one cold and rainy February evening and drove, with the windshield wipers doing double time, to Vancouver, Washington. I had stopped by the store to pick up some groceries and diapers and was intent on delivering them and checking in on Mariela and her baby boy, Caleb. I realized how exhausted I was as I hauled the two heavy bags of groceries, diapers squeezed under my arm, up the grimy staircase littered with cigarette butts. I took a deep breath, closed my eyes, and settled myself before knocking on her apartment door. "Stay calm; be positive; remember that you can't control this situation," I reminded myself.

Mariela had given birth three months earlier by C-section after a long and difficult labor where the doctor finally decided the large baby could not be delivered vaginally, given Mariela's small adolescent body. Her eyes had been wide with fear as I soothed her, looking away while the doctor cut into her young belly to extract a healthy boy. The nurse had handed the swaddled infant to me but reading my trepidation correctly, said only, "Here's the little guy; he is perfectly healthy," in a tone that lacked congratulations. When I left the hospital that cold night many hours later and walked alone through puddles in the dark parking lot, I felt none of the joy usually experienced after a birth. Wrung out after spending many hours by Mariela's side,

I entered a new chapter of my life. I was a grandmother at forty-three and much more scared than joyful. I sat in the car before starting the engine and tried to imagine what lay ahead for me.

"Dear God, give me strength to deal with whatever comes," I said with tears already forming before I finished my short prayer. It had been one thing to let the chips fall when my teenager was beyond control and her life was in chaos but quite another when an innocent life was wrapped up in that adolescent turmoil. My responsibility for the baby I had just witnessed being born hit me hard. I feared it was a matter of time before she handed him over to me when the novelty of being a mother wore off. Nothing in me wanted to raise her child, and yet I wasn't sure if I'd have an option. There was no one else.

I visited regularly, as I was doing on that rainy February evening, which was almost her assigned birthday of February 14. She was almost sixteen years old. "Thanks," she mumbled when she finally answered the door and saw the bags of groceries. She looked young and fragile holding the baby boy. She seemed exhausted and sad.

"Can I come in? Can I help you in any way?" I asked. Clearly, she was distressed, but I knew she was loathe to admit it.

"I'm fine, everything is OK, I don't need anything else." She dismissed me at the door, and I slowly turned to head for my car but then turned back quickly.

"Are you sure I can't do anything to help you?" I was relieved to be heading home after a long day but distressed I couldn't do more to help her. I couldn't imagine what it was like to be caring for a baby at her young age. I had been twenty-two, married, and with a few resources when I had a baby, and I had found it overwhelming. What could it possibly be like for her? It was a huge disruption to the life I wanted for her, but I knew I was helpless to change the course.

"You need to stop always checking on me. I have a family now, and I'll ask for help when I need it," she snarled when I called to see how they were doing a few days later. Trying to respect her move toward independence, I crossed my fingers and stayed away other than driving her and the baby to appointments and dropping off groceries a few times a week. A caseworker and a nurse visited often to check on the healthy, full-term boy who was considered "high risk" due to his mother being only sixteen. I was reassured by their involvement.

One Saturday morning, I drove the forty minutes to the small apartment with a few bags of food and things for Caleb. I had been struggling to balance my involvement, to help when I could and let her call the shots of our involvement with each other. I knocked and waited then knocked again. She opened the door slowly while wiping her tears with a sleeve. Her hair was uncombed, and her baggy sweats were soiled. Caleb was crying in the background, and I could see that the house was a mess. "Here's some food. How can I help you?" I tried not to look alarmed.

"You don't do much to help me—why start now?" She sneered through her tears. I could correct her and remind her of my continual efforts, but I ignored the comment. I was determined to remain nonreactive. Then her tears fell in steady streams as she told me through sobs, "Miles left. He was tired of staying home with me and the baby and wanted to hang out with friends. I told him if he left to forget coming back. We had a big fight…the neighbor called the cops. I'm done with him. I hate him." She allowed me into the apartment, and I went immediately to Caleb, picked him up, and asked her to sit with me so we could talk. "There is nothing else to say." She had stopped crying, and I wondered if she would say more or shut down. I waited a moment, settled Caleb with a bottle, and looked at her.

"You and Miles are both young, and the realities of parenting are difficult. Babies need so much, and Miles wasn't ready to make those sacrifices. I'm so sorry it didn't work out." Would she say she too was done parenting? I braced myself for the declaration that didn't come. I understood that under the weight and drudgery of daily life together, their adolescent relationship had fractured. I had been braced for this outcome.

I sat on her battered plaid couch and looked around the small apartment. It was a mess, and I made a mental note of what I could do to help her organize and clean. I remembered again my own days as an isolated young mother, trying to cope with being alone with a baby all day. Chris and I had just moved to a new city after graduating from college; he worked all day for meager wages, and I was home with a fussy baby, feeling incompetent, isolated, and exhausted from lack of sleep. It had been a sad and confusing time. Friends and family had extoled the joys of motherhood, and I had wondered when I would start to enjoy being at home with an infant. I felt trapped and defective and guilty for feeling that way. To compensate, I had tried hard to be a perfect mother. I was diligent at everything I did; it wasn't an option not to try hard, not to bear down and hide my feelings, and not to toughen up to handle my solitary efforts in my new role of mother. I could imagine how difficult it must be for her, alone with few resources and angry at the world. "It's hard to be a new mom," I said.

Now she was weeping again. "I heard he's been seeing another girl." Her mascara made trails down her broad cheeks. I tried to comfort her but was tentative, having experienced many times the violent swing that turned her anger on me. Her wrath stayed focused on Miles as she spewed out slurs and insults, repeating that she was done with him. I stayed for a while, held the sweet baby, and felt my heart open to him when he smiled and responded to my care. *Don't get too attached to him. Keep an emotional distance,* I reminded myself as I smiled back.

Mariela's caseworker and the State of Washington tried to make Miles financially responsible, but he had dropped out of school and was unemployed, and his single-parent mother supported herself on welfare. He rarely dropped by to see his son, and when he did, there was shouting and accusations, leading to Mariela screaming that he couldn't see his son again. A public health nurse continued to make frequent home visits to assess the situation of mother and baby due to her age and the baby's vulnerability. Mariela was encouraged to attend parenting classes. I offered to babysit so she could go, but she only went a few times.

It made sense for the agencies working with Mariela and Caleb to coordinate with me, since we were all on the same team trying to support her and ensure Caleb's safety. I called the caseworker several times offering help or trying to obtain information but got the same response: "Mariela has not given permission for us to talk to you... sorry." Once I stopped by her apartment while a public health nurse was visiting. Her wary observation of me was telling. I ignored the nurse's chilly reception and asked Mariela about the baby as I handed her a bag of groceries, diapers, and a new baby outfit. When Mariela left the room briefly, the nurse looked at me directly, her voice low. "I'm confused. Mariela told me she had no one in her life to help her. She said you abandoned her, but it looks like you're quite involved."

"You could ask her for clarification in front of me if you'd like," I suggested. The nurse skillfully asked Mariela if it was true that she had no help, no relatives, no interested parties in her life.

"Oh, her." She nodded dismissively toward me. "That's my adoptive mom, but she doesn't help much." This familiar refrain always stung. I said nothing. After the nurse left, Mariela scowled. "Don't try to butt into my life. I'm doing OK and have other people to help me. I don't need your help, and I don't want to live with you, so don't ask." I hadn't asked, and I didn't want her and her baby to live with me, but with this clarity came guilt. What kind of mother doesn't insist that her adolescent daughter and her baby move into her house, try hard to make it work, do whatever it takes? I often chastised myself. Then, I'd remember what it was like when she lived with me before she had a baby, her opposing every limit, her constant hostility, her throwing things, the tension of trying to manage my reactions. My heart raced with the thought of it.

I stopped by her apartment several times each week to babysit Caleb while she worked on GED classes at an alternative school, or I'd swoop in quickly to leave things on the counter and say hello to her and the baby while checking on how he seemed to be doing. Caleb was a happy baby who was developing normally, and I was hopeful that things were going to be all right.

During Mariela's early years of teen motherhood, my determination to help Mariela be successful motivated me to drop what I was doing to babysit, shop for her, help her move, and buy her needed furniture and supplies. I frequently heard from her when she was in need of something and rarely heard from her when things were OK, which only meant there was no active crisis.

One Saturday morning as I got ready for a run with a friend, I got a call from her. "That jerk of a neighbor complained about me to the landlord, so I'm moving. I don't need his shit." She jumped in without a prelude.

"But where will you go?" I asked, desperate for an answer that made sense. Her caseworker had helped find this rent-subsidized apartment, and I was fearful there may not be another.

"I'm moving in with a girl I met. She's my age and has a baby too. We'll share the rent and help each other." Her track record with relationships of any kind wasn't good, but I refrained from mentioning this. She met people easily and could turn on the charm, so people warmed to her quickly. Just as quickly, in her estimation, they would become "bitches" or "assholes," and she'd be done with them. She was as fickle and conditional with them as she was with me. People were wonderful or horrible and rarely anything in between. No one passed the test of total unconditional positive regard for her, and soon the relationship would be a thing of the past.

"This is an impossible situation," I told a man I was dating who encouraged my sharing with his caring and empathic listening. "My seventeen-year-old daughter has a baby, and she's as hostile and manipulative as any conman. If I could, I'd take a long break from her while she matured on her own, but I can't do that. I'm all she has, and I hold on to hope that she will do better. I have to keep my feet planted with her; I made a commitment and I love her." Saying it out loud helped to fortify myself. He nodded and smiled, but I wasn't sure this man who had never been a father understood how it felt to be trapped by this kind of love and commitment.

"You may love her, but it sounds like you don't like her," he said, and his attempts at support were appreciated. We dated off and on for months, but in the end, I left a relationship that I couldn't imagine would endure. My commitment to Mariela was as much as I could manage.

Chad and Jill were dealing with their own challenges of college and being young adults. My ex was remarried and difficult to contact for help. After the breakup with the sweet and comforting boyfriend, I dated several men who offered fleeting support and distraction, but I revealed little about the distressing part of my life that consumed so much of my energy.

My own mother was confounded about Mariela raising a child on her own, and she frequently asked about her in our phone conversations. "How can she possibly be doing OK with that baby? She's just a child who has hardly had any mothering herself." She was giving voice to all my fears, but my silence did nothing to encourage her to be quiet. "This is the outcome I feared for her and for you... What a terrible thing that she got pregnant. I can't believe you let that happen." My mom had never been supportive; her comments were now brutal. "I thought you needed your head examined when you decided to adopt her." Her judgments left my blood boiling.

"Couldn't she for once have some empathy for me rather than kicking me when I'm down?" I said to a dear friend.

"Your mom has never been your ally. Why do you keep expecting her to be different than she's always been?" she replied.

I smiled at my friend and covered my sadness about my mother like an expert. "Hope springs eternal," I quipped.

Once, when sitting with the pain caused by my mother's criticism, I realized I was stuck in a pattern of expecting my mom and others to change for the better due to my diligent efforts at meeting their needs. Maybe they would be able to see I was worthy of love if my efforts at caretaking proved successful. Through my efforts, I hoped to obtain connection. Mariela was stuck in an equally stubborn pattern of expecting the worst of others with no hope of connection. It was my first inkling that both of us were caught in dynamics that didn't allow change or growth.

My parents visited several times a year for a week or more, and it was fascinating to watch Mariela and my mom interact during those visits. Given my mom's negativity about my decision to adopt Mariela, I imagined she would express some of it toward Mariela. Instead, she and Mariela laughed and joked with each other, played cards together, and enjoyed their special time, which excluded me. It was maddening.

One evening when my parents were visiting, Mariela and Caleb joined us for dinner. Mariela and my mom sat in the dining room playing cards, and I played with Caleb nearby. I noticed how late it was and said, "Mariela, it's about time for me to drive you and Caleb home. I have to work tomorrow." She and my mom sneered at me and joined forces to disregard what I said.

"We're having fun. Lack of sleep never killed anyone," my mom quipped, then ignored me and continued to play the game. Mariela burst out laughing and turned back to the game too. I was angry at their lack of respect and felt helpless to do anything without exposing my impotent wrath. It was clear that I couldn't impose my will on either of them, and they seemed pleased to put me in my ineffective place.

My therapist and I had been honing the skill of being nonreactive to deal with Mariela, and I was ready to try it out with my mom when she called a month or so later after I had put in a long day at work. She slid into the well-worn admonishment of what I had gotten myself into by adopting Mariela.

"What did you expect? Of course your life is hard with her. She's a damaged kid raising a kid," she said.

"I'm going to get off the phone now, Mom. These aren't easy times for me, and I need encouragement and support."

"You're so sensitive. My God, I guess I can't say anything to you. I was only saying what you must already know." Her quick retort left me no option but to end the conversation while trying to sound neutral and in control. I said goodbye and was reduced to a scolded, helpless child, doubting myself again. It took days to regain my stability.

When I returned to my therapist, he supported my efforts and emphasized that I just needed to practice tolerating my feelings when I stood my ground. "You must work at detaching from Mariela and from your mother; stay involved but set limits and boundaries; don't allow yourself to be abused; take long breaks to take care of yourself, and then find ways to repair your sense of integrity and wholeness. Be around people who know and love you!" he added with compassion.

I left his office each time energized and hopeful that I was on my way to coping better with the difficult people in my life. I practiced becoming truly open and vulnerable with dear and trusted friends and kept my emotional distance from those who depleted my energy. Mariela and Caleb were a special, more difficult case. I had made a commitment to them, and my job was to discern how to be supportive and loving and to protect myself from Mariela's anger and projections. She gave me lots of practice over the months and years that followed.

I dropped by her apartment with a bag of groceries one late afternoon after work. I hoped to spend a few hours playing with Caleb and talking with her, but I kept my expectations in check. I was open to however the visit went, I told myself. Caleb, now almost two years old, had his tiny fist around a pound bag of jellybeans that he proudly carried around the filthy apartment, his little fingers in and out of the bag and his mouth in rapid succession.

"Um, he could choke on those. Maybe I could fix you two some dinner." I tried to hide my judgment and keep my tone positive.

"Don't you be telling me how to deal with my son. I can fix him dinner; I don't need you judging me."

"I'm only concerned about his choking. I'm just trying to help."

"Leave me alone," she bellowed. I stayed and played with Caleb, but Mariela continued to fume and mutter under her breath, so I left and walked briskly to the car, turned on the engine, put my head on the wheel, and cried, unable to drive. This was impossible. I didn't deserve this. I was exhausted from work and from the weight and worry of dealing with her. "I just want to be done with you forever," I sobbed. "I wish to hell I never met you! I've had a belly full of you and want out!" I sobbed and said all the things I would never dare express to her. After a loud rant on the drive home, I resolved to stay away from her for at least a month. It felt good to curse her and wish her out of my life. Once I was home and alone, I calmed down and set an intention to try harder to be nonreactive and focus on the safety and well-being of her son as much as I was able. Beyond that, there was little I could do. I vowed again to give myself a much-needed break from her.

I didn't hear from her more than a month, but she was never far from my thoughts, a constant static of worry I couldn't turn off. My self-imposed break came to an abrupt end when I heard from the visiting nurse I had met months before in Mariela's apartment. "I've stopped by many times, but no one comes to the door, and she is not answering the phone. Do you know where they are? We are concerned and thought you may have heard from her." The well-meaning nurse's voice was concerned but detached, professional. I confessed that I had not been by to check on her for a month, feeling the judgment she had once had about me reinforced by this admission. All this time I had been enjoying the break from her, assuming the county program was involved and keeping watch. I hung up after assuring the nurse that I'd contact Mariela right away.

The phone rang and rang, and after many attempts, I cursed myself for not calling her sooner. Now feeling frantic, I drove to her apartment, gripping the steering wheel tightly and telling myself that of course they were OK. I held my breath and knocked on her door. I leaned my ear against the door and could hear Caleb whimpering inside. I called for Mariela, but there was no response. My heart rate quickened as I considered my options. I asked Caleb in the calmest voice I could muster to open the door. I could hear Mariela snarl at him, and he moved away from the door. I begged her to open the door.

Then I heard her chanting, a rhythm of words I couldn't understand. I continued to feign calmness as her chanting continued, her son now hysterical in the background. A middle-aged neighbor in dirty clothes that reeked of mildew opened his door, a cigarette dangling off his lips, and looked at me curiously. "I haven't seen that girl and her kid in weeks. I think she's using drugs or something. She just stays in there making strange noises with that little kid crying. I'm thinking it's time we call the police to see what's going on."

"Yes, please call. She needs help." My voice shook. What could possibly have gone so wrong in the time I had taken a break from her, I thought, feeling sick with guilt and angry at myself for turning my back.

The police officer arrived and asked me what was going on. "Does she have a history of mental problems or drug problems?"

"No, I mean, I don't know. I don't think so." I sounded like a pathetic, uninvolved mother to myself, but I resisted the urge to say more. He turned away from me and knocked on the door and told her to open it, but there was no response. He asked me to stand back, and then he pushed it open with force. I rushed in after the police and saw Mariela cowering in a dark corner of the apartment with Caleb by her side. It was at least one hundred degrees in there, the windows and shades all closed. A chair was pushed against the kitchen counter, and the cabinets bare except for a few cans. An almost empty cereal box and several empty cracker boxes strewn on the floor revealed what they had been eating. Or what Caleb had been eating.

It was clear that two-year-old Caleb had been fending for himself. Only a few long-ago-expired items could be seen, or rather, smelled, in the opened refrigerator.

Mariela, spacey and disconnected, ignored us. I approached her tentatively, but she looked right through me. She began to chant again with her eyes closed while rocking back and forth. Caleb came to me and asked to be picked up, keeping a wary eye on his mom. Her chanting intensified; lost in a trance, she still didn't look in our direction.

The police officer made a call. "I'll be transporting a mental to the psych unit."

"Hold on," I pleaded. "Let me talk to her." I tried again to get her attention. "Mariela, look at me. What's happening? Let us help you," I begged.

"I know what I have to do," she responded flatly.

"What?" I pleaded. "What do you have to do?"

Then she was back at it, chanting in a language I had never heard.

The police officer was becoming impatient and moved closer to her. Caleb, sensing a threat to his mom, started to cry. This agitated Mariela, and she stood up and started to walk to the back of her dark apartment.

"I need to take you to the hospital for some tests," the officer said as he followed her. "Just cooperate and come with me, and we won't have any trouble." He looked at me. "Does she have a history of violence?"

"No, not at all, well, yes, she can get nasty... I don't know."

With that, he put his hand on her arm and tried to direct her toward the door, warning her that she must cooperate, or he'd have to use handcuffs.

"Take the child out of the room, ma'am." He looked at me.

While I trembled in the back room with Caleb holding tight around my neck, I heard Mariela yell and try to resist the officer. Within seconds, he had her handcuffed and led her quickly out of the apartment. Several neighbors opened their doors to see what was going on. I watched through the grimy bedroom window as the officer put her in the back of the police car. I wanted to rush to her, to tell the police this was a mistake, that my daughter was not a mental patient, to beg him to be gentle, but I did nothing. The police car pulled out of the lot, and I held tightly to her wailing son and stifled my desire to cry with him.

When his sobs stopped, I drove him back to my house and focused my energy on comforting him. I tried to put the scene of Mariela, handcuffed and shoved in the back of a patrol car, out of my mind. I felt guilty as hell for being a part of what happened, for my failure to reach out to her sooner, for my feeble efforts to take care of myself while her life spiraled out of control. Authorities had hauled her away after I had failed to help her for a month. I was brimming with self-recrimination and seeping with guilt. I turned my attention to Caleb, whose needs, I told myself, I would meet.

He was ravenous, pouncing on food like a famished little beast, and wouldn't let me out of his sight. He whimpered and reached for me in his sleep. The next day he was clingy and starved for food and connection. He didn't ask for his mom. Expecting him to be inconsolable, I had prepared something to tell a two-year-old child that might be comforting. Sitting with him on the couch, I took a break from the book I was reading him and looked into his little face. "Your mom is in the hospital and getting better. She'll come back soon to take care of you, and she'll be all better." He didn't seem at all convinced and turned his attention back to the book we were reading, neither of us swayed by the story I had just told about his mom.

The following day, I left Caleb with Miles's mother, his other grandmother, and went to the psychiatric unit, a place I had visited during my years working in a large community mental health center. As I walked down the long, tiled corridor, my footsteps echoed my despair, and I reeled with disbelief. I was visiting my seventeen-year-old on a locked unit of a psychiatric unit, and her two-year-old son had spent the previous night with me. I would never have imagined this scene when my fantasy life was rich with hope about the fulfillment of adoption.

I checked in at the reception desk and asked to see the psychiatrist assigned to her case. After a tense wait in the reception area, I saw a thin, middle-aged man with a bow tie and neatly coifed hair motioning me to join him in his office. Assuming he would want to hear about Mariela from a mother's perspective, I spilled out the story of her traumatic past, her current stressors, her behaviors that made no sense, and my hypothesis about the factors that may have caused this psychotic break. He listened and nodded halfheartedly, then stopped me by holding up his hand.

"I spent some time with her yesterday at admission and it seems to me that her psychotic break is due to an onset of schizophrenia. She has all the symptoms. I've started her on a strong antipsychotic medication that should take effect soon. Can you take her home and make sure she stays on the medication?" He didn't wait for a response from me, and he was not interested in further discussion about her origins or the trauma she had experienced in Guatemala. He had done his assessment and delivered his opinion.

"She's only seventeen years old and has been through a lot. She was speaking in her original Quiche language before the police brought her here. She has seen terrible things and suffered a lot of trauma and neglect in Guatemala," I tried to interject quickly, frantic to give him a fuller picture.

"That may all be true, but this looks like the classic case of an onset of schizophrenia to me. We'd like to discharge her in a day or two and need to know if you can take her home." He repeated his interest in getting her discharged as soon as possible.

"She has not been cooperative with me for many years, and I have no control over her. I can't see how I could now force her to take medications."

As if this was beside the point, he addressed me firmly. "You will have to for the good of her child. We will make sure she gets follow-ups with the local mental health clinic." He showed me the door.

"I don't think she's schizophrenic. It's not that simple. She is complicated and…" I tried once more to interject her history of trauma, her losses, a final attempt to influence his diagnosis.

"It is a provisional diagnosis; it could always change," he said, now in his own effort to move me in the direction he wanted—literally out of his office. Back in the hallway of the hospital, I felt dizzy with disbelief. I had just been given a life sentence, and with all my heart I hated this doctor who had so glibly delivered it. I must have believed that if he could change his mind about her, deliver a more hopeful and less dire diagnosis, I could go on with my life. He turned around to address me once more. "There are services to help her; our social worker will set these up. You can go visit her now. Oh, yes," he added, "ask our social worker about family support groups. They are helpful."

Years later, I would recount this conversation, the arrogance of the psychiatrist, the lack of empathy and support, and the way my hands tingled with a desire to pick up something and hurl it at him. He was wrong about her diagnosis. She was more complicated than he concluded, but I wouldn't know that for many years.

I walked through the day room filled with mental patients lost in animated conversations with themselves, meandering aimlessly, cursing unseen demons, or sitting alone mystified. I wanted to wake from the nightmare. Mariela looked up from the corner where she was sitting but showed no sign of recognizing me. A blank expression of lost bewilderment spread across her face. She looked every bit the part of a mental patient who had lost touch with reality. She wore borrowed, oversize clothes, her hair was matted and unkempt, and she mumbled to herself.

"Hello, Mariela, can I sit with you for a while?" I sat next to her tentatively before waiting for an answer. I was braced for an angry response, but her reactions were dulled by heavy medication, and she simply nodded. Her vulnerability made my heart ache, and I longed to hold her and tell her she was going to be all right. I touched her shoulder gently and asked if I could comb her hair, not at all certain that I could get a comb through the matted length of it. She nodded passively and handed me the comb she had been holding like a foreign object about which she was puzzled. She had scoffed so often at my attempts at tenderness and affection that I was accustomed to keeping a physical distance.

I sat behind her and began to gently pull the comb through her tangled hair. Her shoulders relaxed, and she was my small and vulnerable girl again. Tears pooled then streamed in lines down my face. I struggled to compose myself. I ached for her and for myself. My love for her was a burden I carried and couldn't unload. She was difficult to love, hard to understand, and yet I loved her. This gut-wrenching experience of sitting in a mental ward combing the hair of my lost little girl would forever etch itself in my memory.

She was somewhere else, as distant as the moon, oblivious to my tugging at her hair. She began to hum as she gently swayed; then she formed the words of a song in Quiche, her mother's language.

Chapter 13

Mariela

> "It's your road and yours alone. Others may walk
> it with you, but no one can walk it for you."
>
> Rumi

Shauna, a Black teenage mother of two with an attitude like Mariela's had given Mariela the idea of moving to New York City. "I'm so sick of living here. I need more color, more excitement, and I need to get away from people breathing down my neck," Mariela had complained to Shauna, who was her only friend, as they talked about the landlord they both hated. Mariela had been hanging out in Shauna's apartment, as she often did, with Caleb and her new baby boy, Antonne, born only months before. Shauna was perming Mariela's straight hair as their four children played on the floor next to them.

"Girl, I'm telling you, New York City is great. I should have stayed there. There are people from all over the world, and everyone mixes, Blacks and Browns, and you can do your own thing—anything goes in New York City. And there's lots of help, especially for single moms," Shauna said as she wrapped a long strand of Mariela's thick hair around a curler.

"I just want to get away from this place. There is nothing here for me. I want to leave the two boys' daddies behind and the annoying mom who adopted me and the bills I can't pay. I've been here way too long, going on thirteen years," she said. Shauna didn't know much about her, and Mariela wanted to keep it that way. She was twenty-two years old and had learned to keep friendships casual, not expecting anyone to stick around long.

Mariela saved and borrowed money, enough to buy two bus tickets, relieved that the baby was free. She didn't tell her mom or the daddies that she was taking a bus all the way to New York City with her two kids. She was fed up with their sticking their noses in her business and tired of dealing with them. She figured she'd be better off without people who wanted something from her. It was easier to get perfect strangers to help her out, and she didn't have to account to them about anything.

The bus started the long journey east, and she was pleased with her decision. The Northwest had never felt like home. She tried to nap whenever she could on the long, mind-numbing bus ride and had just nodded off when her four-month-old's squirming woke her. Caleb, now seven years old, used his brother's fussing as an excuse to whine that he was hungry. Their needs were never-ending, but sitting on a cramped Greyhound for four days and nights was a torture they had to deal with. "Just hush, this isn't easy for me either," Mariela snapped at them. She reminded Caleb, as she had many times before, that when she was his age, she had no one to complain to and had fended for herself. The stories of her orphanage days always silenced him.

Her two kids leaned or sat on her for the three thousand miles it took to get from Portland to New York City, and she did her best to keep them from driving herself and other passengers crazy. Four days on that crowded, stuffy bus hurtling headlong toward the other side of the country gave her plenty of time to think about why she was leaving.

When the bus stopped at some godforsaken town so passengers could get off, stretch their legs, smoke, and buy snacks, she asked an elderly lady if she could spare some money so she could buy food for her kids. She could see by the look of pity on the old lady's face that they'd have enough to eat that day.

At last, the sky darkened and the kids slept, the little guy stretched across her lap, Caleb leaning heavy on her shoulder. She rested her head against the cool glass of the bus window and watched as stars became visible above the wide open plain. They were jewels in the sky like she remembered from the open window of the orphanage in Guatemala. She smiled to herself; she was taking her destiny into her own hands, leaving Oregon and striking out on her own. Sure, she was scared. But she had felt scared all her life. And alone. She liked the idea of putting distance between herself and the mistakes she had made and the people who had hurt and disappointed her. She was hopeful that her decision to leave was the beginning of her luck changing.

The thirteen years she had lived in the US had passed in a blur. She thought of the nine-year-old girl who arrived wide-eyed and scared, a hurt little kid hoping to find love. Looking back, she felt stupid for thinking she'd find a mother who would love her deeply and forever. She was not the kind of person a mother loves and holds on to. She had been left on the streets before she lost her baby teeth. She had felt broken and lost for as long as she could remember anything.

She had done her best to give the American family a chance, but trusting that anyone wanted her or would be good to her was impossible. It didn't make sense that they would love her. It was easier to hold on to what she knew—that she was not lovable—than to change that story and be rejected and left again. No matter how many times her mom said she loved her, it never seemed possible or real.

"You're part of our family now. Forever. And we are all so happy that you are. You are loved, sweetie," Charlotte used to say many times a day. Those words, meant to be kind and loving, had bounced right off her. Charlotte poured in the kind words, and they ran right out. She couldn't believe the luck Chad and Jill had, born to parents who loved and kept them, feeling secure in that love, never questioning that they belonged. She tried to own that feeling, but it didn't work. She had always felt unsure of love, never believing someone would stay, never feeling important enough to bind someone to her. She had given up trying. There were no more tender parts to expose, she made sure of that.

The darkness out the bus window was a relief from the constant monotony of vast nothingness in the middle part of the US, the dreamed-about country full of riches and ease about which all the kids in the orphanage endlessly talked. She had seen the truth of it. People in this country were no happier even with their riches. Had she been happier in the US with all the things money could buy? She wasn't sure of anything except that she hadn't been happy in Guatemala and wanted to leave, and she wasn't happy in the US either.

The car lights whizzing by made her eyes heavy, but as usual, sleep didn't come easily. Thoughts of the past rushed in, a scramble of events in her sad and sorry life leading her to this bus trip going east, toward something she hoped was better. Leaving Oregon was scary but long overdue. She was done trying to work things out with that family in a city covered in clouds and filled with white people.

"I've spent a shitload of energy trying to fit in and belong, and I'm done," she had told Shauna in a moment of weakness when she revealed something of herself. "I need a life that I make for myself."

A counselor she had seen briefly after her discharge from the psych hospital had told her that she needed to practice letting some people through the wall she had constructed to keep herself safe. That young, pretty counselor made it sound easy. But after her frightening loss of sanity and hospitalization against her will, she had shut tight a heavy and impenetrable wall. When she had packed her things to move in with Miles, she cussed out Charlotte and her Mayan mama, both of whom had failed her, and in her mind, they often blended and took the form of an unattainable yearning, of rejection and hurt. She hated them, sometimes with a firestorm of rage, often with a whimpering emptiness she kept to herself.

A familiar well of anger heated her body and made her heart pound, and she had to remind herself that she had already put her anger into action. "I'm the one leaving this time," she said softly to the little boy who leaned on her now. Her thin and helpful boy was her special treasure and helper. His daddy had gone off without her or his son, back to his teenage fun times. Her four-month-old's daddy made it clear he wanted nothing to do with her after a few months, joining the ranks of people who had walked away from her.

"Those damn caseworkers thought I couldn't take good care of my kids, but I proved them wrong," she told Shauna as she had packed to leave. "Eventually, they had to drop my case and let me be. They couldn't prove I was a bad parent."

Shauna had laughed. "Yeah, girl. It will be good to get those people out of your life."

Now, Mariela was taking her two kids to a better life across the country, far from the problems that exhausted her and far from the mental health clinic and people checking in on her.

Passengers rushed off to light up cigarettes when the bus stopped, the smoke drifting into the bus and taking her right back to the mental patients, always desperate for smokes, with whom she had spent a week on the psych ward. Five years earlier, when the police showed up at her small and shabby apartment, she and Caleb, then two years old, were living alone, trying to make it while she attended an alternative school a few days a week. His daddy was long gone, just as her mom had predicted.

It was a miserable time; she was pissed most of the time, and staying at home with a baby was both stressful and boring. She thought the baby would bring happiness, but instead she had been fed up. When the baby looked at her with tears in his eyes as if she had something he needed, it made her want to run. She wondered what she had to give him. But she didn't run because he was all she had, and she loved him in a way she hadn't thought possible. Now, there were two kids who made her weary with their constant needs.

Her memories of the weeks leading up to that policeman hauling her away were blurry and left only vapor trails she had a hard time following. The unique smell of the hospital remained caught in her nostrils for months, and she could even recall it now, the sharp, biting mixture of too many disturbed people held inside windowless rooms, mixed with the odor of cleaning fluids. The time spent in that place shattered and tore down all her well-constructed defenses. She could still remember the staff walking quickly and officially around the unit in their importance, a few of them taking her into their small offices to talk. They were all dead set on cracking her open to see what was inside her disturbed mind. She had been furious at her mom for having her hospitalized and for keeping her son away from her. She swore she would never forgive the betrayal, nor would she continue to call Charlotte Mom.

In the weeks before the hospitalization, she remembered feeling scared of everything, like when she was a child in Guatemala. The gnawing ache of despair made her life feel hopeless. If not for Caleb, she would have seriously thought of ending her own life. She hadn't really wanted to die; she just didn't want to keep living. One day when she returned from the store juggling a bag of groceries and her young son who was crying (he was always wanting something from her), she searched her purse for keys to her apartment but couldn't find them. A neighbor who lived upstairs heard her cussing under her breath and Caleb crying and offered to help her. He got extra keys from the landlord, let her in, and joined her in her small apartment for an afternoon of smoking pot. She thought she may have had sex with him then but wasn't sure.

She often felt like she floated away and observed herself from above when she had sex. It became a regular thing: smoking pot, having sex, laughing together. It made her life more interesting, and she looked forward to the escape. Then something went all wrong, and she became suspicious of him. He seemed involved somehow with the soldiers who had frightened her in Guatemala, and she suspected he was trying to set fire to her apartment. She yelled at him and ordered him to stay away from her. She barricaded her door against him and others she suspected were trying to harm her and Caleb.

She wasn't sure what happened after that; things got more muddled, and she felt more in danger. It didn't seem safe to go outside; people were hiding and watching her, the barricades were her only protection against the world outside. Inside the apartment, it was a deep, dark jungle and she navigated the trails through it like the ones she had run on in Guatemala with her mama. She closed the curtains to hide from menacing soldiers crouching just outside in the jungle. It had all seemed so real, so terrifying. She wandered around her apartment scared of everything, with Caleb crying at her heels.

The language of her mother's village, buried deep inside, came back to her, and she prayed and chanted. The cold and hard pavement of the marketplace where she had waited for her mother's return settled deep inside her, and she couldn't get warm. The sorrow of her mama's leaving washed over her and left her drowning in tears and sadness. *Why didn't she come back?* She chanted her mantra of despair, and her young son joined in the chorus of misery.

Then there had been a hard knock on the door; a soldier was telling her to open the door. She heard Charlotte's voice and couldn't understand what was going on. What was she doing with the soldiers? They broke into the apartment, ended up handcuffing her and leading her to a waiting car. Charlotte was crying while she held on to Caleb, trying to assure him that everything was going to be OK. Mariela had screamed in Quiche, Spanish, and English, her words flying out the car window and lost as the car sped away.

They kept her in the hospital for a week, made her attend group meetings where she was supposed to talk about her feelings. Nurses handed her medications several times a day. She kept to herself, trying to figure things out. Slowly, things started to fall back in place, and she convinced the doctor and social worker that she was ready to return to her apartment. They told her she had a break with reality and would need to stay on medications and see a therapist at a local mental health clinic. They told her that a caseworker would be stopping by regularly to check on her and her son, and they acted like they were doing her a favor. She was pissed that they implied she couldn't take care of her son, but she knew she had to cooperate. Charlotte agreed to stop by regularly and stay closely involved. She definitely didn't want Charlotte's help or interference, but she had nodded in agreement, knowing better than to argue.

Charlotte seemed apologetic about what had happened; she was careful about what she said and tried to gently coax her to take care of herself. The way Mariela saw it, Charlotte had been involved in having her taken to a mental hospital, and there would be no forgiveness for that. It was all the proof she needed that Charlotte couldn't be trusted and would betray her again, if given the chance. She decided to put more distance in their relationship. Charlotte asked too many questions and pried, pretended not to judge, and hovered, ready to swoop in and wreck her life and take her son.

When Charlotte asked, pretending it was a casual question, about drug use, she got furious, ordered her out, and slammed the door. Not that she hadn't wondered if her drug use with the neighbor was responsible for her coming unhinged and spiraling into a state of utter confusion. Maybe she had used more than pot without knowing it. The edges of the present and past had blurred. What was real and not real became hazy and indistinguishable; it was like barely escaping a horror movie in which she was the main character.

She had chanted in Quiche, her forgotten language, buried deep inside her, and Charlotte had been a witness to all of it. She had frayed and disintegrated, and Charlotte thought talking about it would help. She had been a bleeding open wound, and she was unwilling to expose herself further. Charlotte never gave up trying to inch her way closer to molding her into a new and recovered, better version of herself. She knew she was too damaged and defective to fix, and yet this woman who still wanted to be called mom was intent on trying.

The bus swerved around a corner, and the motion brought her

back to the present and the discomfort of the long journey. While she was thankful her kids slept, they were draped all over her, trapping her to the small seat. Other passengers, their heads slumped in sleep, some snoring with mouths gaping open, sat around her in the dark bus, and she wondered how many were riding this bus away from their loneliness and despair.

The baby started to wake, and she quickly shoved a bottle in his mouth. Both boys were good, and they were hers, but it took every ounce of energy she had to take care of them. Still, she was damn sure they had it better than she had ever had it with her Mayan mama. She struggled to reach a few M&Ms on the seat that the kids had spilled earlier in the day. She plopped them into her mouth as her mind wandered back to what led her to this long bus trip.

Her landlord evicted her after discovering the disastrous state of her apartment when she went to the hospital. She wasn't able to convince another landlord that she was reliable on her own but talked Charlotte, who was eager as always to help set her life straight, into cosigning the lease. "You are welcome to just move in with me for a while until you get back on your feet," Charlotte had suggested, but it had seemed like a half-hearted offer, and it was out of the question anyway. She wouldn't live with Charlotte again and be under her control; she noticed how Charlotte had looked relieved when Mariela snarled, "No fucking way."

Had she ever leaned on her mama as her children were doing now? She doubted it, or at least had no memory of it. She remembered only struggling to get her sad mama to notice her, wondering what she did to make her mama turn away, then leave. Her childhood in Guatemala was a vast and empty desert where the mirage of love was yanked away before she could find it. She had thought she found it with the American family, but that inkling of love hadn't taken root. It had been as elusive as the love she hoped for with her empty shell of a mama in Guatemala. She was an adult now with kids of her own and had learned that love was too much to hope for, a childhood fantasy better put away now that she had left childhood behind.

Creating her own family was supposed to solve a lot of problems, but it had just given her new ones. A bitter brew of fear, emptiness, and anger left her exhausted and feeling hung over much of the time. She was full of self-loathing but hated everyone else for treating her like crap because of her defects. Her little kids needed her, but they pulled from an empty well and found nothing, compounding her shame and sense of failure.

The bus pulled into a depot outside a city. These American bus stations all looked alike, squat buildings with neon signs, doors leading to dirty bathrooms, vending machines, a case of corn dogs and stale pizza. Exhausted travelers moved in a trance; barely awake, they lit up cigarettes and stretched their legs before finding a seat on a bus that would take them somewhere they wanted to go. She was one of many travelers heading away from a life that had ceased to work and toward an uncertain future that contained more possibility than the sorry cast of characters she was leaving behind.

Charlotte, with all her talk and supposed good intentions, was not to be trusted. Sure, she had sometimes helped and maybe even cared about her, but it seemed clear that Mariela couldn't measure up to Charlotte's expectations and never would. Charlotte had told her many times that she could become whatever she wanted, but Charlotte could never understand the invisible anchor that weighed Mariela down. Being around Charlotte was a reminder of her defectiveness. And it was exhausting to keep pushing back and protecting herself from Charlotte's interference and judgment.

Chris left her and the rest of the family, married a younger woman and had little to do with her or her kids. She had lived with him briefly before becoming pregnant and moving in with Miles, but after she had Caleb, he threw up his hands and gave up having much to do with her. He hadn't even invited her to his wedding. She had almost forgotten she ever had a father until years later when he reached out to her by asking them to join him and his new wife at a fancy restaurant. When they were settled at the table, Annie, the wife, had started in asking questions. "Where are the fathers of these little guys?" she asked, directing her attention to Caleb and Antonne. "How do you support yourself?" Her expression of judgment and distaste was obvious.

Mariela shot her a hateful look across the table, wrenched a french fry out of Caleb's hand, picked up the baby, and walked out of the restaurant, but not before she screamed, not caring who heard, "You stupid bitch, keep your opinions to yourself, dumbass." She hadn't cared about wrecking the relationship. Chris was nothing to her, and his wife was even less. They must have felt the same way; she never heard from them again.

Her adoptive brother and sister, Chad and Jill, saw her once in a while when they were visiting Charlotte, but they were distant and awkward with her. Charlotte was always trying to get them together, like they were real family and belonged together. She couldn't get this idea out of her head: her three kids, all together. At one time, Mariela had almost believed she was part of this family, but that was when she was young. Her unbearable longing to belong was a childish dream that had died, and she had been foolish for ever having it.

In the seven years after Caleb was born, her life was a blur of moving from one roommate to another, evictions, taking classes at the community college, keeping ahead of agencies whose job it was to check on her, and brief relationships with men whose problems were bigger than her own. And there was always Charlotte trying to shape her life and move her toward some success. After a string of disappointing and sometimes dangerous relationships, she had met a nice Jamaican man at the local laundry mat. He was a tall and gentle man who was ten years older than her and worked full-time. He was sweet and had a big, broad grin and cool accent, and he treated her well. He asked her questions about herself that she avoided answering when she could, and when she finally revealed things about herself, she painted a glossy, abstract picture. She wanted this Jamaican man to like her, to stay with her. She was tired of being alone in the world.

It wasn't as if she believed she could trust him, but slowly he convinced her that his intentions were good enough, especially when he played on the floor with Caleb, who was six years old at the time. He roughhoused, played games, and truly seemed to enjoy her sweet son. It created a scene that she desperately wanted, and she did her best to impress him, which wasn't difficult in the beginning.

Things went well for a few months, and she was happy, even a little hopeful, but she doubted that this good thing would last. She started to feel edgy with him, unsure she could trust him, angry that he needed something from her. She felt frantic about losing him, then would get angry and wound up over nothing. She churned inside and spewed out venom, and it was beyond her ability to tamp it down. She knew her anger made her less than desirable too, but her helplessness made her more prone to attacks of rage. She criticized and accused him, rejected him before he could reject her. In the end he gave up and left, just as she suspected he would.

Several months later, she called him to tell him she was pregnant. She hadn't been with anyone else and knew he was the father. This news didn't bring him back, but he did agree to get a paternity test after the baby was born and give her financial support if the baby was his. This could have made her happy, but instead, it became proof that while he was willing to do the right thing, he wasn't willing to be with her under any conditions, even if she had his kid. The sting was familiar; no one wanted someone as defective as she was.

She didn't tell Charlotte about the pregnancy, not wanting to hear her fretting and judgments. But it slipped out when she came by to hang out with Caleb on his sixth birthday and noticed the rounded belly.

"Mariela, are you by any chance pregnant?" she had commented, her jaw set, holding her breath.

"It's my life. It's none of your business."

She noticed Charlotte taking a last, sad look at her belly before she said goodbye to Caleb that day. "Take care of yourself," she said with that crushed look. She had at least learned to keep quiet, Mariela thought. She knew what Charlotte wasn't saying out loud, though: *Oh God, another child, and she can't take care of the one she has.*

"Screw you. I'm sick of you judging me!" Mariela yelled after Charlotte left. Then she plopped onto her couch and burst into tears. Charlotte had a way of looking at her like Mariela had broken her heart and shattered her dreams. Was this supposed to be evidence of her love? Mariela wasn't sure how love was supposed to feel, but this guilt-inducing display of utter disappointment was far from it, she was sure. Caleb had comforted her as she cried that day. At six years old, he took his place on the couch and rubbed her back. "You are my good little boy, the only one who really loves me," she cried.

A week later, Charlotte had called and offered to take care of Caleb to give her a break. "Yes, I could use some help, but don't be interfering and telling me what I should and shouldn't do," she warned. Mariela felt good about taking the upper hand but also knew her hostility wasn't entirely deserved. Charlotte was trying to help and still cared about her. She couldn't push this stubborn woman away, yet there was no way to make peace with her either. Like so many things in her life, she was caught in a vise and had no idea how to free herself other than what she was doing now on this long trip east, cutting ties.

She was taking Caleb away from his grandma who had been good to him over the years. She had tried her best to keep the two of them apart, fearing a bond would form that was stronger than the one she had with either of them. Now that she was moving to the other side of the country, Charlotte would, no doubt, miss Caleb, and the baby too. That thought caused a stew of menacing feelings that she quickly pushed away. *Screw it,* she thought. *Charlotte has her own kids who will have kids soon. And they would be her* real *grandkids.*

An older neighbor had tried to help Mariela and her kids before she packed up her things and left the small apartment without even saying goodbye. Fran was a sweet lady, and when her husband had died, he'd left Fran with too much time on her hands and no kids or grandkids to visit her. She knocked on their door every few days with something warm she had baked or a book for Caleb to read.

"Here, sweetie, I thought you and your kids would like these oatmeal cookies I made." She stepped inside with the wonderful aroma accompanying her. "How are you getting along? Can't be easy having two kids on your own... If you need to get out by yourself to do some shopping, you tell me, and I can watch the kids," she volunteered, smiling warmly. She let Mariela borrow things and even helped her with money and groceries at times. Fran was easy; she didn't ask questions or ask for anything in return. Their relationship was simple and based on Fran feeling good about helping her and Mariela needing that help. Mariela could present herself in any way she pleased with the kind and generous woman, and she had perfected a narrative and repeated it so many times that it felt like the truth.

"I'm from Guatemala. My parents were killed in the war there. People adopted me and brought me here but never loved me. They kicked me out when I was fifteen, and I was desperate. I got pregnant with Caleb; then his daddy left. Then I fell for a man who I thought really cared about me, but he got me pregnant and left. I've had to do everything on my own, and I just need a little help to tide me over."

It rarely failed. Most people didn't ask questions, didn't want to pry, respected her privacy, gave her help, and looked at her like she was the victim of a stacked deck. The women in Fran's Baptist Church invited her to church and then took up a collection to help her out. She didn't have to ask Charlotte for help for a long time.

Charlotte wasn't with her when she had her second baby, a boy she named Antonne to please his Jamaican daddy and try to persuade his financial support. She had decided not to include Charlotte in the agony of birth, where she felt more vulnerable than she liked. The nurse and social worker met with her after the birth, took notes, made suggestions, and scheduled follow-up visits from a visiting nurse. The daddy wanted to play an active part in his baby's life but not in hers, and this rejection stung. She didn't make it easy for him to see his son.

That was when she got the idea to move to New York where she could make a new start away from people who had rejected and judged her. If her kids' daddies didn't want her, well, the hell with them; they wouldn't have their kids either. And her adoptive family could go to hell. The story that they had never cared about her had become reality to her, and she decided she didn't give a damn about them either.

She gave her belongings away; there would be people in New York to help replace things. She was a survivor, as a counselor had once told her. She said goodbye to only a few people, avoiding people like Charlotte, the boys' daddies, and even Fran, who might question her decision and want her to stay. She asked the few people she told if they could help her out with some spending money for the long trip with two kids. She was shedding old skin, leaving what didn't work, starting over, she told herself when the trip she had planned scared her. She would reinvent and become a better version of herself in New York. She would no longer be the lost girl from Guatemala, the discarded Mayan daughter who should feel lucky to be adopted. *To hell with all of them,* she thought, speeding along the long dark highway going east, away from the mess that was her life and toward a future she, and she alone, would create.

Chapter 14

Charlotte

"Seek the wisdom that will untie your knot. Seek
the path that demands your whole being."
Rumi

My phone rang, and I tensed, thinking it could be her and I'd need to brace myself and manage my reactions. I had been enjoying a leisurely Saturday morning, drinking coffee after talking to a friend on the phone. I was still in my running clothes after an early-morning jog. Running had a cleansing effect on my psyche; when I ran, I forgot about troubles and simply focused on breathing deeply while listening to my feet on the pavement beneath me. The leaves were deep red and golden yellow; the rain hadn't yet knocked them off into faded wet piles. I loved running this time of year, and talking with a dear friend had gotten my morning off to a great start.

It was my brother calling, not Mariela, but I was preoccupied during the brief conversation with him. I had been expecting a call from her after not hearing from her for many weeks. When I didn't hear from her or she failed to return calls, I worried about how she and her young kids were doing. Although our conversations were rarely satisfying, and I was often anxious to get off the phone, I was reassured hearing her voice. I had become accustomed to bracing myself to hear a one-sided barrage of how she had been wronged. She shared a litany of troubles and frequently ended our conversations by asking for money. Evictions, threats to discontinue electricity, fights over money with the fathers of her two children, missed appointments with caseworkers…there was always something causing turmoil. She was an expert at shifting all blame off herself, feeling victimized, and then becoming irate when I asked questions for clarification or wasn't forthcoming with the desired help. Our phone conversations left me exhausted and fearing that her needs and demands would define the rest of my life. There would be no peace, no freedom from worry, no ability to get on with my life as my ex-husband seemed to have done so easily, I often thought with bitterness.

For several years after my divorce, my life was in turmoil. Then I began to adjust to being single and found some aspects of it enjoyable. I moved to Portland to enjoy city life and be closer to friends and activities. Chad and Jill graduated from college and were doing well, but I was still hopelessly ensnared in Mariela's life. My decision to adopt her had begun to feel like a life sentence of my own making. I often found myself thinking, *If only I hadn't…* Then I'd stop myself before going further with that dead-end thinking. I did adopt her, and I didn't know how to stop caring about her, loving her. She no longer referred to me as Mom, saying that after my betrayal of putting her in a psychiatric hospital, she no longer considered me her mother.

"My mom left me in Guatemala when I was a kid, and I don't need another one. Besides, you called the cops on me—what kind of mom does that? I can never forgive you for that!" This was said in anger, but stung all the same and was a reminder that whatever I had managed to build with her was crumbling. She wasn't one to understand another's perspective, show empathy or understanding, or get over being wronged. Our connection frayed so much as time went on that I couldn't imagine how a thread of it remained, and the promise of reaping the bounty of a mother-daughter bond was looking more and more beyond my reach. I held on to that whisp of hope that our relationship would heal and even grow someday. I didn't know how to cut the ties of our fragile bond, even if I was the only one holding on. And I wondered if she would ever call me Mom again.

The motivation driving my desire to get it right with her was revealing itself as I became more acquainted with my inner workings. I was the kind of person who honored my commitments and didn't walk away from responsibility even when the going got rough. Demonstrating and living this value was important to how I saw myself. It had been driven into me and my brothers in the Catholic, military family in which we were raised. I came from a family of conscientious hard workers. As the only girl in the family, I was taught to be selfless and good, caring for others and subjugating my needs. Feeling accountable for things that happened, even things out of my control, caused me to judge myself harshly and simultaneously defend myself against being wrong. Mariela frustrated my desire to prove myself good or right on a regular basis almost from the beginning of our story together.

In the months after her discharge from the psychiatric hospital, she slowly improved and eventually showed fewer signs of a major mental illness. I breathed easier as she benefited from the services of the mental health clinic and other helping agencies. I was never sure if she continued the medications prescribed by the psychiatrist who diagnosed her as schizophrenic. I had always doubted if she was schizophrenic; her illness, whatever it was, wasn't following the typical course of schizophrenia, and there were so many other confounding variables that made a diagnosis difficult.

I consulted with a well-respected psychiatrist friend with whom I worked. "Hey, Carla, I'd like your opinion on something. It's about my daughter." Carla was happy to weigh in with her professional opinion, as long as no one took advantage of her willingness. With her permission, I started, "I could have my head in the sand on this, but at seventeen, wasn't it premature to label her with a major mental illness? She's definitely got issues with attachment that make all relationships difficult, and she saw terrible things happen in her country that no doubt left her with some PTSD, and then there is the neglect and sexual abuse she probably suffered on the streets and in the orphanage, not to mention the horrible abandonment by her mother..." My voice had become high-pitched and desperate as I listed the ways she had been damaged. Hearing myself list her life injuries, I couldn't deny that Mariela was on a long, uphill battle against excessive odds. But, I reassured myself on a regular basis, trauma experienced in early life was amenable to treatment.

"I agree with you, Charlotte, she is much too complex to label with a single diagnosis, especially one like schizophrenia. The single best way to determine that diagnosis is to wait and see how she does. If she isn't on medications, I would suspect at some point in the near future, there will be another psychotic break, especially if she's under stress," she said with a gentle and caring demeanor that made her well-liked among the staff at the mental health clinic where we worked. "With her history, she will probably need professional treatment to work through a lot of this, maybe for many years. She's fortunate to have you to stick by her. And she could be very resilient. It's amazing what some people overcome." She smiled, no doubt sensing I needed this encouragement.

So, I went about my life, telling myself that the story wasn't over, hoping her resilience and strength and support from others would buffer her from the ravages of mental illness. I was pleased that thus far she seemed to be free from psychosis and able to function on her own with support from the services that were in place for her and her kids. When I didn't hear from her, I chose to relax and enjoy the break. She was constant background static in my life, never fully out of range, but just beyond my awareness if I focused my attention elsewhere. I was busy with full-time work and caring for my now-widowed mother with failing health by flying once a month to New Mexico, where she lived close to my brother. I spent time with my adult children and dated various men then debriefed the encounters with women friends. I enjoyed outdoor adventures like skiing, hiking, biking, and running the streets of Portland alone or with friends, our feet pounding to the sounds of our laughter and talk.

My inner life was replete with frequent self-incriminations, guilt that I didn't do more for Mariela in equal shares with guilt that I did too much in the face of her frequent abuse of my good intentions. The complex internal landscape couldn't be easily explained, and support from friends was often not forthcoming. So, I used discernment talking about tribulations with Mariela. Many of my friends had heard enough about Mariela to inform their opinion that I should draw a clear line in the sand, minimize contact with her, and let her go.

"You've done enough for her. You gave her a chance at a good life; she's a young adult and beyond your control. Take care of yourself and move on." They nodded in unison, agreeing, and making it sound easy. I liked the idea of it, but I wasn't even close to cutting ties with her.

"I hear what you're saying, and I'm trying to set limits," I responded, knowing that my process was jagged and at times defied logic. Mariela was holding her own at twenty-two, living in an apartment with her two kids, and seemed to have a few friends. I created a space for her in my life by providing support through regular check-ins on the phone, some financial help, and occasional visits to see her and her kids. My role with her became that of a supportive listener who had very little influence, a sounding board without a voice. I listened, always holding my breath, afraid to hear a break with reality, the return of psychosis that I so feared.

When a full month went by without a word from her, I became concerned and called, bracing myself for a calamity. A recorded message said the number had been disconnected. I panicked. Had something again gone terribly wrong when I turned my attention elsewhere? Within an hour, I was on my way to her apartment in Vancouver. A young woman finally came to the apartment door after my persistent knocking.

"Uh, hello, do you happen to know where the previous renter went?" I tried to make my voice calmer than it was.

"Oh, her, she moved out three weeks ago, left a big mess and no forwarding address." She squinted as she inhaled on a cigarette, her hand still on the doorknob, ready to cut me off.

An elderly neighbor came out, introduced herself as Fran, and looked me over, puzzled. "You looking for Mariela and her kids? I didn't know she had anyone in her life who cared about her. That poor girl doesn't know what she's doing, just running from her problems. I thought I meant something to her; I tried to help her." Fran bent to pick up the small dog at her feet. "Sweet little kids, but their mama has problems. Of course, she told me what happened, about being left by everyone. I guess you can't blame her, alone in the world."

I listened and felt the accusation fall squarely on me. I adopted her, and yet she still felt alone in the world, unable to feel the love still very present in my heart. The guilt of not being enough slammed against my urge to defend myself to this woman who stood in judgment of me.

"I'm her adoptive mother. She's not an easy person to help." I averted her accusing gaze. I wondered if I was being honest. Was she that difficult, or was I just not trying hard enough? Mariela had this effect on me. My own motives became suspect when confronted with a different reality, so like my mother's criticism, which I always took to heart no matter how off base. When in doubt, I doubted myself. These two significant people in my life were all too happy to offload their problems and to drop blame on me, and I dutifully picked it up, willing to shoulder it.

"She rode the bus with those two kids to New York, and I haven't heard a word from her." Fran's tone was chiding as she shut the door, seeming to blame me for Mariela's departure from her life. I turned and walked through the parking lot where I had parked many times to drop off groceries, to play ball with Caleb, to take the kids for a walk to give their mother a break. After years of trying to comfort and reassure Mariela that I'd never leave her, she had left me without a trace. I stumbled into my car and gasped for the breath I hadn't realized I'd been holding.

A torrent of mixed feelings swirled around me on the drive home, equal parts relief, sorrow, and guilt. She was gone, three thousand miles away, out of my life. She and her children lived across the country, and I was free at last. Ignorance will be sweet bliss; what I didn't know couldn't hurt me, I thought. I won't be faced on a regular basis with agonizing decisions about how to help her and her kids. If I hadn't felt so guilty, so miserably culpable, so inadequate, I'd have celebrated. *What kind of mother celebrates when her kid and grandkids move away with no forwarding address?* I asked myself. On the forty-minute drive home, my car was awash with tears, and the air was thick with self-incrimination. I walked into my house limp and emotionally exhausted, collapsed on my couch, and allowed myself a huge sigh of sad relief.

Naturally, my friends jumped back in with their feedback when I told them that Mariela had left the area.

"Let her be; you've done enough."

"She's made her choices, and she can live with them."

"She's out of your life," a good friend said emphatically, as if it were a done deal.

I heard from Mariela a month later. She announced that she was in New York, and I told her I had discovered she was gone through her neighbor, trying to cover my hurt and an array of other feelings that hadn't been sorted. She said proudly that she went straight to a social service agency where she was given resources and a place to stay. No one would allow a mother with two children to live on the streets. She had predicted correctly, and help had been forthcoming.

"Is everything OK with you and the kids?" I asked.

"Of course, everything is just fine. I like it here. I've already met good people who will help me out." Her tone of angry dismissal was not surprising. She seemed intent on letting me know that I was dead to her.

I could have offered to fly out and help her, offered advice and counsel, or sent her money. But I did none of these. I clutched the phone tightly and held on to resolve, saying in a tone I didn't recognize as my own, the words caught momentarily in my throat, "I love you. I only want the best for you and your kids. Call me once in a while to let me know how you're doing…" Then I said goodbye. Had my heart closed to her? Did my utter relief at her leaving prove what she had suspected all along, that I didn't love her? I put my hands on my heart and let myself feel what was true. I loved her, but my love was more a burden than a joy. I was depleted from trying to help her in the face of her volatility and rejection, and I needed a break, perhaps a permanent one, I thought.

So, I took pleasure in my full life and turned my attention elsewhere, enjoying the distance in miles between us. It meant I didn't have to make endless choices about how or if to help her. I assumed emotional distance would follow. I had yet to learn that emotional distance is a process that takes spiritual work.

Mariela's needs had been so relentless that I feared I had failed to give Chad and Jill what they needed and deserved from me. They were both married and busy getting established in their lives. Being with them was joyful and easy. I wanted to focus on getting to know myself while enjoying a much-needed respite from juggling too many balls, several of them spiked and painful. Though not all of them had been stilled. Once Mariela's needs were not front and center, I could more fully focus on my elderly mother, a responsibility that was similar to the one I had with Mariela, emotionally draining, necessary, and often painful.

My brothers and I had moved our mom into a care facility close to Santa Fe, New Mexico, where my older brother, John, and his family lived. The agreement that Patrick, my younger brother, and I made with John was that we would relieve John and his family regularly. We all agreed that our mom was difficult and exasperating, and while it was our duty and desire to care for her, it was also a burden, and one we should all share. Dad had died four years earlier at eighty-five, after a protracted battle with cancer. His death meant our mom was alone, needy, increasingly negative, and often demanding.

My dad had been the easier parent for me, and I had often felt aligned with him against my mom's hostility, which was regularly aimed at one of us. I had grown up seeing him as the nice parent who needed protection from the angry wife who picked on him. It was, of course, considerably more complicated than my youthful assessment. I traveled to New Mexico every six weeks or so, playing the part of dutiful daughter and helpful sister, trying to put my heart into it. Those visits, meant to be caring and supportive of the parent who had caused me so much anguish, left me depleted and sad. Often on the flights home after spending hours at her bedside listening to mind-numbing tales of negativity, I cried as I wrote in my journal, trying to process my feelings.

My mom was in her mid-eighties and had gone blind due to multiple eye conditions and botched surgeries to repair them. Her mind was sharp, and her opinions, spoken from the bed where she stayed much of the time, were often harsh and grating. Her inability to see created a dilemma. I had empathy for her loss of sight, but it was wearisome listening to her complain about it in endless ramblings about how awful her life was. I said to a therapist once, "I have never felt *seen* by my mom." Then I realized that blindness and the brittleness of her personality meant being seen and felt by her was truly unattainable. Time had run out for that. My job had become one of acceptance and forgiveness and making peace with her as she was.

Once, as I traveled to see her, I set clear intentions to open my heart, to listen with love, to say only affirming things, to see behind her words and focus on good memories. I made a list of all the ways she showed love. She had taken me horseback riding, I reminded myself, when I was a total horse fanatic as a young girl. Her benign neglect had allowed me to venture out freely while growing up, and that had given me confidence. She bought me ice skates from a thrift shop after I begged for them. She made all of us laugh with her songs and funny expressions. I hadn't been coddled or spoiled. I didn't expect too much from others, and being easy to please was a good thing, I told myself. But sooner or later, this line of thinking brought me back to what I didn't get from her. I always doubted her acceptance and love. It would take practice to let go of that.

One visit I surprised her with quality headphones so she could listen to music and books. When she put the earphones on and heard the calming music, she smiled. "I like this. I've always loved music since I was a girl. My daddy used to play the piano for us kids before he died. Those were happy days, all seven of us kids around the piano with mama holding the baby. There was always a baby." She had switched from her usual diatribe of the people in her life who had wronged her and gone way back in time as she listened to the music, remembering her early years, as I sat beside her.

"This is good, Mom. Tell me more about those days," I encouraged her. She listened quietly to the music that had stirred something in her; then her eyes, no longer able to see, filled with tears. "Everything changed when Daddy died and we went to the children's home. mama got so depressed and skinny trying to take care of all of us during the Depression with no husband, no help. They took mama to the mental hospital and had to split us kids up. I stayed in that damn children's home a long time, and that was no picnic, I'm telling you."

"I'm sorry, Mom. That sounds really hard." A spark of compassion ignited, and my heart softened. Why had she waited all these years to talk to me about this part of her life? "I wish I had known about this earlier." It was then I realized that her grief had shifted from her shoulders onto mine, and I had carried it. She had been left with a well of bitterness and anger, the only emotions she expressed.

"Why the hell talk about something you can't change that makes you feel terrible to remember? Bad things happened in that home that I have never told anyone. And I'm too old to care now. Mariela dealt with some of the same shit, I bet," she said. "It's the same everywhere. Kids get hurt when there is no one around to protect them."

Her expression was sad as she talked. She and Mariela both possessed a small, hurt child inside. Both felt defective and angry about their lives. Neither of them could be vulnerable or show empathy to others.

"You're right, Mom, Mariela has dealt with a lot, many of the same things you had to deal with. The two of you have always seemed to know that," I said, my eyes filling with tears. I looked at my mom; the angry wind that often blew from her was finally silenced by her vulnerability. I touched her thin, wrinkled hand, surprised at its softness. She and Mariela were gravely injured early in life and hadn't healed from the damage inflicted by life's cruel circumstances. Both had wounds that couldn't be seen, covered over with scabs, that had affected their lives and the lives of the people who loved them. I had fallen quite naturally into a role of continually trying to change both my mother and my daughter so I could prove myself worthy of the love I desired. Both these maddening women were teaching me a complicated life lesson. If I was unhappy about this self-imposed role, it was up to me to change it. I had a choice, I realized as I continued to hold my mom's hand. I could give myself the love and compassion I sought and learn to stand my ground solidly while keeping my heart open to both of them. In that moment, the task seemed achievable.

"I'm going back to my hotel soon, Mom—what can I do for you before I leave?"

"My feet hurt like hell. It's a constant burning sensation. Could you rub them for me?" she asked. My mom, who hadn't hugged me since I was old enough to remember, who never told me she loved me, was now asking me to show affection and care for her. I was being put to the test already. Could I keep my heart open?

"OK, Mom, looks like there's some nice lotion here. I'll give you a foot massage," I managed to say, still unsure I could be so tender. I had the lotion in my hands, ready to apply it to her feet, and I looked at her, blind and vulnerable laying in front of me. Then I rubbed her feet for a very long time as she hummed a tune from days gone by.

Chapter 15

Charlotte

"These pains you feel are messengers. Listen to them."
Rumi

Mariela called from New Jersey one Saturday morning after many weeks of my not hearing from her. She sounded excited, "How about we go to Belize and Guatemala?" She posed the question as if she had never had anything but the warmest regard for me. I stopped folding the warmed laundry I had just removed from the dryer. I sat down on the bed, eager to hear what would come next. I wasn't sure what to make of her request, but I wanted to know more.

"You want to make the trip now with me and your two kids? Soon?" I tried to clarify. Years earlier, I had promised to take her back to visit her country, but this was before she had children, before she was hospitalized, before she had so much resentment and hostility toward me.

"I'm twenty-three years old, and my kids are good travelers, so why not now? I need to see where I'm from."

The idea intrigued me. I presented it to my good friend and fellow mental health therapist, Barbara. "Why not take the chance? This trip could help repair our relationship and begin her healing from the trauma she experienced in Guatemala?"

She responded quickly, "You are nuts to even consider it. I know what you hope for, but she's not ready to meet you halfway. Embarking on such a trip could make things worse rather than better between you."

"I think I must have amnesia when it comes to her. I'm always so willing to turn the page and begin a new story," I admitted. "It's an opportunity to bond with her and for her to experience her culture and come to terms with her history," I countered. "I can't deny her that. It may be *the* thing that will help her turn a corner. I'm not ready to give up hope. And I think I've learned how to keep my expectations sufficiently low," I added in an effort to convince Barbara that I hadn't lost my mind.

I took the time off work, bought tickets, and made plans to meet Mariela in Belize City to begin our adventure. I had fantasized that after some days enjoying the beach together with her children, we would head to Guatemala where we'd explore some sites and cultural experiences, visit the orphanage where she had lived, maybe even look for her village, and re-create a loving bond based on our meaningful times together. I hoped to really get to know her two boys and step into being their grandmom, which had been difficult due to her hostility and the emotional and physical distance between us. Antonne was now crawling and giggling and getting into everything, and Caleb, her eight-year-old helpmate, was always watchful of his mom.

I waited nervously for her arrival at the airport, not knowing what to expect. I wondered if the time away from each other may have created a different dynamic between us. She appeared exhausted and overwhelmed as she approached with Antonne on her hip and Caleb following at her heels. She didn't smile, and she stiffened when I embraced her. It had been a long flight with two children, and I suggested we relax in the hotel.

"What do you think of us leaving Belize in a few days and taking the bus through Guatemala, stopping at Tikal and other interesting places on the way to the highlands?" I asked her. She stopped me before I could share more details of the plan.

"I'm not really interested in visiting that country. I just want to stay here and chill on the beach with my kids." She walked away from me, speaking over her shoulder as she left, "You're the one who wants to go to Guatemala. I hate everything about that country. It means nothing to me."

I couldn't hide my shock; surely, she was joking. My heart raced, but I put on a practiced calm face. "We've come this far, and we're so close." I tried to sound more positive than I felt. "Wasn't it your idea to visit Guatemala?"

"I changed my mind. Go ahead if you want to go. I like the beach, and me and my kids want to stay here." I struggled to adjust my thinking; staying in Belize would make for a much easier trip, and we could have a good time together without the stress of traveling in Guatemala. Maybe this was just what we needed to create some good feelings, I thought. And dragging her and two young children through Guatemala, battling her resistance, was out of the question. She would win any power struggle. Her resistant tactics far surpassed my will, and I didn't want to risk an ugly battle with her two children along. After considering my alternatives, I changed my expectations, my new skill born of necessity, telling myself if we managed to have a good time together in Belize, that would be success enough.

We stayed in Placencia, Belize, a quiet Caribbean beach village with turquoise water lapping against white sands, small clapboard houses on stilts, and beach shacks where delicious fresh fish was grilled to order. The waves were background music from our quaint two-room cottage surrounded by palm trees. The heavenly locale and peaceful setting would surely soothe our rough edges. But a constant irritating tension buzzed between us, and despite efforts, I had difficulty relaxing with her. I was on guard but tried pretending all was well. I was determined to have a fun trip and create a lasting positive memory. If she became negative or confrontational, I could ignore her or meet her negativity with empathy and understanding. I set my intention to be nonreactive, practiced breathing in calmness, and arranged my face to appear happy and serene.

The skies were a perfect blue on the second day as we walked on the beach together, adoptive mom and grown daughter with her two children, eight years old and nine months old. The ocean breeze made the temperature perfect. I carried her baby son on my shoulders, played in the sand with both kids, romped in the shallow waves with Caleb, and for the first time felt like a grandmother to them. Mariela was withdrawn and pensive and didn't join us in the water, but I focused on the kids, resolving again not to react to her ever-fluctuating moods.

A muscled Garifuna man, dreadlocks hitting his bare shoulders and sarong tied low on his hips, strolled on the beach toward us, then stopped. He winked at Mariela, looked her over, leaned in close to her, and said something I couldn't hear. They laughed, and he flashed a broad, seductive smile at her. They faced each other and talked and laughed as I continued playing with her kids. I hadn't seen her this animated and pleased in a very long time. I told myself that her enjoyment of his flirting was a good thing. Then, she turned away from him to face me. "Hey, Charlotte, come here with my kids." I approached them and introduced myself to the tall man hovering over her with languid eyes. Mariela said, "We're going for a walk together with the kids. See you later. You can go do your own thing." She dismissed me with a scowl.

He moved close to me. "Here, I'll carry that baby." He reached for Antonne, who tightened his grip on my neck.

"Hey, give him the baby; he wants to hold Antonne," Mariela demanded.

I protested, then reluctantly handed Antonne to the stranger, then looked to Caleb. He stepped beside his mother and the man holding his baby brother and looked across a wide divide of sand at me standing alone. Ten minutes earlier, Mariela hadn't known the man, and now she was ready to walk off with him. *How is this possible?*

"What are you doing? Can we talk?" I begged Mariela as I moved away from the stranger, hoping she would follow. She stood firm.

"We're going to go have some fun together. What are *you* doing?"

He looked at me with his own smirk and turned away as he flung a muscled arm around her, and the four of them strolled off together. Caleb, perplexed, turned and looked at me, but hung on to his mom.

Mariela looked up at her sexy new friend like he was a prized possession. He pulled her tighter, and she melted into him. All morning, with growing unease, I had ignored her indifference tinged with annoyance toward me and had countered it with an upbeat and positive attitude. Then, she discarded me the minute she had an option to be with someone else. *Did I mean anything to her?* I fumed as I watched them walk away. *I mean very little to her.* The full weight of this obvious realization—that until that moment had been denied—stopped me in the sand.

My relationship with Mariela existed because of the work I did to sustain it. If I did nothing, we had nothing. Our relationship was an illusion I kept alive in order to deny an unhappy ending to my adoption story. Another realization quickly followed: I had protected myself for years from the collapse of my core fantasy: *With enough love and care of another, I would be loved in return and have the connection I desired.* The fantasy continued, *If I could just get it right and be what she needs, she'll know she's loved and will then be healed and return my devotion.* I exposed my lifelong prescription. The familiarity of it was frightening. I thought I had turned the corner when I sat at my mother's bedside, yet I was still struggling with this damn story of trying to be enough.

My entire childhood had been built on striving to find the key to please my mother and win her affection. Now, in my adult years, I was locked into a similar pattern trying to prove something to Mariela. With that insight came a flood of tears, an utter helpless sense that there was nothing more I could do. *I can't change who she is. I can't will it to be different; it's beyond me.* I cried and walked, kicked at the sand, walked some more, and finally swam in the warm waters of the Caribbean. *She will never be the loving, attached child I dreamed of,* I repeated through sobs that mingled with salt water. *I can't heal her, I can't heal her.* I sobbed. *And my mother will never be the mother I wanted and needed either.* There was relief in letting the despair and helplessness wash over me, my wounds of disconnection finally exposed.

My tears mixed with the clear, warm water as I swam back and forth along the shore. *This is what I've been avoiding; this is it, feel it fully, live with it, accept it. I can't change who she is.* As my arms slid through the water and my legs kicked me forward, I felt my own strength and vowed to change myself. I would no longer force my will. What a hopeless narrative I had been living, first with my mother, then with my husband (now long gone), and then with my Guatemalan daughter: wounded people I had needed, hurt people I had tried to heal. I cried as I let the water soothe me.

My body cut through the water with increasing ease, but despite the pleasurable sensations, I came back to the present reality that Mariela and her children had walked away with a stranger in a foreign country. *Don't fret; remember you can only do so much. Focus on enjoying the day by yourself,* I reminded myself to stay calm as I walked around the small beach village, scanning the streets for any sign of them. I went back to our cottage to see if she had returned, found it empty, then walked some more, read, swam, stopped at a fish shack, and tried to eat the delicious fresh fish sandwich I bought, then returned to the cottage, and still she hadn't returned. Her leaving had provided me hours alone to sort out feelings. I tried to feel grateful for that and made an attempt to soothe myself again.

But by late afternoon, I was feeling frantic. I could no longer sit still. My newfound resolve from earlier in the day to "let her be, accept her, understand your limitations" evaporated, and I was back in a stew of helpless rage about her putting her kids in danger under my watch. I had no idea where to look for her. I asked the first person I saw, a woman slumped on a chair selling her crafts on the street, if she knew a man who met the description of the one who had walked away with Mariela earlier in the day. She laughed ruefully and said that I was describing many of the men who hung out at the beach watching for American and European women.

"Your women love our sweet-talking Garifuna men with their long dreads and bare chests, and he'll get her money and more, that's for sure." She laughed again as if describing who would be the winner of a card game.

"Could he be dangerous to her?" I stammered.

"Depends what you say is dangerous," she said with a knowing grin. Mariela was a tough survivor, but she was no match for a seasoned gigolo and scammer. I felt desperate to find her before dark and asked her if local police were nearby. "Sure, we have police in Placencia, but they don't really do much; they sit at a desk in the muni building a few blocks away. Hey, good luck to you." I couldn't tell if she spoke with disdain or complete indifference, but it was clear I would not be getting more help from her.

Not much business was conducted in the small ramshackle building I assumed to be the municipal building. I entered an open door and saw a man sitting in a chair with his feet propped up on his desk, barefoot, and eyes at half-mast. On his desk, a flimsy sign read: Police Section. He sat up straight when I approached, surprised at what looked to be his first business of the day.

"I'm visiting your town with my daughter and her children. She walked off with a man this morning and hasn't returned." I sounded pathetic even to myself.

"Yes? Is there something I can do for you?" He yawned.

"Well, I'm afraid for her. She didn't know him; she has two young children," I said with as much respect for his position as I could muster. "He introduced himself to her as Washington. Do you know him?"

"Ma'am, you need to relax. She's not missing till she's been gone a few days. Maybe she just needed some time without her mama." He winked and leaned back in his chair.

Shaken and unsure what to do next, I turned and left, wanting to make some rude final comment to keep myself from feeling so miserably stupid. I refrained, thinking this man may be the only help available should she not come home later in the evening. I walked slowly back through the town, already intensely disliking Placencia and its unhelpful people, who seemed so intent on putting me in my place.

Back in the cottage, which was more confining by the minute, I paced, floorboards squeaking, and cursed her. Then I noticed that her suitcase and other belongings were gone. She had returned to the cottage in my absence. The emptiness mocked me. The sky darkened, and the constant breeze turned to heavy wind and howled in rebuke of my new resolve to let her be. Within fifteen minutes, the palm trees swayed and thrashed violently against the small cottage. I stepped outside and was slapped by a ferocious wind.

Within minutes, the pelting rain against the front porch had me rushing for cover. I stood at the window thinking any minute I'd see them running toward the safety of our dry cabin. She couldn't possibly be outside with her children in the dark, in this fierce storm, the thunder and lightning violent reminders of my insignificance and lack of control. Palm branches broke on the roof and all around the cottage, creating a barrage of noise and chaos. *Damn her*, I repeated, cursing her and myself for being here with her. Why hadn't I listened to Barbara when she said this was a crazy idea? Why had I held on to the ridiculous belief that this trip could make a difference? The howling wind felt like ridicule in the face of my naïveté. I had been manipulated and used again. "Never again, never again..." I cried as lightning lit the room and made me duck for cover, even though I was inside. Exhausted, I said a prayer for their safety, lost again in the familiar pattern of resentment and anger followed by guilt and confusion. Impossible to sort out how I felt or what I should do, despite the crashing branches, I fell asleep for a few fitful hours.

The birds were singing a magnificent chorus when I awoke alone in the cottage. Before my feet felt the rough wood planks beneath me, anxiety overtook drowsiness. Pale light filtered into the window, and her empty bed taunted me. My first thought was how to solve this problem of my missing daughter and the two grandchildren I was getting to know. The few hours of sleep had given me a needed reprieve, but now I was again in the full throttle of anxiety. It occurred to me that one option would be to simply wait for her to return today, and if she didn't, I would be within my right to leave Belize and Mariela be damned. It felt good to imagine having the power to make such a bold move. I was indignant and wanted to stand up for myself. But I knew better than to let this become a battle of wills where her children became the ultimate losers. My concern for them stopped me. Again, she had me in an impossible position, and I cursed her.

A middle-aged man dressed in a torn T-shirt, ripped shorts, and flip-flops was outside the cottage, slowly picking up branches from the storm, humming to the reggae music that played on his radio. I approached him, reminding myself not to look crazed. "Um, my daughter and her two children didn't return last night after walking away with a man she didn't know. I don't know where to look for her; do you have any ideas?" I asked, trying to relax the tension I knew lined my exhausted face.

"Oh yeah, that can be a problem. These men know how to get what they want from American women. Most of them just want a little money and a good time."

"He introduced himself to her as Washington. Do you know anyone by that name?" I was still trying to appear less shaken than I was.

"Sure, we all know each other here in Placencia. That Washington, he's a real player. He comes on to lots of women. That's how he gets by, you know."

"Does he live near here? Where can I find him?" I tried to keep my voice steady.

"He lives with a few other guys in a run-down house on stilts on the main road that goes out of town. No one has addresses, but his house is the bright-blue one with a lot of bicycles out front."

"Am I safe to go there?" I asked, already knowing that this was my only option.

"Yes, you be safe enough. More than likely, he'll be stoned."

I waited until I could no longer tolerate pacing and imagining the worst. It had been more than twenty-four hours since she walked off, and I was still trying to absorb the significance of her doing so.

I walked on the long, sandy path out of town, lost in thought. It was slowly sinking in through many layers of denial just how unattached she was. My connection to her kept me trying to build a relationship, forgive her, seek her out, hopeful that things would change so we could be something to each other. How had I completely deluded myself that she shared my love and connection? I had allowed myself to believe that under her tough exterior and unhealed heart was a vulnerable person waiting to be healed by love and devotion. What if she was simply not capable of forming an attachment, not just with me but with anyone? If this was the case, I didn't even have to take this personally.

All these years of trying to get it right with her, and I was just now seeing the reality of my experience. It took standing alone on that beach, left behind, scared, and not knowing what to do that brought me to this place. A reciprocal, loving relationship with Mariela was my construct, a wish fulfillment, a fantasy that I chased, believing it existed, just beyond my reach. If only I could help her understand; if only I could convince her of my devotion; if only I could demonstrate my love. At that moment I realized how many of my beliefs began with "if only…"

And then came a realization that had me shaking my head in dismay: I would have identified this pattern and faulty thinking long ago in any of my clients. I had been too close to the drama to see it clearly. Tears filled my eyes as I thought of her as a small girl desperate to be loved but probably never believing it was possible. Our lives together had been fraught from the beginning with me trying to persuade her with a love that she didn't trust or believe. She was twenty-three years old and living her life full of turmoil and upheaval far removed from my influence. *Had she ever been under my influence?* I wondered. Her early years had impacted her so significantly that what I offered in the brief time she lived in our family seemed a pittance. My internal dialogue, meant to soothe and release me from habitual struggle against odds stacked against both of us, helped strengthen me for what lay ahead that day.

I looked at the waves rolling onto the beach, the timeless rhythm and beauty, and felt the strength and purpose that had nothing to do with me. It was as much folly to try to change and control that which was outside my control as it was to think I could control the rhythm of the waves. The forces at work were deeper and stronger than my will or any action I could take. Mariela's story was unfolding as it would, whether I liked it or not. For a moment, the future seemed less scary. The story was in process, and all I had to do was let go and see what happened.

This new insight quickened my step, and for moments, things felt as if they would fall into place according to another power, not my own, and I was comforted. A calming sensation, the first I had felt since she walked away, washed over me. I was only responsible for my actions and keeping my heart open; she was responsible for her own life, and those of her children. I loved her despite everything and would continue to love her, but I wanted to let go of forcing an outcome.

As I walked in the warm sand, I looked to my bare feet supporting me as they pressed into the sand and left prints. *I have to take care of myself. I can't walk away from myself in the service of her.* With all my obsessing about Mariela's behaviors, I had failed to ask what worked for me. This trip was not working; it had been a bust from the beginning. Mariela was not yet interested in finding her roots or healing her childhood trauma. That was my idea for her. I wanted to find Mariela and tell her we would go home; there was no need to stay longer. I would tell her that I had nothing to prove, that I'd always love her, but I'd work on acceptance rather than change. I'd tell her that I had to take care of myself, and her life was her own to live.

I walked calmly with this emotional resolve. "Please, Lord, let me hold on to this resolve as I deal with the crisis looming now," I whispered an earnest prayer, a habit from my Catholic upbringing, as I walked, still looking in all directions for a sign of her.

Sweat pooled at my waistband; my hands trembled, and the heat made me lightheaded as I walked. It was already in the nineties, and a fierce sun drilled into me accusingly. My thoughts, which only moments before had steered me toward emotional resolve, now spiraled into the possibilities of peril. Would she be raped? Would her children be abused? My imagination of dreadful outcomes held me hostage, and my new awareness of only moments before moved to the background.

I had to find her, and going to Washington's home was my only option. A wave of anger took the place of the resolve I felt moments before. *Why the hell am I in a godforsaken town in Belize putting myself in danger while desperately searching for an adopted daughter who doesn't care if I live or die?* I didn't want to stay in the village a minute longer than I had to. I decided to pack up, pay the bill, and hop on the bus that left hourly and travel along the road out of town where I had learned Washington lived. I felt propelled by anger and determination to find her and get the hell out of Belize.

A short time later, I climbed aboard the bus, and as it lumbered slowly down village streets picking up passengers, I rehearsed the ultimatum I would give her. My new insight that she was not attached to me left me unbalanced and unsure how she would respond to my pleas that she come with me. Can you threaten someone who really doesn't give a damn about losing your affection? Can you withhold something from someone when they never trusted you had something to give? Was there even a shred of bond between us to count on? What good was an ultimatum when we were not playing by the same rules? The futility of my endeavors sat solidly in my lap.

Heat, fear, and anger were a wicked brew causing sweat to pour down my back as I turned for a final look out the bus window at what I had once dared to imagine would be a healing paradise. *Why had I been so easy to manipulate?* Full of shame and a sense of my own stupidity, I willed myself to stop my self-bashing dialogue. *I did it out of love for her.* I tried to comfort myself. *And because I'm pretty damn naïve.*

As the bus roared out of town, I saw the row of dilapidated houses on stilts that sat on the beach. I asked the driver to let me off when I saw the bright-blue one with five or six bikes propped up against it. This was certainly the home of the man I had last seen her with, his arm around her, beaming at his good fortune. Trash and discards littered the front of the house, but from the back there was a perfect view of the turquoise water lapping below. Lugging my backpack off the bus, I stopped on the street to resolve myself before approaching the house. The important thing was to determine if she and her kids were safe and unharmed; then I'd go from there. Reggae music pounded through the thin walls. A screen door at the top of steep, uneven steps was all that separated me from the confrontation.

It occurred to me at that moment that I didn't have to do anything. As soon as I knew she was OK, I could leave Belize by myself, call it a bust, let her suffer the consequences of being stuck there, and figure out for herself how to get home. It was tempting, and if she didn't have two children depending on her, I might have done it. Instead, with heart pounding, jaw set and determined, and fear and anger fueling my steps, I walked up the uneven wooden stairs. I let my heavy backpack drop at my feet before shouting above the music, "Hello, hello, Washington, I'm here looking for Mariela. Hello? Hello?" My voice sounded thin and shaky, so I took a breath and tried again. "I'm looking for Mariela. I'm her mother."

"Don't you be coming around here yelling and making a scene, lady," Washington was at the door, glassy eyed, shirtless with his shorts dangerously close to falling off, long, matted hair falling over his brown shoulders. He leaned against the door frame and looked right into me.

"Is Mariela here? I'm looking for her and her kids." I tried to cover my mounting fear of being in a face-off with this man, on his turf, at the top of a steep set of shaky stairs. The docile man of the day before was gone, replaced by a man defending his territory.

"If she's here, it's because she likes me. Maybe she's tired of you—did you ever think of that?" he leered, his words lazily falling out of his mouth.

I was thinking about what to say next, when Mariela came from behind him, holding Antonne. I couldn't see Caleb, but I was immensely relieved to see that she and the baby looked fine, sleepy and messy, but alive.

I thought I saw relief on her face but couldn't be sure. If it was, she immediately transformed it to scorn. "What are you doing here? Get a life!" she spewed at me, and just as quickly she looked to Washington for approval, and he put his muscled arm around her. Caleb appeared at the door, looking like he wanted to run to me, but he hesitated. His face looked like he had been crying, and he seemed confused and scared. I motioned to him to come stand next to me, but he looked to his mom and instead stood beside her.

I couldn't waste any time. The bus left on the hour from Placencia and would be passing here again in forty-five minutes or so. My plan was to be on it, heading north to Belize City, hopefully with Mariela and her kids.

"I'm leaving Placencia, Mariela. It didn't work out for us here. The bus comes by here, and I hope you and the kids will join me."

"You can't tell me what to do. I'm a grown woman. Maybe I want to stay here with Washington." She leaned into him. He was a foot taller, and it didn't work well to have their arms around each other's waists. He winked at me as if to communicate, *I can't help it—the woman wants me.*

I hoisted my backpack onto my back, steadied myself, then started down the uneven stairs with shaking knees. I turned around when I reached the bottom and said in my sturdiest voice, determined not to grovel, beg, whine, or otherwise try to convince her of my devotion, "Mariela, I love you and your kids, but I'm leaving Placencia on the next bus. You can decide what you want to do. If you choose to stay here with Washington, I wish you the best. But think about what you're doing. You only met him yesterday, you don't know each other, and you have two kids to think about." Old habits die hard. I was slipping into lecturing, and she was digging her heals in, ready for a battle of wills. I stopped myself. "I've said enough. I'm going to wait on the road for the bus to come. I hope you join me."

Something had shifted in me. I walked away but heard Washington whistle and say in a loud voice so I could hear, "Shit, that woman talks a lot." Then the music from the radio blared again as I collapsed on the curb to wait for the bus. I grabbed a handful of sand and let it slide through my fingers. Tears welled in my eyes, but my resolve was intact. I had played all my cards, and the rest was up to her. She would either come with me or she wouldn't, and only time would tell.

I checked my watch for the tenth time. The bus was due, and there was no sign of her. So, this was my answer. She would be staying here in Placencia, and I would be going home without her and her children, I thought miserably. Villagers rode by on bikes and seemed not to notice me. Others walked lazily in the hot afternoon sun, greeted me, and continued on their way. Behind my sunglasses, my eyes brimmed with tears.

I heard the bus before I saw it. Having just picked up a few passengers, it was accelerating toward me. I still didn't see Mariela, so I stood and grabbed my backpack, then turned toward Washington's house. Mariela was descending the stairs and walking slowly toward the bus, holding the baby, with Caleb trailing a few feet behind. Scowling, squinting in the bright sun, she looked right through me. I kept my face blank, determined to allow her to join me without feeling like she had lost a battle of wills. It was clear that my victory, as she saw it, would come at a great cost.

"I'm glad you came," I said flatly as she boarded the bus.

"Fuck you" was her only response. I took a seat, and she went to the back of the bus to sit as far from me as possible on the six-hour journey to San Ignacio, where we would spend a few days before our rescheduled flight was due to leave. We had cut the trip short by ten days; there would be no healing trip to Guatemala. I had no idea how to reconcile that and wasn't sure I wanted to. My goal was to spend the last few days without incident, then get safely home. I couldn't resist trying to help her with the kids; they were restless and hungry. She rarely interacted with them, but when I tried, I got a sharp rebuke from her.

"Just leave us alone. Go stick your head in a book and forget about us."

"How about if I have them sit with me so I can read to them?" I replied.

"They don't want to." She dismissed me and turned away.

I could hear the baby fussing and wanted desperately to help, but when I tried again, she barked, "I said to leave us alone." Frustrated and angry, I did bury my head in a book as she had suggested but couldn't concentrate.

Considerably more tenacious than I, she was determined to punish me and rarely talked to me for the next few days. Being held hostage by the fear of her angry outbursts kept me sidestepping and measuring everything I said; in reality, I had no control of even that. She was angry, and I was the target, like it or not. No one else stuck around long enough to incur her fury.

Occasionally, the ludicrousness of the situation struck me. She was furious with me and demonstrated that in all her actions. Yet in my estimation, I was the offended one. She left me on the beach, sick with worry and unable to find her and her kids. I had purchased the tickets that were changed. I was walking on eggshells to prevent an outburst. "She's impossible," I fumed under my breath.

Our last few days in Belize had some moments of pleasure as I played with her kids and enjoyed their youthful enthusiasm. When she wanted a break from them, she'd urge Caleb in my direction or hand the baby to me. At her whim, she would take the baby and call Caleb back to her without explanation. I couldn't help notice that Caleb seemed unnaturally eager to comply with her instructions.

Caleb was already showing signs of trying to predict and take care of his mom. Her approval was erratic and kept the eight-year-old anxiously trying to obtain it. Her attention to him was incidental and not based on his needs. As I watched Mariela relate to her children, I understood how the loss of her mother in the upheaval of the Guatemalan war had profoundly shaped her ability to parent. She was not overtly abusive, but she neglected their basic needs for security and emotional comfort. Already, Caleb seemed considerably more concerned about taking care of his mom than having an expectation that she would take care of him. And she depended on him to take care of baby Antonne more like a partner than a child.

"Can I help you take care of Antonne instead of Caleb? He's just a kid—let him play." I tried to intervene.

"It's good for him to help. When I was his age, I took care of lots of babies in the orphanage," she snapped back at me as she handed the fussy baby to Caleb, who knew better than to protest.

I was more than ready to leave Belize and Mariela when the day came for us to fly out. The trip had been a disaster; she was more hostile now than she was before we ventured out together on what I hoped would be a healing, bonding trip. We had connecting flights in Dallas and were there for a few hours together. Then she would fly to New York, and I would return to Portland. I bought her a meal in the airport, walked her to her gate, gave her children a quick embrace, and then looked her directly in the eye. I had avoided confronting any of her behavior while we were out of the country in fear of her acting impulsively or dangerously when we were so far from home. Being held hostage like this didn't sit well with me, and I'd had enough. Brimming with frustration and anger, I finally expressed it.

"It's been a long week with you. I had hoped we might have some fun together. I've had it with your attitude, your anger, and you blaming me for everything that has gone wrong in your life. And I'm tired of trying to make it right for you. You are in charge of your own life. I'm done letting you abuse me," I said with one quick breath before she could interrupt or walk away.

I needed to be heard; I needed to tell her it would be different from now on. I wanted to show her how angry I was and how hurt I felt.

"So, get out of my life then," she replied, apparently unmoved by my tirade. "Who needs you? You're not my mother, so stop saying you are. I have a mother. And she was better than you could ever be." Now her eyes were filling with tears.

I knew her tears would trigger compassion, which would soften my stance and make providing her with emotional comfort my primary concern. This had been a pattern. She was returning to New York soon, and it could be many months (or years) before I'd see her again. I wanted to be adult about it, express my real feelings, which were negative, but let her know I loved her. "Listen, I love you, Mariela, but I don't want to go on this way. It's not good for either of us."

She would not make it easy to tie things up neatly and with understanding and compassion for each other. "Get the hell out of here. And don't be calling me. I'm done with you." She yanked Caleb's hand and pulled him toward seats at the gate. Antonne started to cry, no doubt scared by the anger, and she shoved a bottle into his mouth as she sat down.

I stood speechless. There was nothing more to say, nothing more to do. She didn't seem to need resolution, understanding, or patching up to protect the bond of love. I turned to leave, my knees shaking, only now aware that our conversation could be heard by all those standing around. I didn't care. To hell with all of them. They had no idea what I was dealing with. Let them think I was a deplorable mother.

Before turning a corner in route to my own gate, I took a final look at Mariela sitting at the gate with her two children. She looked untroubled by our final words.

Chapter 16

Mariela

> "Don't grieve. Anything you love comes around in another form."
>
> Rumi

Mariela stood at the doorway to her community college class talking to Jennifer, the tall, slim, pretty sociology teacher who had taken an interest in her. "You know, you should return to Guatemala if you can, since you haven't been there since you were a kid," Jennifer said with enthusiasm. "I'm fascinated with Mayan culture. I went to Guatemala several years ago, and it's truly amazing." It was a new experience for Mariela, to have someone so interested in her, so keen to learn more about her country and her life. "What a wonderful opportunity it would be to return with all you know now," said the educated, poised woman not much older than herself. Mariela decided then that she'd call Charlotte and present the idea Jennifer had inspired.

Mariela hadn't told Jennifer, whom she admired, that she had two kids, no money, and supported herself on welfare. She liked the part she was playing of being a fascinating Mayan student. She had been in the class for a few months, arranged by a caseworker in Jersey City, where she had found better services and cheaper apartments than those available in New York City. The same caseworker had arranged day care for Antonne, still a baby. Caleb was now in second grade. She felt like a new person having started over on the East Coast with new people who didn't know her past, a clean slate, and now a college class, meant to help her feel success and hope for the future.

She had called Charlotte one Saturday morning from her small Jersey City apartment and shared the idea of going back to Guatemala—and also to Belize, which sounded exotic with its warm tropical beaches she had seen when she looked up the country on the library's computer. She was surprised and pleased when Charlotte, despite everything that had happened, agreed to consider the plan.

"It will be fun to spend some time together in your country," Charlotte had said with that hopeful tone in her voice. Who knew what Charlotte expected to happen on the trip? *What she hopes for is her business,* Mariela thought. In truth, the country of her childhood haunted her and represented little more than loss and pain. She had no people in Guatemala, no favorite places to visit, no connections. She had stopped speaking Spanish long ago and had no desire to think of that strange language, Quiche, that had poured out of her when she lost touch with reality.

During the years she lived in the orphanage, she had fantasies of walking the streets of Guatemala City, seeing her Mayan mama, and the bitter then loving reunion they would have. She still had recurring dreams of running after her mama who disappeared into the crowd of a marketplace. The terror of losing her ghost mama would wake her, shaking and confused. In another dream, her mother held her so tight she felt smothered, her face pressed against her huipil that smelled of maize. In those dreams she wanted to get away so she could kick and hurt her mother. She screamed, "Why did you leave?! What did I do?" and woke up with ragged breathing and these questions still bitter in her mouth.

Maybe going back would settle her nightmares, and if nothing else, she would get a much-needed break from single parenting and going to school. So, with the inspiration and encouragement from Jennifer and with Charlotte's agreement to pay the way and go with her, she made plans to first visit Belize, then continue on to Guatemala, the country that haunted her dreams. Getting distance from Charlotte had given her some hope that maybe they could travel together peacefully. Being with Charlotte often evoked some miserable feelings that seemed visceral and beyond her control. Was it anger, resentment, bitterness? She wasn't sure what stirred up those feelings, but she hoped she could control them on their trip together.

When they were together in Belize, Mariela felt Charlotte's penetrating blue eyes on her, trying to figure her out like she was a puzzle with a missing piece. Charlotte had known her at her worst as a desperate little girl, then as an unhappy teen mother, then as a mental patient. She resented the vulnerability she felt with her adoptive mother.

"Would you stop judging me and trying to control me? I don't need you! Isn't that obvious to you?" Mariela had yelled at her during the trip. Then at the airport when they were going their separate ways, Charlotte got red faced and shaken as she unleashed her anger before turning to go to her gate. Mariela wondered if the relationship was too broken to repair after that. That thought scared her, but she dismissed it quickly. She told herself that she could live without Charlotte, but she doubted if they were really done with each other. They had a hold on each other that was beyond explanation. Charlotte was the closest thing to a mother she had, and the only person Mariela had been able to turn to for help. She wasn't sure she wanted Charlotte completely out of her life. *I just have to keep her at a distance and not allow her to have control over me,* Mariela thought, her strategy for all relationships.

She had been tempted to stay in Belize with the sexy, slightly dangerous guy she met there. She figured that she could move in with him and share the costs, which were nothing in Belize. They'd take care of each other and her kids—that's what she'd been thinking, letting herself imagine his strong arm around her, enjoying a simple life like the one she had as a kid in Guatemala. Simple food, fresh air, people she would come to know in the village who liked her and saw by her coffee-colored skin that she belonged with them. The dream had taken hold, but only briefly. Her Garifuna boyfriend had asked to borrow money, and she had given him all she had. On the one night she spent with him, he had left with her money and come back with beer and pot, with no intention of giving her change. She was pissed but didn't let him know it. She didn't want to destroy her dream of a home in Belize with this man. But when Charlotte gave her the ultimatum, Mariela knew she'd get on the bus with her. She hated Charlotte for spoiling her dream and blamed her for the unhappiness and frustration she felt. She returned to Jersey City without ever going to Guatemala. She was relieved about not going. She wasn't ready to visit that damn country.

After that disappointment of a trip, she returned to her apartment and the community college in Jersey City, happy that she had chosen it as a place to live. It was teeming with immigrants, people down on their luck, artist types, students, people of all colors and languages. She fit into the blend, and no one asked where she was from. All shades of people from light brown to black, most speaking English with lots of different accents. Saris and hijabs were as common as blue jeans and suits. Being invisible with no pressure to fit in felt good. It wasn't unusual for people to speak Spanish to her on the streets, assuming that was her first language. She never spoke back to them in Spanish, wanting to deny the language that had replaced her original Quiche, the language that came between her first one and the English she now spoke without an accent.

She learned to fit in with people collecting food stamps, housing benefits, WIC, and getting help to pay electric bills; everyone was looking for help, and there was no shame in it. People were friendly and spoke to each other openly, chatting and sharing tips while they waited in lines for assistance. It seemed they were all on an overcrowded party boat trying to stay afloat. Everyone was hustling something to survive.

She was enjoying a life beyond being a struggling single mother. Riding buses and subways alone gave her an opportunity to talk to men and create a new identity, one more to her liking. Distance from her old self, the one full of shame and dependent on the family who picked her up off the streets, emboldened her. Most of the time, she didn't give Charlotte and her family a thought. When Charlotte called occasionally to see how she was doing, Mariela was a closed book and planned to keep it that way.

She grew comfortable hanging out, drinking coffee, and watching students rush by as she sat in the library or student center of the community college. She imagined being one of them and paid close attention to the way they talked and acted. She started to mimic being carefree or studious or preoccupied, depending on the image she wanted to project. One day as she sat in the college community center, she noticed a nice-looking Black man watching her while he worked cleaning tables, his muscled arms flexing as he moved chairs around. She smiled at him, and he smiled back with a quick wave. She started to watch for the nice-looking maintenance man each time she sat in the student center. He circled around her doing small jobs, straightening chairs and sweeping, occasionally catching her eye and smiling. His shyness was appealing. It was clear to her that he wanted to meet her.

When he finally came to her table and grinned shyly at her, she saw that he was older, maybe forty or even forty-five. He introduced himself as Hasan. He smiled, the lines around his eyes deepening. He had intense but kind brown eyes, kinky dreadlocks tied back, warm-brown skin, a muscular body, and a friendly face. She liked the fact that he was older and was responsible enough to work full-time at a real job. So many of the guys she met did nothing but stand on street corners hustling and bullshitting each other.

She and Hasan talked off and on, mostly joked around; then finally he asked her to go for a walk when he got off work later in the afternoon. They became regulars, seeking each other out, talking about their days, holding hands, and laughing. One day he told her he had something important to tell her, and she listened carefully. What was he planning to tell her, and would she be expected to reveal herself more fully to him?

"I'm a Muslim. It's an important part of my life. I go to the mosque and follow our traditions." He looked more serious than she had seen him.

"Oh, is that why you use the name Hasan? Is that why you seem so different than the guys I usually meet? That's not a problem for me," she added quickly. She knew nothing about Muslims other than what she'd heard about them flying into the World Trade Center. But Hasan was a local guy and not one of those fanatics, she was sure. She couldn't see how his being Muslim would be a problem for her.

He continued, "I'm not married and don't have children, but I like the idea of it." What was she to say to that? She liked this man and wanted him. He was a grown-up, worked full-time, prayed, took life seriously but knew how to laugh and have fun. And he liked her. It was time to tell him about her kids. They were a secret she couldn't keep.

"I have two kids at home, an eight-year-old boy and a little boy almost two," she said casually, like they weren't much trouble at all, an afterthought.

"You have two kids! That's great! When can I meet them?"

Hasan met her kids that week and seemed happy to include them. He roughhoused with them on the floor, taught Caleb simple card games, played hide-and-seek with both of them, and when they all walked together, held on to their small hands. She marveled that he was so good with them. On Fridays, he prayed at the mosque and returned feeling serene and ready to spend the day with her. When he asked her to wear a headscarf, she didn't mind. Her identity was changing, and she was thrilled to be with this good man. He wanted her and her kids, and she wondered how she had finally gotten lucky in her life. He told her he would someday like to marry, and she assumed they would. She vowed to show him only her most fun-loving and charming side. She'd keep her angry, impatient, bad-tempered side underground, she decided, to keep this good man in her life. It wouldn't be easy to hide her dark side, but she was determined. And being with a good man such as Hasan would surely rid her of her demons.

Hasan worked long hours and often stopped by the mosque, coming home exhausted to a clean apartment and a home-cooked meal. She agreed to take Caleb to the Islamic school for instruction and joined other Islamic women at the mosque to pray. Memories of going to Catholic mass, kneeling and praying in long rows of orphans, resurfaced. Orphans got flicked on the back of the head if they dared squirm or whisper, but even so, she had liked the routine, the sense of belonging to something. She was unsure if she believed what she was taught about Islam, but it didn't matter. It was a comfort to sit silently with others who did. Hasan beamed to see her, his woman, sitting in prayer, and he began talking about having a baby together.

Charlotte called one Sunday for the first time in weeks. Mariela was cooking, her kids were playing near her, and Hasan was trying to repair their vacuum.

"Hi, I've been thinking about you. How are you? How are things going?" she said in the light and breezy way that Charlotte used to start conversations.

"I'm good. We're all here. I've got the family I never had." Mariela was anxious to let Charlotte know that she could create her own good life. She knew this would be hurtful; Charlotte still liked to say that Mariela was part of their family. What Mariela really wanted to say was "I needed you, but you were never enough. I've replaced you and don't need you anymore." Finally, she was truly in control of the relationship with Charlotte and not a needy kid begging to belong. She had her own kids and a man who had chosen her; this was the way a family felt. She smiled to herself.

She looked at her small, clean apartment as she talked. Her children were happily playing, and her man was waiting for good food she had cooked in her kitchen. "I'm happy," she told Charlotte; then she realized it was the first positive emotion she had shared with Charlotte for many years. It surprised her that she wanted to share this. Had Hasan finally made her happy enough to forget the burden of her losses? When she got off the phone with Charlotte, she busied herself chopping vegetables as she hummed a tune.

Hasan was delighted when she became pregnant, lovingly stroking her swollen belly, and as she became bigger, he did more to help her around the house. She smiled to see him so involved, and it was a real smile from her insides, not the fake pulling up of her lips she had always done to win favor. She had wondered how he'd respond to her losing her shape, but he was proud they had created a child, and he doted on her. He was with her when she delivered a beautiful baby girl that they named Yasmin. He was thrilled with his child and looked at her like she was a miracle to behold. Her first two children had been born without much involvement from their daddies, who left when the babies were young. This time, Mariela said to herself, there would be someone to take care of her and help her with their child.

She was so accustomed to withholding from Charlotte that her instinct to tell her about the new baby surprised her. Maybe Charlotte would be happy for her and even send some money to help out with expenses, she thought, before she made the call.

"Hello, I've got some news. Hasan and I just had a baby girl. Everything is good, and I wanted you to know."

Charlotte said nothing for a minute. Was she shocked, disappointed, worried? There was no way to tell, Mariela thought.

Then Charlotte finally broke the silence. "I'm so happy for you. Girls are wonderful. I'd like to send you something. What do you need?" Mariela had been correct about Charlotte wanting to help. She reminded herself that Charlotte did come through for her. She could depend on that.

"Hasan works, but now with three kids, we could use some money more than anything." She wanted to end this pleasant conversation before it changed to something different. Mariela didn't fully understand her resentment against Charlotte, but it was there, right below the surface and ready to erupt at the slightest provocation.

"I'm happy to put a check in the mail to you. How are Caleb and Antonne? What do they think of their new baby sister?"

Mariela could feel the conversation shifting and Charlotte taking control of it, directing it to discover more, to get into her business. "They are good. Everything is good, other than our tight budget with three kids. Listen, I've got to go, I hear the baby crying." She hung up and was glad to get off the phone before she said something she'd regret.

When Yasmin, her little girl with black ringlets framing her cute face was three, Mariela discovered she was pregnant again. She wasn't happy about it, but Hasan was thrilled. Being a father gave him a chance to redo his own sad and scary childhood. He told Mariela after they were together about a year that his father had left when he was a young boy, and his overburdened alcoholic mother gave him and his four siblings just enough care to keep Child Protective Services from removing them. Mostly the kids raised each other. He said that he would make sure his children, and the two older ones who weren't his, would experience the security and love he never had. He liked being a parent, but he never made it look natural or easy. He had to work at it, and so did Mariela, both of them learning how to show love when they had received so little as small children.

Mariela's pregnancy made her tired and moody. She was bored and overwhelmed with the life that had pleased her not so long ago. Her life had become dull drudgery with Hasan and the three kids, and soon she'd have another baby to trap her in their apartment. She complained to Hasan, "I want a life too. I never got an education, and I want to go back and take some more classes. How about you watch the kids a few nights a week while I take some classes at the community college?" He agreed. Hasan wanted her to be happy, and he said taking care of the kids a few nights a week wouldn't be a problem.

She loved being a student and often asked Hasan to watch the kids on the weekends too, so she could study. She was discovering that she was a good student, and her teachers encouraged her. For someone who hadn't finished high school the usual way (she had a GED), she was pleased at her progress. She thought things were going well.

Hasan, however, was beginning to be critical when he came home to a mess or when there was no dinner laid out for him. He expected her to take care of the kids, keep up with the shopping and laundry, take her classes, and pray at the mosque, like a good Islamic woman. His salary barely kept them out of poverty. His approval was important to her, but in short supply, and she resented him for it. Anger and edginess seeped into their small living space, and she couldn't shake it. Hasan, who was supposed to be the end of her loneliness and despair, was the cause of it, she fumed.

"Why are you late again? Don't you want to come home to me and your kids?" she'd rant and follow him into the kitchen, her heart racing with anger. His actions were pulling up fears of rejection from the depths of her, which transformed to anger and resentment.

"Mariela, you've got to back off. I've worked hard all day. I'm tired. Leave me alone, please," he begged.

"What, you think I'm not tired taking care of the kids all day?" she screamed. "I told you, I need a life too." She needed his compassion and patience, and he needed the same in equal measure from her. Neither of them had a reserve to pull from.

The arguing became predictable and stopped only when he walked away from her, out the door, which caused her to feel panic and fury at the same time. Several times when he left, she thought she'd seen the last of him, but he'd reappear, pick up the baby, tell her he needed some space, that was all, and they'd have some peace for a while. Then she sensed he was judging or rejecting her, and the vulnerable feelings elicited were unbearable. He had the power to shatter her and walk away. The feelings, similar to what Charlotte provoked in her, left her wrecked and dripping with resentment and hostility.

After their baby was born, a boy they named Ameer, she told Hasan she was done having kids. The new baby in addition to the other three left her too depleted to fight with Hasan. She could feel herself shutting down, closing in, walling off from him and even her children. She called Charlotte one day, in an attempt to reach out for help, but she didn't know how to ask for it. She was done groveling and needing her but didn't know what else to do. As soon as she heard Charlotte's voice on the phone, she started to cry. "Please help me; I'm scared," she wanted to say but couldn't. How could she need this woman and hate her for it at the same time? Her feelings were knots too tight to untangle. Mariela told her things weren't going well with Hasan and left it at that.

Chapter 17

Charlotte

> "Life is a succession of lessons which
> must be lived to be understood."
>
> Rumi

After the ill-fated trip to Belize, awareness about my predicament with Mariela shifted. Those tumultuous days of traveling together gifted me with a new perspective. Before the trip, I had seen her as a victim of circumstances, her personality formed by grief and loss, and amenable to change through love. The well-meaning therapist who worked with Mariela when she was an adolescent had solidified this belief when she looked over her glasses at me and said sincerely, "Your job, Charlotte, is to heal her with your love and commitment." Only later did I realize that I kept that message in my hip pocket and lived by it. The therapist's attempts to empower me left me with an inflated sense of my ability to change Mariela's life course. It was an immense burden to believe I could right the wrongs of the past by simply loving her enough.

After our trip together, a more complex picture of Mariela emerged, and I stepped back to try to make sense of it. The trauma of her early years had indelibly shaped her. What her genes contributed would remain a mystery. I was a latecomer to her life and development, but I had been doggedly determined to rewrite her whole story with the ending I desired. Slowly, I came to accept that her life journey was in her hands. I was a loving witness, and that was difficult enough. My stubborn hope that she would be healed through love and devotion was the mechanism that held my grief at bay. As long as I had hope, I could avoid sinking into the sorrow of my helplessness and loss. I realized I had used the same unconscious mechanism to cope with my narcissistic mom and my immature husband. The insight was flickering, and my hope for change was a life raft not easily discarded.

Mariela's behaviors were maddening, and I was angry that my well-meaning efforts weren't appreciated and didn't affect or influence her. If divorce from a child was possible—as it is with a married partner with whom there are irreconcilable differences—I would have asked for one from Mariela: "I loved you, I tried to hang in there with you. I committed myself to standing by you, but I give up. I can no longer do this," I'd say. "It's over, and I wish you the best. I will always hold you in my heart, but I'm done." Then, I'd do the work to emotionally move on.

But there is no legal avenue for dissolving the ties that bind a mother to her child. People do turn their backs on their kids all the time, I argued to myself, for less than I've had to deal with, but I knew that would never be me. I was attached to her and wasn't ready to give up trying.

One day as I walked during my lunch hour through the leafy streets near our clinic, I admitted a truth to my dear, unflappable friend Barbara, fairly sure she wouldn't judge me. "The truth is, I don't like her. She's aggravating as hell, and I wish I could get a pass out of her life," I said. "I'm tired of being on her sinking ship, and I want off." Saying these feelings out loud was scary. They were statements of fact, rather than sentiments seeped in guilt and remorse.

"God, I don't blame you a bit, but you're the type who makes a commitment and sticks with it. You didn't leave your unsatisfying marriage even after it was clearly broken. You're like the patron saint of lost causes," she quipped, studying me for a reaction. We had been through a lot together, and our relationship could handle this kind of talk. "Seriously, you've got to practice setting limits with her. She drags you through shit, and you just hang in there with her. You may be dealing with her for the rest of your life. Do you want to be rescuing her when you're in your fifties, sixties, or even seventies? This may never be the relationship you hoped for, you know."

"Yes, of course, I know. You're right," I said, agreeing too quickly to a comment that broke my heart and scared me to death. Finally, I began to scrutinize the destructive dance in which we were caught. Mariela was unconsciously committed to her sad role as victim of circumstances beyond her control, and I was devoted to her story, which kept me stuck. Neither of us knew how to bow out. I was trapped in a box of my own making that said good mothers don't give up on their kids; good mothers are devoted to their children's success; good mothers work harder to help their kids. This well-practiced dance where we frequently stepped on each other's toes maintained our ailing relationship, despite being injurious to both of us.

While still stuck in that delicate dance, I had started to date a psychiatrist to whom I had been introduced by a friend. Jack was a nice-looking, divorced, intelligent man whom I found appealing but remote and difficult to know. We were spending more time together, and he seemed more interested in asking me about my life than sharing much about his. Initially, that was a welcome switch from the many men I dated who talked incessantly about themselves.

"I was thinking about your adopted daughter," he said one evening as we sat in his sparse living room, devoid of objects that would help me understand who he was. "I wouldn't be surprised if she has a significant attachment disorder, given her abandonment, her institutional care, and what you've told me about her behavior."

I was all ears and appreciated that he was interested enough to be curious about her. "Yes, I've been reading about attachment disorder, and she definitely has some traits."

"People with attachment disorder have extreme difficulty trusting, being dependent terrifies them, they lack empathy for others. If

Mariela as a young child never had her needs met by a loving and reliable parent figure, then she would have a very hard time building a secure and stable bond and trusting another caregiver, you. Ultimately, people with attachment disorder have a distorted perception of how relationships work." He seemed to enjoy explaining the diagnosis to me, and I was more than happy to focus on the perplexing topic that had affected my life.

"So, I wonder if she can ever recover from that early trauma and loss," I said, not sure if I wanted to hear his response.

"It's rather doubtful that she can completely recover; it depends on the degree of deprivation, her resiliency, when she began to have corrective caretaking responses in your home, and many other things. And, given our jobs, Charlotte, we have to believe that a good therapist could make a difference for her at some point."

I told him about a recent, somewhat hopeful conversation when Mariela had asked how I was doing, a rare inquiry. Typically, Mariela talked about difficulties in her life, and I listened, offering support. When she asked about me, I was pleased and jumped in with an opening for further conversation. "I've been better. Work is really hard right now; our caseloads are huge, and our budgets have been cut."

"I couldn't do that kind of work," she said. "It sounds awful to listen to people's problems all day." We laughed, and I agreed that it could be challenging, thinking ruefully that listening to her problems had taken a huge toll on me and had defined our relationship for years. "You are a good listener, so I bet your clients like you." I was stunned with her positive regard, such a rare commodity. I told Jack that my hopeful heart would invariably soften at those times. Then the next time we talked, she was inexplicably bitter and angry at me.

"Sounds like you get right on her emotional roller coaster with her," he said. "Hang on tight. I bet she can give you quite a ride." He continued, "She's not trying to drive you crazy. That's her internal world, which you try to make sense of from your perspective. You make the mistake of thinking that she thinks and feels like you do." He looked at me with empathy, as I let what he said sink in.

"You're right. She's unstable. I never know who is going to show up when we talk. I'm constantly trying to figure her out."

He laughed. "Hey, that's your problem. Have you ever thought that perhaps you can't figure her out? Her emotional life is wildly different from yours." His eyebrows furrowed as he looked to see if I followed his thinking.

"You're right," I said. "I suspect she knows just how to look like she's attached, like she cares, but it's a thin veneer to get her needs met without real and genuine regard. It makes me sad to think of her being such a fake with her emotions," I added.

"But she's not a fake. That may be all she's capable of at this point in her life."

I let this new way of seeing her settle in. Jack and I often talked about her during our brief romantic relationship that would later become a friendship. He remained helpful as I entered a new phase of deeper understanding of Mariela and myself in relation to her.

Another time when Jack and I were having coffee, he asked about Mariela. "She sounds like she also has some characteristics of borderline personality disorder." He was in the habit of talking about others, I suspected, to keep the focus off himself. "That's not unusual, for people with attachment disorders caused by early childhood trauma to also be borderline."

I was very familiar with this diagnosis. It was a dreaded psychiatric label that meant a client would manipulate, baffle, act out, often against themselves, and see everything in black or white, and it was very hard to treat. In relationships, people were either idealized or denigrated, shifting from one to the other quickly. All of us found it difficult to work with clients who had this unfortunate diagnosis.

"My God, you're right. Why haven't I seen this before?" I had been embarrassingly blind when it came to Mariela.

"Because you're too close to see it. And besides, who wants to see that? Denial is a marvelous thing."

I recalled her stories from the orphanage days when Mariela pretended to care about someone in order to get something from them. "I knew how to get the teacher to give me more time or more paper to draw on." "I pretended to love the social worker, but I really hated her." "I never liked that girl; I just acted like I did, so she would help me do my chores." These were learned and necessary survival skills, honed on the streets and in the orphanage, I had thought, not realizing that these traits had been woven into her being. It was painful to realize that although she appeared to care about me at times, genuine emotion beneath the behavior was minimal or lacking. The sweetness behind her greeting, "Hi, how are you doing?" would quickly turn to venom, if her following request for money was denied.

Work with a skillful therapist helped me continue to shift my perspective and gain insight into my painful dynamics with her. My relationship with her didn't get easier, but over time I learned to use less energy untangling knots I couldn't see or understand. When I finally understood that Mariela's personality may not be amenable to change until she did some very difficult work with a therapist, I loosened my grip. I had lost influence over her long ago, and knew she'd seek out a therapist only when and if she was ready.

My marriage falling apart and my inability to change Mariela exposed a crack in the façade of perfection I had honed since childhood. I had spent a lifetime trying to be "good" and loving to others, believing that was the ticket to be loved myself. Over time and slowly, I made room for being real rather than perfect, applauded my genuine effort rather than my accomplishments, and valued openness rather than playing a prescribed role. Once my primary roles of mother and wife were revealed as flawed, I had to learn that I was more than the roles I had played, most of them an effort to be loved and accepted. Beneath my capable and secure exterior was a doubtful child I had to learn to love and accept.

"God, I worked hard to hold things together, and for what?

Things fell apart despite or maybe even because of all my efforts," I said to Barbara as we shared dinner one evening.

"Yeah, I do that too. That seems to be what women do—well, women like you and me, until we learn it's not a winning formula for happiness." Barbara said with wisdom gained from life experience. "Char, you can't blame yourself for your marriage or your adopted child not working out. Sometimes there is nothing to be done to keep things from unraveling. You seem to think you can fix things through sheer will. Not everything can be fixed, and who knows what needs fixing anyway." She smiled.

Slowly, this new way of thinking was taking shape through the help of friends and therapy. The compassion I had for others was expanding to include myself. I began to accept my limitations, my foibles and quirks, and my misguided attempts at control. I started to focus on being better so I could become the person I was meant to be, not the person I thought others needed me to be. I began to feel lighter. I said "I don't know" much more, and I laughed at myself with good-natured affection.

"I'm a work in progress and a slow one, at that." I laughed with Jack one day when we met for lunch.

"Yes, we all are. It comes with the territory. Healer, heal thyself, you know," he quipped.

In the years that followed, when Mariela lived in New Jersey with Hasan and her kids and I was single with no kids at home, I stayed busy with work, friends, dating, and connecting with Chad and Jill, both married with careers. I also jogged each dawn before work and trained for triathlons. When weeks went by without hearing from Mariela, I allowed myself to feel relief and had a mantra I said to myself, *Things are unfolding as they will. It's beyond my control. Love and peace to you, dear Mariela; please feel my care and wish for your well-being.* This mantra brought me a measure of peace and was significantly better than gripping the phone with dread and believing I could change outcomes.

My life was busy and full, and despite this, often when sitting on a beautiful summer evening enjoying music with friends, my thoughts would turn to her, and I'd wonder how she was doing in her small apartment in Jersey City with her children. My thoughts of her and the guilt I carried about her not doing better would darken my mood and bring a cloud of guilt even on the most pleasant of evenings. *How am I to find happiness or contentment in my life until she is doing better?* I'd ask myself. *Will her chaotic life continue to cast a long shadow over mine? Why did I purposely bring her into my awareness when I knew I would be flooded with guilt and recrimination? Should I be doing more for her? Is she getting the help she needs to overcome her traumatic past? Why, oh why, did I let my naïve desire to change a life ruin mine?* And on it would go until I remembered to take a deep breath. "Let it go; let her go," I'd repeat, and more and more often I was able to bring myself back to the present pleasant moment quickly.

One of my passions had always been the study of different cultures and traveling to learn more about them. I decided to embrace this passion by heading to South America. I reasoned I could enjoy an adventure and experience internal growth and change with the change in landscape and culture. My first trip as a single person was to Ecuador where I spent a month practicing Spanish and exploring small and scenic Andean towns. The Indigenous people of that country reminded me of the Indigenous people of Guatemala I had seen on our trip to adopt Mariela. I felt a connection with them as I rode local buses and explored Andean sites and culture by myself. The journey of self-discovery was challenging and expansive. Then, a few years later, I traveled with a medical group to Bolivia to work in an altiplano eye clinic with the Aymara people, another Indigenous group. Jill, now a registered nurse, joined me on the mother-daughter volunteer adventure.

As I sat in a wind-swept and barren high-altitude clinic taking a break from using an eye chart to check villagers' vision, I noticed again how similar the physical characteristics were among the Indigenous people of Latin America. A young mother waiting patiently with a child strapped to her back looked at me and smiled shyly. Her sturdy arms were hairless, and I remembered newly adopted Mariela giggling with fascination as she compared our hairy arms and legs with her own bare ones. This memory filled my eyes with bittersweet tears and pressed on my bruised heart. *There are no guarantees in life*, I said to comfort myself as I gazed at each beautiful, stoic Aymaran person whose vision was clouded by cataracts due to their long days in bright, high-altitude sun. I felt both sadness and love for my elusive daughter. I managed a wry smile, thinking how easy she was to love from this distance.

I wondered how any of the strong and resilient Bolivian villagers would do if uprooted and forced to live elsewhere. How would they manage far from their culture, language, community, and people who looked like themselves? The women with their short, strong bodies, thick, coarse, black hair, almond-shaped eyes, and high cheekbones looked like Mariela. I was tall, lanky, and pale with curly hair and couldn't have looked more different. And yet, I thought, we all just want to be loved and held and cherished. As I sat in the chilly clinic in Bolivia, I thought of Mariela living in New Jersey with the obstacles she had to overcome, the adjustments she had to make, and the hurdles I had unwittingly expected her to jump.

I had thought I was doing a generous and good thing by taking her to the US, but her life had been difficult and filled with turmoil and adopting her had created a heavy burden on my life and my children's. I had focused on all she would gain by living in the US after losing her family in Guatemala. I had underestimated all she would have to give up. She was a sad and unattached kid when I met her, and leaving her country had severed her remaining moorings. It would be her life's work to put the pieces of her life together again in a way that made sense. I felt the shame of a privileged do-gooder as I sat writing in my journal while Jill wrote in hers in our shabby hotel room that evening. *Did my intentions justify her losses?* I asked. My thoughts swept me into a loop of remorse, guilt, and sadness.

We were near the Equator, where it turned dark at 6:30 p.m. like clockwork, so we wrote in journals for an hour in the sparce light of a small table lamp. Truly letting go of the struggle to prove myself through Mariela, I wrote, allowed a sense of powerlessness and grief to surface. That evening after Jill and I said goodnight to each other and huddled under thick wool blankets, I allowed myself to quietly weep. The tears soaked the graying pillowcase as I grieved my incapable mother, my unfaithful husband, and Mariela's inability to attach. I wept for the lost energy of my life that had kept me trying to fix situations and people beyond my control. I looked over to my beloved daughter, Jill, who had already fallen into an exhausted sleep in her small, hard bed, and felt immense gratitude for her and for Chad and their families. While there had been losses, there was also so much for which to be grateful. *Why focus on what hadn't worked?* I asked myself. *Go ahead and cry, Charlotte, but never forget how truly blessed you are.*

Still, the questions tumbled around my mind. *What if Mariela is never OK? What if her life is always full of turmoil and loss? What if she is destined to be lonely and unhappy no matter what I do or don't do?* A truth settled into the sadness. I needed to open to this grief and make room for it. Like Mariela's early loss, my loss of the imagined beloved and healed daughter would be the ache I may always carry. I would not let it define me. I fell asleep uplifted by a peaceful presence of my own making. Who says I get to write the happy ending? No one gets to do that. I smiled, patted my heart, and eventually fell asleep.

The next morning, I opened the window to a bright-blue sky and a resolve to enjoy my day and keep my heart open, not just to others but to myself. I talked to the steamed-up mirror in the tiny bathroom after a barely warm shower, "Hey, you, you really tried hard. Mariela's story isn't over. You did your best. Don't be so hard on yourself, sweet woman." I smiled at my reflection that looked more and more like my mother's, a startling fact with which I still had to make peace. I was starting to get the hang of riding the waves of self-incrimination and letting them fall away, rather than holding on and going down with them.

Months later on a drizzly fall day in Portland, my good friend and hiking partner, Ann, and I walked a trail and talked about dating. We hiked together each weekend and often talked about our latest encounters with a man on whom we had high hopes or another who had fallen off our list of hopefuls. I was a runner, biker, skier, hiker, and dragon boat paddler and met men easily. I sifted through them, determined to keep the upper hand and not allow myself to be vulnerable again. That frantic dating phase, as I called it, was fun and allowed me to gain experience with a variety of men, but it ran its course after a few years. "It's like having nothing but dessert all the time—great when you are having it, but a sugar hangover after, and not satisfying or fulfilling." I smiled. "I think I'm ready for something deeper, maybe even commitment." Ann looked at me with raised eyebrows. She was as surprised by my pronouncement as I was to hear it from myself. "Did I really say that? My brain must be overheated by this climb." We laughed.

I had recently told a nice man I had been casually dating for a month that I didn't think we were a good match. We had been sitting in my living room with the fireplace flickering on our faces. He had taken it well; I knew how to end things before they got too involved. But each relationship that didn't work out led to a line of thinking that there would never be someone for me and I better get used to being single. Despite feeling the breakup was the right thing to do, I felt sad and lonely about it.

I had gotten skilled at rapid-fire dating one man then another, deciding quickly if I wanted to stay involved. Thus far, most of them hadn't met enough of my list of must-haves or there had been major deal breakers. When someone did meet my unrealistically long list of qualifications, he'd invariably tell me that he couldn't see our relationship lasting. "Dating is an exhausting and often heart-wrenching process of finding the nerve to end it with someone or being dismissed yourself," Ann had warned me. I had yet to realize how truly unavailable I was for the long-term relationship I said I wanted, but going through the process offered distraction for years.

Finally, I slowed down on the dating treadmill and turned my attention elsewhere, spending time with women friends and family and doing things I loved. Cycle Oregon, a long-distance weeklong biking adventure, was one of those adventures. While attending a Cycle Oregon event in 2001, I looked across the room and saw a male friend standing with a man who caught my attention. I walked right over, and my friend introduced the man. I was immediately drawn to Bill, a divorced, athletic man with grown kids, tall and handsome and with an energy that pulled me in. I didn't understand the pull but didn't try to. I wanted to get to know Bill. I acted immediately, letting the friend know the next day that I'd welcome seeing Bill again and asked him to relay the message with my phone number. My boldness surprised me. I was typically not that forthright disclosing my interest or making myself vulnerable. It was the first of many times I'd be vulnerable with Bill.

"I haven't heard from that guy who intrigued me, but I don't regret putting myself out there," I told Ann weeks later.

"Nothing ventured, nothing gained. Excuse the cliché."

I had resigned myself to not hearing from Bill. Then he called. He later told me on our first date that he had started to date a woman in California and wanted to see if that was going to develop into anything serious before he contacted me. That same night, on our first date in an Indian restaurant, he used a pen to draw a timeline of his life on the table's butcher paper and encouraged me to do the same, his visual way of helping us see each other's lives. What I initially thought was an odd way to get to know someone became a delight. There was a map with places we had lived, high points in our lives, low points, changes, beginnings and endings, scribblings, drawings of our children, and much more. When we finished, we had a complex drawing that illustrated all the ways our lives had intersected through the years, our similarities and differences, and a lot of laughter and chemistry.

He had married for the first time the same year I had, we both had grown children, and our biological children were the same ages. I told him about Mariela, leaving out the details that I figured were too much for a first date. We had both recovered from difficult divorces. We discovered that both of us had attended Catholic schools and were Irish, we had moved west to get away from crowded East Coast conventions. We both loved the outdoors, camping, biking, skiing, rafting, exploring, traveling, and reading. We laughed often and talked for hours. I looked at him across the table and felt I knew him from another place and time, and I knew I wanted this man in my life.

I was still wary of commitment, linking it with pain and entrapment. My fear of being hurt kept a tight rein on my emotions, cutting off the energy of a fully opened heart, but I didn't understand that then. Our paths had been similar enough to believe we were meant for each other, but under our barely contained enthusiasm for each other was a layer of anxiety, a blockage intended to keep us safe but that failed to allow love to fully take root and flourish.

This dilemma of wanting what I feared gave me an appreciation of Mariela's lifelong dilemma. My fears, while not as entrenched, kept me paralyzed, nonetheless. It took seven years of dating and jostling for control, assessing my vulnerabilities and safety, and a separation from each other to further define what our relationship meant to us, until finally I felt ready to plunge into the deep water of matrimony. It wasn't easy to navigate the rough waters during those early years of marriage, but love and therapy were our life rafts. Bill was surprised that behind my mild, accommodating manner was a woman to be reckoned with and not someone who would easily bend to his will as his mild-mannered first wife of thirty years had done. Our solid foundation, love, and mutual passions sustained us, and I eventually opened fully to love's gifts.

Bill's job took him out of town often, and this was difficult for me. I wanted our relationship to progress the way I imagined. Again, I was trying to force my will in order to ease my anxiety and fear. The frequent partings and transitions put stress on our relationship, but we navigated this dynamic and learned from it. I learned to be appreciative with what we had, to let go of trying to impose what I wanted instead. This well-honed strategy couldn't be put aside easily. Over time, I learned to see that my struggles against or for a certain outcome had caused me to impede my flow of energy and joy, a real losing strategy with Bill, Mariela, and all the relationships in my life. There was much to discover about Bill and about myself in relation to him and others, and the years that followed were rich with growth and a deepening love.

One Saturday after an early-morning jog, Mariela called. I had started cleaning our home, determined to enjoy some quiet time alone while Bill was out of town. As soon as I heard her voice, I regretted picking up the phone. She sounded terrible. Her relationship with Hasan was rocky, I knew, but I hoped they could hold their eight-year relationship together. Her partnership with Hasan had taken me off the "hot seat" of being the only committed, caring person in her life, and I held on to hope that she and Hasan would discover a path to work through the tough times about which I had heard a little. I had liked Hasan when I met him at our extended family reunion in Pennsylvania earlier that year when he and Mariela and their four children, ages eighteen, eleven, six, and three, joined the reunion. He fit in well and seemed unfazed by the chaos of all the young children and varying ages and personalities of my large, extended family. I hoped he would become a permanent fixture in Mariela's life, adding the stability and sense of belonging I thought could be the psychological glue to sustain her.

As she, Hasan, and the kids prepared to leave the reunion to drive back to New Jersey, I said, "Goodbye, Mariela, I'm happy for you.

You have a wonderful family." An energy best described as love and hope surged through me. She was edgy during their visit, but overall, I considered the family reunion a success and a demonstration that she had a large family that accepted and loved her. She was almost thirty-three years old, had successfully taken some college classes, and had managed to hold a long-term relationship together. She had someone else in her life to lean on and engage with in her dance of hostile dependency. I had stepped back, enjoying the hiatus from her emergency phone calls. I was thrilled that she had a partner who seemed like a good man, and I appreciated my life free from constant worry about her. I trusted that she and her kids were doing OK and felt immense gratitude.

Then she had started to call more frequently, often complaining in endless streams of hostility about Hasan. "I've had enough of that idiot. I don't need that man in my life. He's nothing to me, and I'm better off without him." I had talked to Hasan several times since the family reunion. At first, he asked about her to better understand her; then, it seemed clear he was on the brink of throwing in the towel.

"That woman drives me crazy. What's wrong with her, anyway?" he asked. "She's a mess, never happy; she's selfish and mean, and I'm not sure I can take it anymore." I tried to encourage and support him without saying much about her. I dreaded the day when the full weight of her needs and difficult personality were back on me. "Hang in there, Hasan. She's not easy, but she can do better." I hedged the hard truth that she had always been difficult, and my hope that she would do better depended on the stability their relationship provided.

Now, I sat down, knowing this would not be a quick call. She started talking in a low, flat voice, her shame and sorrow barely concealed. "Hi, could you help out with rent this month?"

Several weeks earlier, I had told Mariela that Hasan had called me and was concerned about her. I knew I was duplicitous talking to both of them, but I also planned to extricate myself quickly once they reconciled. She had scolded me. "Don't be talking about me to anyone, you hear? It's none of your business. And you can't believe a word that man says."

Despite knowing she was loathe to share her personal life, this time I asked directly, "Are you still with Hasan?"

She paused a minute after my question. "He's an idiot. He left, and he's not coming back. I hate him; that's all I'm going to say. I could use help to pay some bills, but if that's too much to ask, never mind." I heard her desperation and sadness and the usual dismissive tone.

The wonderful respite from my entangled dilemma of how to best help her was over. "I'm happy to help you this month," I responded, wondering if I was doing the right thing. Would she ever be fully independent? Would I ever be able to turn away from her and not feel responsible? I wondered how she was going to get by. "How are the kids?" I braced for anger or sarcasm, but it didn't come.

She sounded dull and sad. "They're OK." My desire to support her and keep her from nosediving while she moved toward what I hoped would be full adult independence was at odds with the sense that I was enabling her dependence on me. Setting limits and boundaries was a topic I frequently taught clients, a foundation of healthy relationships. But when it came to my personal dilemma of whether to rescue Mariela and her four children, I had a hell of a time doing what I advocated for others. I marveled how quickly I could get pulled into her drama, or perhaps it's more honest to say *our* drama. It was difficult to set limits with her when I suspected her kids weren't getting what they needed. I imagined being trapped by this pattern of helping just enough to keep her afloat with financial infusions, always careful not to encourage her dependence on me.

I asked my therapist, "What the hell am I supposed to do? If I refuse to help her, I feel like shit, and if I give her money, I feel like a manipulated idiot."

In his usual calm and thoughtful way, he said, "Think of it like giving to your favorite charity where you are not quite sure where the money is going, but it feels good anyway to help if you can." That advice got me out of the quagmire of indecision about whether it was good or bad to give her money.

Mariela and I entered another phase of more frequent talking, much of it about current upheavals in her life. She had taken a job working at a tollbooth for the New Jersey Turnpike, and it seemed like a good fit for her. She put her hand out and took their money with a brief "thank you"; that was all the interaction necessary. She didn't like the job but stuck with it for many months. I was hopeful that with my occasional help and the help of social service agencies, she could avoid a downhill slide.

A month or so later, I was listening to music at an outdoor concert on a beautiful summer evening, a light breeze blowing and calypso music beating in the background. The subject among my women friends had turned to serious relationships. "I'm scared of getting hurt again, but I so want to be with a man I love and respect," said Joyce, a beautiful woman fresh out of a painful divorce. "You have to risk getting hurt again, and who wants that?" Joyce smiled wryly as she redid her long red hair, a habit, especially when talking about serious subjects.

"It took me a very long time to make a commitment to Bill despite loving him. Once you've been hurt and had a marriage fall apart, it takes a while to risk again," I said. "I wanted to be sure I was with a man I could trust, who was vulnerable, open, and connected, but I was afraid to entirely be that way myself. I kept a part of myself walled off and safe."

"Yea, Charlotte, you were one tough customer," Kathy said, laughing. "I don't know why it took you so long to see you and Bill were perfect for each other, well, as perfect as it gets anyway." Kathy liked Bill a lot and enjoyed an easy bantering with him on rafting trips we had taken together.

"I was paralyzed by fear," I joked, knowing there was truth in that statement. I had taken this quandary of commitment to my therapist.

"Trust is at the heart of all relationships," he said. "We are wired for connection and attachment, but it's also terrifying, especially once you've been deeply hurt."

Driving home from that session, still processing my feelings, I allowed myself to imagine what it must be like for Mariela who had this dilemma as bedrock and beyond her awareness. If I had been scared of being hurt and abandoned, it had to be terrifying for her. It explained her frantic attempts to pull someone to her and then push them away with hostility with the first inkling that they were not there for her. This pattern left her and everyone around her exhausted and confused. I imagined how painful Hasan's leaving had been.

Mariela's breakup with Hasan sent her into an emotional tailspin of fury and grief. "I should just kill myself, nothing works for me," she cried one day as we talked.

"Please go talk to someone who can help you," I pleaded. "Can I help you find someone? I'm happy to pay for a therapist." I heard my desperate attempts to get her help, to keep her from encroaching on my life with her pain and unresolved grief, which I felt so completely unable to change.

Each time she called, there was an angry barrage. "I swear I hate that man and hope something bad happens to him like he deserves! I'm not going to make it easy for him to see his kids, and I'll make sure he pays his child support." She shifted from angry threats to dejected misery. I listened until it no longer felt helpful for either of us; then I tried to nudge her toward an understanding that above all else, she had to focus on her kids' best interests.

"What are you saying? You don't think I'm a good mother? I know what my kids need, and I don't need you to tell me." Just like that, she turned her fury on me. Of course I had huge doubts about her ability to mother, I always had, but now that she was alone and distressed about Hasan leaving, I was genuinely worried about them. I wondered constantly if I should alert Hasan of my concerns. It seemed like a betrayal of her, but then I remembered what I had said to her about keeping the best interests of her children the primary focus. I tried to stay out of it, but I finally felt I couldn't leave the welfare of her kids to fate.

I paced across my kitchen reaching for the phone, then putting it down, and reaching for it again. "I have to do what I can for her kids," I said to Bill. "It's not like I'll ruin the wonderful relationship I have with her," I added, realizing that she would be angry at me no matter what I did.

"Hello, Hasan." I was determined to be straight forward. "I'm concerned about the kids. She's my daughter, but we both know she can't be good for them with her depression and angry, volatile moods." He listened but didn't respond. He wasn't going to make this easy. "Your kids need you now more than ever. I know it must be hard with her, but are you planning to see them often, um, stay involved with them? Is there anything I can do to help?" I added when he still hadn't responded.

"I'm just happy I'm not living with her anymore. That woman needs help. She's all over the place with yelling, shutting down, crying." He told me he was going to court to see if he could get custody, but he doubted he could; he worked full-time and couldn't stay home with the little ones, and there was no clear evidence that she was harmful to them. The court had scheduled the hearing in a month. "All I can do now is stop by and pick them up every other weekend, but every time I do, she rants and yells. She can be good with the kids, then turn around and yell at them for nothing or refuse to talk to them." He sounded exhausted and sad. "You could help by coming out here and staying with her and the kids."

I had asked how I could help, and here was my answer, one I didn't want to hear. I was speechless for a minute.

"Uh, do you think that would help? I don't have much influence on her," I stammered, the guilt leaving a knot in my stomach. Hasan and I were planning behind her back, excluding her. It felt good to have an ally but wrong to be talking about her with someone she now hated. I had to look out for her kids and of course, I should go to her and be helpful. If Jill or Chad needed me, I wouldn't hesitate. Overcome with guilt, I cleared my throat to respond. "Well, yes, I suppose I could fly out," I finally said, knowing he could hear the tightness in my voice.

Nothing in me wanted to go to New Jersey and expose myself to her anger and despondency. But I felt responsible to at least try to patch up some holes in her life.

"I don't think you should go out there," Sherry told me later. She was a coworker and devoted mother of three who knew about Mariela's past trauma and my fervent desire to get her pointed in the right direction. "You allow yourself to be flung around by her moods and manipulations, and you go from feeling hurt and angry to forgiving and hopeful. That just can't be good for you. Why don't you work on expecting nothing from her and just stay grounded no matter what she does? You don't need to go running to her; it won't solve her problems." Sherry's advice sounded reasonable and logical and simpler than it was. I was nonreactive and grounded when it came to dealing with acting-out clients and had even learned to be that way with my mother, but Mariela was different. I so badly wanted her to be different than she was, to be healed and happy, that it interfered with my ability to keep a safe distance from her turmoil and not make it my own.

I had started to fantasize that my going to her and being in her physical presence would be the healing act she needed. I could put all else aside and devote a week or two listening to her, reassuring her, helping her cope with being left by Hasan. She had been abandoned; now she would understand that she had me, and this act would be the starting point for a different kind of relationship between us. Just like that, I turned my thinking around, and now I had myself convinced it would be a good thing to visit her. She had that effect on me. I flip-flopped with confusion. Still, I called her. Her response did not surprise me.

"No, I don't want you here. I'm real busy, I don't have time for visitors, my place is a mess, and I don't want you coming around telling me what to do" was her flat response to my half-hearted appeal to visit.

Undaunted, I continued, "I won't get in your way. I'd stay at a hotel and take the kids, so you'd have time alone. I'd like to see you."

Before the words finished tumbling out, I got a strong internal message that what I was saying was naïve and untrue. Jolted out of my denial, I realized I didn't want to go. I was playing a part. Why was I trying to talk her into something I didn't want to do? My lifelong habit of disregarding what I wanted and pushing ahead with what I thought might benefit someone else was again revealed. And I thought I had started to recover from this childhood habit of ignoring my needs in service to others. I realized I had a long way to go. She would be my best and most difficult teacher, and I was still learning.

I didn't hop on a flight to New Jersey as my hopeful heart had thought for a time was a good idea. Instead, I waited and did nothing other than calling occasionally to remind her I cared about her. Her neighbors got increasingly concerned and called Child Protective Services, a caseworker was assigned, therapy mandated, and I stayed in Oregon on the very distant sidelines, where I belonged.

Chapter 18

Mariela

"Why do you stay in prison when the door is wide open?"
Rumi

Hasan was the one who had insisted on them going to Charlotte's big family reunion, despite Mariela's protests that she wouldn't feel comfortable and didn't really belong to that big Irish family that planned to meet in central Pennsylvania. But because he seemed to care about it so much, she began to wonder if the reunion might rescue her relationship with Hasan, which was going downhill fast. As it turned out, that damn reunion was the beginning of the end.

Charlotte's brothers and cousins and their families had flown in from all parts of the US. Charlotte sounded like she wanted Mariela and her family there too, so after arguing with Hasan about it, the six of them had piled in their rattletrap car and headed to central PA, a place she had heard Charlotte talk about, where Charlotte had visited her grandma, cousins, aunts, and uncles as a kid when their family wasn't living overseas somewhere. The farmlands and green hills they drove past reminded her of the lush countryside in the highlands of Guatemala, or what she could remember of them. She hadn't known this kind of scenery existed on the East Coast; pavement and parking lots, ramshackle or sky-high buildings were all she knew.

She had been nervous as hell and felt like she was walking onto a stage without knowing the part she was supposed to play. She was well aware that she had caused trouble and heartache for Charlotte and her family, and now she was asking to be let in like a puppy with her tail between her legs. That familiar feeling of being in the dark about how to behave or feel swept over her and transformed to anger.

To hell with Charlotte and her perfect family, she thought. *I don't owe them anything.* Her need to destroy the relationship with Charlotte for good and be done with it and her need to feel some connection to the only mother she knew were in stark contrast and horribly confusing. This woman who called herself Mom kept opening the door, inviting her back into her life, making Mariela face this awful dilemma, rather than shutting the door once and for all of any possibility.

Since Mariela moved to New Jersey and especially since their trip to Belize together, she had noticed a change in Charlotte. She didn't get pulled into the ups and downs of Mariela's life, didn't ask questions, stayed in her own lane, so to speak. It was easier in some ways, but she could no longer manipulate Charlotte quite so well, and that was maddening.

The aunts, uncles, cousins, Charlotte's brothers, and their families had welcomed Mariela and her family like they had found their way home. Mariela played the part, enjoying the idea that these people were "hers." Maybe they were pretending too; perhaps this was an act on everyone's part to feel less alone in the world. Hasan, who had no relationship with his screwed-up family, was excited to be with people who were friendly and included him. They swam in the lake, had picnics under leafy trees, rented kayaks, and paddled to the middle of the lake, sometimes in circles, laughing wildly at how little control they had over the kayaks. A sudden rainstorm caused peals of laughter from the kids, who romped in newly created puddles.

Then, in the evenings, the food came out, platters of food shared generously by the relatives, intent on feeding each other. Charlotte's brothers, John and Patrick, whom Mariela had met several times over the years, seemed genuinely happy to see her and to introduce her to their grown kids and grandkids. Under the shadow of these very tall men, a scientist and an engineer, both well over 6'4," Mariela had felt short, dark, and poorly educated. She couldn't imagine that they'd want to talk to her, but they had been friendly and nice, and so were their wives and kids. Two of John's grown sons were musicians, and they led the group in songs around the campfire, everyone joining in. In the dark, Mariela's eyes had filled with tears as she gazed through the flickering fire to her kids smiling and Hasan singing with a content expression. Could she trust what she saw? Was this real? Was this what belonging felt like? Would this feeling, whatever it was, be gone in the light of day?

One of John's daughters was married to a Moroccan man, a practicing Muslim she had met at college. They had three little kids, and she wore a beautifully stylish head covering. Mariela was immediately drawn to the blond-haired, green-eyed cousin who now shared her same faith. Charlotte's big family was Irish Catholic, but Pauline's family was included and accepted like it made no difference. She and Pauline sat on the grass and talked while their children played around them.

When it was time to gather for family photos, everyone had motioned for Mariela's family to find a place as they shifted to make room. Mariela held Ameer close to her and smiled at the camera, unsure if it was happiness she was feeling or if she was pretending to be happy as she had so often done. *What did I do to win these people over? Or is being Charlotte's daughter enough to win approval from this group?* she had wondered as Charlotte's sister-in-law smiled at her and asked to hold Ameer. For someone like her who never assumed she belonged anywhere, this inclusion was a miracle not to be trusted.

Jill, now married and with two kids, had been happy to see her and meet Hasan and her two younger children and to see Caleb and Antonne again after a long time. Chad and his family hadn't been able to come to the reunion. Mariela had been tense around the family, not knowing what to expect. She had been the problem child in the family, the one who had caused their mother so much hand-wringing, the one who moved away and hadn't stayed in touch. But they didn't talk about any of that.

"It's been a long time. I'm so glad you came, Mariela," said Jill, smiling and then inviting Yasmin, a chatty six-year-old, to play with her little girl, Emily, a few years older. Mariela liked Jill, she realized. But she had no idea how to bridge the gap that she had created. The two sisters who had flown out of Guatemala together many years ago tried to reconnect but found it difficult. The kids, who had no trouble connecting, romped, pretended, chased each other, and became inseparable for the few days they were together. She had seen Charlotte beaming several times as she watched her grandkids playing together.

"Mariela, please stay in touch, and come visit us anytime. We'd love to have all of you stay with us," said Jill in the generous way she always had. Jill waved and waved as she and her family drove off back to Wisconsin, where they lived.

The reunion had ended with all the relatives making promises to do it again before too long, kissing and hugging and well-wishing. She hadn't wanted the displays of affection she hadn't deserved or earned, the sweet words that she didn't trust or believe. Charlotte had walked them to the car, tears in her eyes, and reached for her. "I'll miss you. Really. I've enjoyed this so much. It's been good to spend time with you and Hasan and your kids. I love you," Charlotte said, trying to stifle her tears. Mariela couldn't get out of there fast enough.

Mariela had been an emotional wreck when they finally made their exit. She couldn't handle any more of the cloying and affection. How something could feel so good and painful at the same time was confusing, and she had experienced an intense desire to get away from the stew of feelings that overwhelmed her. Hasan tried to talk to her about the reunion on the drive home.

"I can't understand what you got against your family. They are good people, and they try to include you. Did you ever think it's you that has the problem?" he said as if he were doing her a favor to point this out. Meeting her adoptive family had given him too much information about her, too much to hold against her.

"You don't know a damn thing about it." She felt angry that he was poking at what felt like an open wound. She had been tired of sitting in the hot car, exhausted from three days of being "onstage," and she was not in the mood to hear about her problems.

"What the hell is your problem, Mariela? You're never happy. Nothing is enough for you. Can't you ever be happy with what you got?"

She knew he was correct about her not being happy for long. Her moods grabbed her and swung her around so quickly that she never knew where she'd land.

"Just leave me alone, Hasan. I'm too tired to fight," she pleaded. But the kids were asleep in the car, and he needed to talk.

"I'm not sure I can keep doing this. The way you are is wearing me down. And I sure as hell won't marry someone who makes me crazy," he said. "You're impossible. I knew you had problems, and I was willing to deal with them. But what's in it for me? You're too damn difficult."

She felt trapped in the small car with him and his rancor. By the time they got home, she had worked herself into a fury wanting to hurt him. He had tried to stay calm. "You need to spend more time reading the Koran, praying, going to the mosque, and taking care of our kids, and stop feeling sorry for yourself." He carried the sleeping kids from the car and put them to bed. "I've got to get some sleep. I'm staying with friends tonight," he announced as he drove away.

Alone in bed after he left, she cried and fumed, remembering all that Hasan knew about her, all that she had shared to make herself vulnerable to him. She had told the man how she was left in a marketplace in Guatemala, struggled to survive in the orphanage, then gotten adopted by a family who couldn't make room for who she was. He had been angry when he heard her story, wanted to take care of her and make her feel safe again. But over the years, her story failed

235

to move him, and he wanted her to get over it, and then after meeting her adoptive family, he thought she had nothing to complain about. His family had never been that loving, he said. He was tired of hearing her excuses for sleeping in the afternoons while the kids watched TV. She had been a good partner for a while, but it hadn't lasted. He called her an angry, bitter, lazy, and manipulative woman. She lashed back at him but felt a sickening truth. She hated him for being right; the real Mariela was a defective bitch.

The air was thick with tension whenever he was home, so he stayed away more and more, which just made things worse. She was furious and lonely, couldn't wait for him to get home, then verbally attacked him when he walked in the door. She was convinced he was with another woman. One night he came home late and walked straight to the bedroom without saying a word. She accused him of cheating, called him names, cried and slammed doors, and even threw something at him. Hasan walked out the door saying he felt like hitting her, but he'd be damned if he'd do something like that. He screamed as he left, "I can't do this anymore. You need help!"

"If you leave, don't be planning to come back here. You're not welcome here anymore. You selfish son of a bitch. Who needs you?" she screamed with hot tears running down her face. Caleb and Antonne comforted the younger kids and stood waiting to see what would happen, if he'd come back. The kids had seen it all before, and she knew it left knots in their stomachs. They all thought he'd be back; he had always come back no matter how angry he had been.

But this time, he didn't come back. She was furious and shocked that he actually left, even though she had always suspected he would abandon her. Their relationship had lasted eight years, longer than any other she'd had in her life, having been with her real mama five years, four years in an orphanage, and then six years with Charlotte and her family. Nothing lasted for her. She hated Hasan for leaving her but wanted him to come back, just like when she was a young girl praying for her mama to return. When she was convinced that he wasn't coming back, she tore off her head scarf and threw it away. "To hell with this thing. I can do what I want, I don't need you or your lousy religion," she ranted and cried.

The rock-bottom pit of loneliness that had always been there returned with a force that knocked her over. She stayed at home, mostly on the couch, and let the world go on around her. She was alone and miserable with a persistent ache of emptiness. The kids got on her nerves, frayed as she was with hot anger and grief. She was sometimes happy to have Hasan take them on weekends but never made it easy for him. He had left her; he didn't deserve his kids.

The Puerto Rican neighbor named Sylvia, an older woman with too much time on her hands, stopped by regularly. "How are you and the kids doing these days?" she asked casually in her thick accent, but Mariela knew she was checking on her, looking for the cracks in Mariela's life, wanting to involve herself in the drama. She was one of those Christian types who didn't give up easily, all smiles and concern. Sylvia heard Mariela screaming at Hasan one day when he came to pick up the kids, and she rushed over when she saw Hasan's car pull away. "You can come with me to my church, OK? God alone can help you with anger," she said as she stood in Mariela's door, hinting that she'd like a longer conversation. "I've had my fill of religion, and I'm not interested," Mariela said without trying to be polite to the do-gooder with a syrupy-sweet voice who said she'd pray for her before she turned to go. Mariela did allow Sylvia to keep the kids a few times so she could get a break from them.

Once when the apartment manager heard Mariela yell at Hasan as he was putting the kids into his car for a weekend visit, he said to Hasan, loud enough for her to hear, "That girl is losing it. She's got herself some big problems. She needs help." Mariela saw the way the men looked at each other, conspired against her, and the memory resurfaced of being dragged by the police to a mental hospital. She wasn't going to let that happen again. She stayed inside and kept to herself, suspicious of everyone, afraid and alone, but determined to keep her head down and not draw attention.

One afternoon, she dozed on her ragged, brown couch that a neighbor had helped haul from Salvation Army. The kids were playing on the floor as the TV droned in the background. When the phone rang, she jumped to get it. She was hoping for a response from an application for more electricity assistance, but it was Charlotte calling to check on her. She felt a wave of relief that someone out there in the world gave a damn about her, but what good was that? Charlotte lived across the country, and besides, Mariela didn't want to open up to her. She was torn between wanting to cuss her out for not being the mother she needed and crying her eyes out because she needed her. Mariela wanted to tell her how awful she felt, how she needed help, how she even thought of ending it all if it wasn't for her kids, but she said none of this. There was nothing Charlotte or anyone could do.

There had been some small talk, Charlotte expressed some concern and asked a few questions, then Mariela ended the phone call, which she was sure was unsatisfying to both of them. After hanging up, Mariela retreated to the couch and lost herself in thought. She wondered again, as she often did, about the bond so many people talked about between mothers and their children. Had her Mayan mom been bonded to her? Obviously not, she thought, or she couldn't have left. Was Charlotte bonded to her? Was she bonded to Charlotte? She didn't think so but couldn't be sure. How was it, she wondered, that some mothers loved their children, stayed committed to them, and that some children were lucky enough to have these kinds of mothers? She had always hated the stories about mothers and their beloved children. It meant her own flesh-and-blood mother was a lousy piece-of-shit mother or that she was too defective to have a mother be bonded to her.

She thought of Hasan trying to convince her that Charlotte loved her. "You're crazy not to see that the woman cares about you. Who cares if she's related to you? And I'm not sure being blood is always such a great thing anyway." His own mother had died when he was in his twenties, long before he had made peace with her.

"I just don't care much about her," she had responded. "I wanted her love when I was young, but I never trusted it and couldn't love her back." Charlotte had expected some special connection that seemed impossible, like wishing for rain in the desert. It pissed Mariela off that Charlotte expected something from her that she had no ability to give.

She heard her kids playing on the stairs outside the apartment and thought about them. She kept them at an arm's length, especially as they got older and had their own personalities and expectations. She sometimes felt guilty about it and wished she could be different. She had started having kids when she was young and never felt like she knew how to be with them. Their needs were a mystery; she couldn't imagine how she was supposed to mother them but knew that she could never admit that to anyone. No one had answered her questions, indulged her, cared about her feelings when she was young. Her kids expected a lot.

She fell further into a pit of despair months after Hasan left. The anger she felt initially had kept her afloat, but once that stream ran dry, she was done caring about anyone or anything. Her kids tried to pull her back into their lives, but she had no energy for them. They got themselves off to school and didn't ask for much. Ameer entertained himself with some toys and the TV. She knew she wasn't good for them, but they seemed to be doing OK. When she was his age, she reassured herself, she was living on the streets. If she followed that thread of memory back, she could feel the cold concrete where she and her mama sat hungry and cold before she disappeared forever. She remembered her mom's glassy, detached eyes. Her kids had it much better than she ever did.

One morning, she was sitting at the kitchen table drinking coffee and staring at the TV. The house was a mess, but she didn't have the energy to do anything about it. There was a soft knock on the door, a pause, following by a louder knock. She had no friends or family that stopped by, and she wondered who it could be. She received a monthly check from Children's Services, but the caseworker had never visited. When it was clear that the person at the door wasn't leaving, she opened it a crack. An overweight, nicely dressed Black woman with an official but friendly smile introduced herself saying she was from Children's Service Department and wanted to talk. Mariela shrugged and let her into the messy apartment. She knew to be pleasant and cooperative when people like this came snooping around.

After some small talk, the caseworker tried to strike up a conversation with her kids, who withdrew, being unaccustomed to visitors. She finally said to Mariela, "A few neighbors are concerned about you and your kids. I'm checking to see if you need some help, if things are OK with you?"

"I'm OK. I don't need any help except for more money. I take good care of my kids. Who told you I was having trouble? I don't bother anybody." She tried to keep her voice from turning hostile.

"You've missed several appointments for your children at the clinic. We need to see them. And I want to offer you some free counseling. It wouldn't be a bad idea for you to talk to someone; raising kids on your own can't be easy. Besides, when we think you need to do something for your children's best interests, I suggest you do it."

Mariela got the message; if she wanted to keep getting financial assistance, she needed to do what they wanted. She wanted to cuss her out and show her the door, but she kept a cool head instead. She made her face a blank slate, but underneath she boiled. Who was this woman to judge? The caseworker handed Mariela a card with a man's name on it, a counselor to call for a mental health appointment. People had been telling her for a long time that she needed to talk to someone. She had tried that when she was younger and hated all the questions, the long silences, the expectation that she would spill her guts.

"Talking to someone about your life in Guatemala could be helpful," Charlotte had said more times than she could count. "Talking about parenting and all the stresses of your life might be good," Charlotte had said just weeks ago. Now it looked like this caseworker was going to mandate it.

She showed up for her first counseling appointment feeling angry about being forced to go and not expecting to think much of the guy named John whom she'd defy for an hour. In her mind, her only choices were to be defiant or to give in, and neither of these choices seemed to fit the situation. John was a short, muscled, Latin-looking man with graying hair and kind eyes behind glasses, the type of man you could walk by a hundred times and not notice. He mostly listened, made her laugh a few times, and wasn't bothered by her anger or tough attitude. She spilled out the well-rehearsed narrative of her losses in Guatemala and in the US, ending with Hasan. John let her words just fall around him; never picking them up to examine or react, he just accepted what she said with a caring nod. He seemed to be looking for something else, and she became interested in what that could be. What did she have to say if it wasn't about this story of her life, being abandoned and rejected?

She continued to see John—what was her choice? It kept the caseworker off her back, and she hated to admit it, but John was an OK guy. She tried to bring him back to her story of wrongdoings and people who had failed her. She wanted him on her side. It was not that he didn't try to understand, he just kept telling her that her story was bigger than that. He offered a different way of seeing Charlotte, different from the one she had all those years.

"It's clear she loves you. She's hung in there with you all these years. She didn't have to do that." He smiled. Mariela wasn't convinced but felt a small opening about Charlotte where there hadn't been one. "You think people are pretending to care, and you don't trust that they actually do. That makes sense since you had to pretend as a kid to get people to take care of you. It's hard to trust that others really care about you. It goes against your story of being unlovable."

He helped her understand that it's hard to let go of a story you've told yourself so long that it feels like a part of you.

Over the following months, her memories weren't recounted with the usual angry, empty feelings. Instead, huge surges of raw emotion escaped, sobbing that wouldn't stop. John was there to comfort and encourage her. At first, she had tried to control the outpouring of emotions, feeling she would get buried in them. It felt like a dam had broken, and the tears and terror she had held back since early childhood poured out.

"Why did she leave me?" she sobbed. "I was alone in the world. I didn't have anybody. What kind of mother does that?" Her face twisted into a tortured look as she wept.

"It's good to cry, to feel the pain of being left. You didn't do anything wrong; you were just a little kid...." John soothed her as she cried.

Then Mariela started to find reasons to cancel appointments. She didn't like the way the sessions with John left her raw, exposed, and shaken. What if all this crying cracked her wide open and she lost touch with reality, as she had when she was seventeen? She wanted to shut down on the pain and hurt again and let it spread inside where it could be contained and controlled.

John called her a few times, encouraging her to come back. It was his voice that made her consider it. He was kind, he wanted to help her, and she missed talking to him. Maybe she could handle it without losing control this time. Maybe she was finished crying. So, she went back to talk to John and found the pain was there waiting for her. She wasn't finished crying or feeling loss and pain, or the anger and bitterness of being left. The well of her sadness was bigger than she imagined.

After each session, she'd go to the nearby park to sit under the trees. She was too exhausted and confused to make her way home on the subway. Sometimes after she sat for a while, she'd feel hopeful, an unfamiliar energy that made her feel lighter. She wanted the sensation to last, but it didn't. Slowly, as she returned to the reality of her life, that sense of lightness and hope dissipated and was replaced by a familiar dread and sadness. When she told John about this, he understood. "Over time, Mariela, you will sustain this good feeling more and more, but you must be patient and stay with the healing process. It's not easy, but it's definitely worth it, and so are you." She wasn't sure what he meant, but for the first time in her life, she wanted to trust somebody.

Chapter 19

Charlotte

Life is a balance between holding on and letting go."
                                                    Rumi

Mariela called one day on the verge of tears, "Caleb is done listening to me. I don't know what to do with him. His other grandma said he could live with her and go to school in Oregon. I can't deal with him anymore. Can you buy him a plane ticket?" I wondered how she'd do without him. She had depended on him more like a partner than a son. But she was fed up with the challenges of single-parenting Caleb and three other kids in a small apartment in Jersey City. He had started to hang out with a rough group of teenagers, many of them dropouts, just as she had as an adolescent. I agreed to buy a ticket and help his other grandmother in Portland get him settled and hopefully on the right track. I was aware I was bailing her out of problems, but I also knew I had to extend a hand to her son.

I hadn't been surprised to hear that her greatest ally was no longer willing to bow to her wishes. Caleb had been regularly challenging her, no doubt tired of his lifelong helpmate role. She was having difficulty parenting and sounded overwhelmed and frustrated when we talked. She had found a job she was trying to hold on to but had a constant litany of disputes erupting at work and in most areas of her life. Some disaster was always nipping at her heels. I listened and looked at the clock, setting an imaginary timer for twenty minutes; then I dismissed myself from her one-sided vent. I hoped that my listening demonstrated I cared and that my clock-watching demonstrated I had my limits. I reminded myself to be present for her during this limited time and listen with compassion.

The calls from her reminded me of the long and negative phone calls I had suffered through with my elderly mom. I had been a dutiful daughter and now was a dutiful mother in an unbalanced, caretaking relationship. I had practiced how to end depleting tirades when I felt used up and also how to keep my heart open for the limited time I could cope well. My mother, who had always been a challenge, had died a few years earlier. I had made peace for myself from my one-sided efforts to accept and love who she was. Learning more about her early life in the year before she died had helped me develop compassion and empathy for her. And it had helped me take her difficult personality less personally. I was perfecting my skill of nonattachment when she died. I had come far enough in this process to grieve her death in a less complicated way than I would have been able to do had I not done that valuable work. Mariela continued to give me plenty of practice in nonattachment, acceptance, and not taking things personally.

Weeks later, I called to check in on Mariela and the three children she had still living with her. "Hi, I wanted to let you know that Caleb seems to be doing OK. He likes the school he's in, and, well, so far so good," I said in the noncommittal attitude I had developed about the adolescent I was getting to know. "How are the kids doing? How are things without Caleb?" I braced myself for an answer, sensing she was hanging in the balance.

"The kids are OK, but they don't even know how good they have it. I'm working and trying to take care of them with no help," she responded. I had learned to let this comment slide over me. No matter how many times I sent her money or showed support and care, it never seemed to register. She held on to a story that no one cared about her. She and my mom were surprisingly alike in that way. Their needs were insatiable, and nothing I did was enough to fill the emptiness they felt inside. It was as if they held out empty baskets and ridiculed my efforts to fill them. I had stopped trying to convince Mariela of a different story and met her statements with practiced equanimity. She and I were in a time of relative ease with each other, primarily due to my newfound abilities of keeping my heart open with boundaries intact. We talked regularly, every week or so, and once in a while she said something that sounded like appreciation.

"I need someone to talk to who understands me," she exclaimed one day, "and you're a good listener. You understand me." Before I could mitigate my response, my heart swelled with hope and expectation. *Could this be the beginning of that relationship I hope for?* I thought. Then for no apparent reason, at least not a reason I could predict or understand, the next time we talked, she became hostile and pulled back with anger. It was a dance I knew well, but it never ceased to rattle me. I learned to recover from the missteps quicker and didn't use energy trying to figure out what went wrong.

Over the years since Mariela had been living in New Jersey, and after her breakup with Hasan, I had worked to stay in her life with emotional distance so that I was not pulled into her fray. It wasn't easy, but as long as Mariela was self-absorbed, angry, or shut down, which was often her default, my emotional distance was successful. I had a much harder time when on rare occasions she showed vulnerability or sadness or when she said things that sparked hope. Then my heart softened, and tears would fill my eyes in a way that astonished me and made me shake my head in wonder at my sudden turnaround. My heart had never shut to her—I had just learned to safeguard it for my own good. I had a strong attachment to her, despite her seeming lack of it to me, and it was probably not alterable.

Occasionally, I began to experience the absence of expectations, the sweetness of living in the moment with no future or past thoughts to disrupt the goodness of the present. These moments were fleeting but occurred often enough to give me hope and solace. Like Mariela's dance of getting closer then moving away with hostility, my dance with acceptance and then struggle was a well-honed routine that moved to its own internal tune.

Caleb graduated from high school with the help of his father's family and me. I had a relationship with Caleb that, while not what I'd consider close, was based on some appreciation of each other. Bill and I met him for dinners at local restaurants, where we'd try to keep a conversation going while avoiding any talk of his mom. Bill had an easier time of it since he could talk about sports teams, Caleb's favorite subject. He was still fiercely loyal to his mom and caught in a bind, as he didn't get what he needed from her but had always been her support.

Mariela called him often and talked about her problems, mostly about those with Hasan, with whom she fought constantly about Caleb's younger half-sister and half-brother. Since Caleb had been a young boy, I had watched him struggle to obtain his mom's approval, attention, and affection and seen how hungry he was for it. My own mother had been a tough customer; I smiled to myself at this awareness, realizing there was no longer a sting in it. While my mom and I hadn't worked out the warm and loving relationship I had always wanted before her death when she was eighty-seven, I had come to terms with her inability to let in love or express it.

How sad, I thought, that she had been unable to show me love. Her heart had softened a little but had never become open and willing to be vulnerable to anyone, even her only daughter, who had fought a mighty battle to obtain her love. I had learned a valuable lesson that despite what I did and no matter how good and loving my intentions, the hearts of others are not mine to open. My work was to chip away at my own walls to let in the love that was all around me. My hope for Caleb was that his mom would be able to see and love him as he needed or that, in the absence of that happening for him, he could loosen the grip on this need and accept what he had and look for others in his life to love and be loved by.

"You're not as easy to live with as you think you are, sweetie," Bill said after we had a frustrating standoff about a matter than seemed inconsequential a day later. "You've got a few blind spots," he added to get in a last jab, since I had just delivered a zinger his way. My relationship with Bill hadn't met my idealized expectations and fell short of the marital bliss I imagined possible. We loved each other and had no trouble expressing that love in a multitude of ways, and yet we were different in ways that often baffled and frustrated us.

When we met, we were thrilled to discover the ways we were similar, but as our relationship evolved, we were shocked to discover all the ways we were dissimilar and all the hard edges we presented for each other. Those edges softened, and we learned to embrace our differences and accept each other the majority of time. It was an ongoing process of intention, openness, and desire to cultivate deeper love. Both of us were working toward the same goal. My relationship with Mariela, however, was a solitary one-sided effort.

Bill and I were relaxing at home one morning, flipping through the newspaper and drinking strong coffee when I noticed a lecture was scheduled at a local community church about an organization helping Guatemalan orphans. "Wow, look at this!" I moved the paper in front of Bill so he could see why I was excited. "I will definitely be going to that program."

A week later I was sitting in a fluorescent-lit church social room with fifty others, listening to a handsome middle-aged Latino talk about Nuestros Pequeños Hermanos (Our Little Brothers and Sisters), a nonprofit organization he was obviously passionate about that helped orphaned children in Latin America. Staying involved with the children of Guatemala, the country that had given up one of its children to me, enthralled me. An opportunity was knocking on my door, and I felt expansive about the prospect of giving back in some way to help orphans in Guatemala. Maybe I could finally get it right, I thought.

Nuestros Pequeños Hermanos (NPH) did not look for adoptive families for the many hundreds of children in Guatemala under their care. Instead, they kept orphaned children with their siblings and ran their "orphanage" like a home, with family units of eighteen to twenty kids, each with four or five "aunties." Extended families were encouraged to visit regularly, if possible. Children went to excellent schools, got regular medical and dental care, and even had access to psychologists. In the countries where these NPH homes were active, sponsors, or donors in Europe, Canada, and the US, helped fund the organization.

One of the hallmarks of the program was that local aunties, caregivers who demonstrated maternal traits and skills, were paid enough so they stayed to provide loving continuity, a tremendous benefit for the children under their care. I was surprised to hear the speaker refer to attachment and bonding issues, trauma-informed care, trust-building exercises, and safety and security for the kids. Several speakers were locals who had visited the orphanage home in Guatemala and were enthusiastic and eager to share what they had seen and learned. The organization needed donations and sponsors, that was true, but they were looking for partners in their work and welcomed people visiting the homes.

I was eager to learn more. I stayed after the program and talked to a friendly, enthusiastic woman with hair just starting to gray around her temples who had spoken highly of the organization and encouraged the audience to ask her questions.

She introduced herself. "Hello, thank you for coming to learn about our program. My name is Gloria. Are you interested in learning more about our program in Guatemala?"

"Yes, I actually have an adopted daughter from Guatemala. I love the country and have wanted to find a way to help their children."

"I'm happy to tell you more about NPH. I really believe this organization is doing the right thing by leaving the kids in their country and supporting them there rather than bringing them here, especially given what we're learning about adoption in Guatemala. You do know about the adoption scandal in Guatemala, don't you?" Gloria asked, her brow furrowing.

"Well, yes, I've heard some things recently about children being taken from parents and then put up for adoption." I was embarrassed not to know more than I did.

"It's been common practice in Guatemala. Thousands of kids who weren't true orphans were taken illegally, then adopted for lots of money. It's a multimillion-dollar underground operation. It's been going on for years, but only recently have people begun to understand the extent of it. Kids are bought or taken from poor parents, kept in shelters or government orphanages, then fast-tracked for adoption to the US, Canada, and Europe. Attorneys and finders, as they are called, make lots of money. Very little of it goes for the kids' care or to the biological parents."

"I adopted my daughter back in 1987, and she was nine at the time," I said, thinking this scandal couldn't apply to me, to Mariela.

"Oh, at that time, no one had any idea what was happening, but later it was determined that by the early '80s, soldiers were instructed to take babies and young kids from destroyed villages because they were worth a lot on the adoption market. Thousands of children were stolen from Indigenous moms living on the streets who were displaced and had no way to find their kids or anyone to turn to for help."

I listened intently, my head reeling with memories of Mariela's stories about her burning village, the trek to Guatemala City, about living on the streets, about being with a woman about whom she was confused, never sure what had happened to her first mom, all of it being a mystery beyond her young comprehension. Maybe she hadn't been left by her mother; maybe she had been lost or stolen and given to the huge orphanage system so she could be sold when a couple wanted an older child.

"Where can I read more about this?" I asked while writing out a check, beginning my involvement with NPH, an organization that I would come to know well over the years. I would later speak on their behalf and do fundraising events for them.

"By the way, how is your adopted daughter doing now?" Gloria said as she took several steps toward a couple standing nearby waiting to talk to someone.

"It's a long story, but overall, considering what she went through, she's doing OK," I said, realizing how many qualifications I had put on my answer. I smiled to myself as I prepared to leave the room, realizing that for the first time, sadness and shame hadn't seeped in, weighing me down as I responded to the inquiry about Mariela. I wanted to do something to help kids in Guatemala. I couldn't change what had happened to Mariela, but I could help the kids in Guatemala now.

I read everything I could get my hands on about Guatemalan history and Guatemalan adoptions after that. I learned that extreme economic and political injustice had ignited a civil war that lasted from 1960 to 1996. The Guatemalan army, backed by the US government, launched an operation that targeted the Mayan population whom they believed supported the guerrilla movement. Pieces of Mariela's puzzle were falling into place. She and her mom and other family members had been victims of this war. The army destroyed 626 villages like Mariela's, killed over 200,000 people, and displaced an additional 1.5 million. Mariela and her mama, Maria, were two of these displaced people whose lives were upended and destroyed.

With so many children orphaned or displaced during the long war, a lucrative "adoption market" had been born. Hundreds of thousands of children were adopted through state orphanages or a private system run by Guatemalan lawyers for huge profits. I thought of the well-dressed, fast-talking attorney who had held out his hand for an unexplained additional fee. The insatiable demand for adoptable children had the unintended consequences of creating a very profitable private and unscrupulous market.

Guatemala eventually overtook China and Korea as the world's largest source of children for adoption. Lawyers learned that they could charge foreign families immense sums for children they acquired through dubious and illegal means. This market for children was promoted as a humanitarian means to rescue orphaned children who were most often not true orphans. Adoption agencies in the US and other Western countries were unaware that they unwittingly took part in this corrupt practice. Well-meaning adoptive parents were unaware that attorneys and others working with them used all sorts of tactics to acquire Guatemalan children, from buying and kidnapping children to defrauding and coercing women to give up their kids.

I was convinced that Mariela was one of these children. Her stories of being taken from the marketplace by a woman who called herself mama and then transferred to a large orphanage where no attempts were made to locate her parent started to help me put the missing pieces of a puzzle together. The parents whose children were taken searched to no avail for their lost children, and the children old enough to remember a parent did the same. But no records were kept, Indiginos had no birth certificates, and families couldn't pursue their claims of stolen children when most couldn't speak Spanish or understand the corrupt legal system under which they lived. My heart ached for Maria, Mariela's lost mother. Was she still alive somewhere in Guatemala? Was there any way to learn more about the disappeared Mayan mother, the missing link in Mariela's life? Could I help Mariela enlarge her story from being willfully discarded to one of being a victim, like her mama, of a cruel and uncaring system? And might that bring her some measure of solace?

Mariela and I talked on the phone every few weeks, but I was unsure how much I should share with her until I knew she was stable enough to deal with it. I had told her about my support of NPH but little else. I still never knew which Mariela would show up.

She mentioned a few times that she was living in a group situation, but when I asked questions, she clamped shut and refused to say more. "Let's just say, I'm getting some help."

"That's great," I said and didn't pry. I had put off mentioning that I was planning a trip to Guatemala until that day it seemed like a good enough time to tell her. Maybe that was now. "You know that organization I'm now involved with that helps orphaned kids in Guatemala?" I started. "I'm going to visit Guatemala, tour around a little, then visit the home I told you about that helps kids. Maybe one of these years, in the future, you could go with me."

"Maybe. But I hate that country that gave me nothing but pain, so why in the hell would I want to visit it?"

"Well, I thought you might have some interest in seeing it again at some point; maybe trying to put some of the past to rest. If nothing else, we could enjoy an interesting visit." I tried not to think of our Belize trip as I spoke. Then, I caught myself. *Stop pushing your agenda; she'll tell you when and if she's ready to explore her past.*

"No, that's what you want to do, not me. You go. Leave me out of it. I'm not ready for any memory trips to hell." She spoke emphatically, but without the hostility I expected.

"OK, then." I was all right with the plan of going alone. It would allow me to focus on my own experience and to fully embrace the country and its kids without focusing on Mariela's healing. Although disappointed that we couldn't yet share the experience, I figured when and if she was ready for such a trip, I'd entertain the idea again. I closed the subject and made plans to visit her country.

Chapter 20

Mariela

"The wound is the place where light enters."
Rumi

She sat on her bunk in a women's shelter, trying to put the pieces together of recent years, what led her to this place after she had a stab at family life with a man who once loved her, a job, and a home. Had it been a cruel trick to think she deserved something more than a shelter, which reminded her of the orphanage, her childhood home?

The life she created in New Jersey had slipped away from her, despite her angry grasping to hold on. Then she had opened her hands and let it all go, relieved to be pulled down where she belonged. The metal bunkbeds in the big, barren room, every one of them filled with homeless or battered women, reminded her of the bunks where she had cried for her mama. The sad and angry women with whom she shared the cramped room brought back memories of the needy, filthy orphanage kids. There was an odd comfort about the shelter, a familiarity of institutional life where she knew what to expect, where she was one of many, all lost, all struggling to survive. The women in the shelter had even thrown a party for her thirty-fifth birthday and teased her about a hard-ass like herself being born on Valentine's Day. She didn't tell them that she had no idea when her real birthday was. Many of the women in the shelter were as mean and angry as she was, and she saw herself in their pathetic posturing.

The years before she ended up at this shelter had been tough. Caleb had gone to Oregon where his grandmas helped him get out of high school and get a job. She missed him terribly. After he left, it was just her and the three kids, and it all got to be too much. She stopped seeing John, the counselor she had once found helpful. She had stuck with him despite his insistence on opening her up, until he told her he'd be leaving the agency. *To hell with him*, she thought. He was leaving her too.

Hasan was always on her case about not being a good enough mother to his two kids, who were still in grade school. He was always threatening to take her to court so he could get custody and stop paying child support for what he considered her inadequate care. Antonne was a skinny and withdrawn teenager who didn't give her any trouble except he often didn't want to go to school. That worried her, but what could she do? His father sent child support from Oregon but hadn't seen his son since she moved East when he was a baby.

One cold Saturday morning, Hasan stopped by to pick up the kids, who weren't wearing coats in the freezing weather, and he yelled to her from his car, "You should know that I filed for custody. You'll get a notice to show up. I'm tired of messing with you about taking care of these kids. Where are their coats? It's too damn cold for them to be out here without coats." He was serious about taking her to court to get custody, and she knew he'd tell the judge about her emotional problems, about forgetting appointments again. "I thought you were doing better. What the hell happened?" Hasan said after he buckled the kids in the back seat of his car and turned to her. "Are you still seeing that counselor guy? He was helping you. What happened to that? I'll bring them back tomorrow night; in the meantime, clean up the place, get some food for them, get ready for the school week." He was like a broken record, always telling her what she could do better.

She had dreaded having to show up in the court hearing to convince the judge that she wasn't a shit parent. She had called Charlotte and asked for money to hire a lawyer, but Charlotte said she wouldn't. She said Mariela would have to fight this on her own. It almost seemed that Charlotte was on Hasan's side and hoped she'd lose her kids. Mariela told her if she lost them, she'd also lose child support, which meant she could lose her apartment, but none of it seemed to make a difference to her. Charlotte wasn't mean about it, but when she said no, she meant it. Charlotte had learned how to draw a firm line in the sand, and she didn't budge. It was aggravating.

She received the summons to the hearing but didn't go, not wanting to deal with the shame inflicted on her by Hasan and the judge. The judge awarded custody to Hasan. They would live with him and visit her on weekends. Hasan arranged his hours at the college where he still worked as a janitor to get off early to pick up the kids from school. His sister who lived nearby watched them when he needed help.

Mariela had only Antonne, and the two of them lived in relative harmony because he was a quiet, sad kid who stayed in his room much of the time. He didn't seem to care if Mariela was home or not, so she began to go out in the evenings to get out of the small, messy apartment that depressed her. Antonne occupied himself playing video games. Mariela hadn't been much of a drinker before this time but learned quickly that when she drank, she relaxed and could meet people more easily, talk and laugh with them, and forget about her dreary life. Going out at night helped her mood, she reasoned, and it didn't hurt anyone.

But things started to go downhill. She didn't pay her rent on time; then her car broke down and she couldn't fix it, so she had to junk it. The school called about how many days Antonne was missing and threatened to get authorities involved if Mariela didn't get him to school. That's when she called his father in Portland, the good man who had been paying child support since she left Oregon when Antonne was a baby. He had always wanted a relationship with his son, and Mariela encouraged him to have Antonne live with him and finish high school in Oregon. Antonne's father and his family agreed to the plan. Mariela called Charlotte, shared a little about the situation, and asked her if she could buy a plane ticket so Antonne could travel to Portland to live with his father, whom he didn't know but idolized nevertheless.

Mariela was relieved not to have kids to care for but lonely as hell. She didn't have real friends. People came and went out of her life, and she often wondered if friends were worth the trouble. It seemed easier to hang out with people she met in bars or to stick to herself. She worked odd jobs, got fired from a few, bummed and borrowed money, and finally the landlord, who had never fixed a damn thing, appeared at her door and said he was done waiting for rent and handed her an eviction notice. The trappings of her life that had anchored her fell away, leaving her alone and desperate for solace, with no soft landing in sight.

One night she sat at the laundromat keeping warm and wondering what to do, when a friendly, funny guy struck up a conversation with her. He was a tall, skinny, very Black Nigerian who seemed anxious to make a connection with her. "Girl, you are so short and so cute. I can't place you—where you be from?"

"I'm from here," she answered with a coy smile.

"That's not what I mean. Where'd your people come from?" He grinned, showing large white teeth.

"Oh, my people came from Guatemala—you know that place?" she asked.

"Yeah, somewhere in the Caribbean, right?"

They talked an hour or so, as the dryers whirled their hot air in the background. Finally, he said he was going home and asked if she wanted to join him. She had been hoping he'd ask. As they walked into his shabby walk-up apartment, she told him that she'd cook and clean for him in exchange for rent, but she knew he'd expect sex too. That was OK with her; she thought he was kind of cute.

What a mean loser he turned out to be. They drank together, but he became violent when drunk, especially when she stood up to him, which she regularly did. He often pushed her against the wall, and in their final violent exchange, he knocked her against a table and onto the floor, where she hit her head.

Neighbors heard the ruckus and called the police, and she ended up in a women's domestic violence shelter where the caseworkers asked her lots of questions, trying to figure her out and connect her to resources. Mariela liked the young, earnest caseworkers who were always available to talk, who asked lots of leading questions in an attempt to flush out how they could best reach her. She was pleased that they worked so hard on her behalf, but the other women in the shelter got on her nerves. It had been a long time since she had had to eat and sleep with a group of lost souls like herself.

During the first months of living in the shelter, Mariela didn't contact Charlotte. She had no idea what she'd say and didn't want to hear Charlotte's sad voice and concern when she heard about the latest downturn in her life. One day in their group sessions, the women talked about their moms, weaving stories of abuse, longing, and even some love. Mariela talked about Charlotte and felt sad as she told the others that Charlotte lived far away but had been there for her over the years. Mariela was surprised to be opening up; maybe it was that the other women were talking about their hurts and losses. After the group that day and before she could change her mind, she picked up the shelter phone and called Charlotte.

"Hey, it's been a long time, Mariela. I think about you a lot and wonder how things are going for you."

"Uh, OK, I mean, things have been tough, but I'm managing." There was a long silence.

"You can tell me what's up, Mariela, I'm here for you and won't judge you, I promise," said Charlotte.

She listened to Charlotte do her usual supportive pep talk from a dark corner of the shelter where she huddled on the phone. She had been living in the shelter for months and was pissed that she couldn't tell Charlotte, but she'd be damned if she felt like exposing herself to

Charlotte's pity and the questions that would follow. She maintained the silence for a minute more; then the tears welled in her eyes. *What do I have to lose by telling her?* she thought, taking a deep breath before starting.

"I ended up in a shelter after I got evicted, I lost my job, I got beat up by a boyfriend, I'm trying to get my shit together. This place is OK. I'm getting some help," she said all in one shame-filled breath. She was destroying Charlotte's vision of what was possible, which had always been better than Mariela's vision for herself.

"Thanks for telling me. You know I'm on your side, rooting for you. I know you've got it in you to turn things around." Charlotte's voice was full of emotion.

Yeah, sure, you do. Mariela thought. *Why in the hell would you?* She had lost her kids, had no one, couldn't hold a job, had been evicted and was living in a shelter, had been with more loser men than she could count, and was pretty sure she couldn't stop drinking. How the hell was she supposed to get "back on her feet," as Charlotte liked to say? *How the hell do you turn a stray into a cuddly pet?* she thought, more convinced than ever that Charlotte was a real dreamer. *What the hell does she see in me that I can't see in myself?* she asked herself again.

Now that Charlotte knew the full story, Mariela called her every few weeks. She moved to a different long-term shelter meant for rehabilitation and recovery from addiction and emotional problems. The women had to attend a therapy group to stay in the shelter, so she agreed to join a circle of women with a group leader to talk about her sorry childhood. She had already spilled her guts to John, and it hadn't really changed a thing. She wondered if she started drinking after that because she couldn't handle being opened up like that and then left with her wounds still bleeding. He had helped her see some things differently, and she got better for a while, but it hadn't stuck. She went back to feeling empty and lost.

Back when she was seeing John, she had gotten the nerve to ask him about her diagnosis, and he had answered in his typical warm and generous way. "Mariela, you are a wonderfully complex woman. You've got some PTSD from early childhood experiences, some attachment issues from being left by your mom, some depression and anxiety, and a tough survivor personality."

"Wow, I sound like a real mess," she said, actually relieved at his lighthearted nature when describing her. He told her she was more than a bunch of labels, which weren't helpful anyway. She could *choose* a different life, but she needed a daily program, needed to learn how to deal with negative emotions and take care of herself, be accountable to other people, and finally deal with the shit she was afraid to look at.

"Lots of people get badly hurt by life, but they *choose* to stay on a path that leads them to a better place," he said.

"I want to believe you, but it all seems impossible. I've been the way I am my whole damn life. I've been a hot mess since I was a little kid," she tried to joke with him.

"Stick with a program, keep coming in to see me, surround yourself with positive people. It's hard work but worth it. You're worth it."

She had started down a path to rebuild herself when she worked with John. Then one day during a session, he cleared his throat and looked intently at her. "I'm leaving this agency in six weeks. My wife got a job in another city, so we'll be moving." He looked sad as he delivered the death blow to their relationship. "I'm going to transfer you to another therapist, who is excellent; I know you will like working with her. I couldn't recommend her more highly," John said, but they both knew she wouldn't see someone else. They had spent hours talking about her fear of abandonment, about not trusting others, about her difficulty attaching.

"What the hell, I'm only half-baked." She tried to use humor to cover her utter devastation about another person in her life leaving. "Are you telling me that your wife is more important than me?" she said, sounding like a smart-ass to cover the injury. He was making a *choice*, as he frequently reminded her when talking about her behaviors, to leave her.

Now, she looked around the circle of eight women in her recovery group in a Jersey City women's shelter. They were all bad-asses who had hit rock bottom on what seemed like the end of a long hard road to nowhere. Glenda, the large, Black, no-nonsense middle-aged woman with short, cropped hair who had lived on the streets herself when she was younger, told her that getting out of the hole she'd dug herself into started by telling her story to others in the safety of the group. Glenda had worked hard to recover and then became a counselor at the shelter. She liked to tell them, "Never think you can't turn it around. I did two decades ago, and you can too." Nothing shocked her; she was just a big bundle of love who wanted to spread it all over the women who sat frightened and hopeless in her midst. Every time one of them spewed out anger and hate, she met it head-on.

"Come on, girl. Let that bad stuff out, so you can let in some light," she said. "I don't give a damn how mad you are, just don't be disrespecting yourself or anyone else. You got a choice. You can hold on to all that hurt and work yourself up so you want to hurt someone else, or you can let it go. The past is done; that stuff is done. It's time to move on and make something else out of it."

Some of the women would tell their stories and cry like babies, their faces contorted in pain as they tried to hold themselves together, then lost control of their emotions. As Glenda leaned toward them with complete acceptance of their emotional displays, she said in her soothing voice, "Go ahead and cry. We're here for you. That's one good bucket of tears, and there will be many more. It's all good, sweetheart."

It touched Mariela in a deep place to listen to Glenda's soothing voice while grown women cried. They sat on tattered couches and chairs in the small group room infused with the smell of stale cigarette smoke. They were a bunch of sad and angry women hurt as kids and crying on each other's shoulders, trying to drop their masks and discover who was lurking beneath the pain.

Mariela observed the other women closely, trying to understand what made them willing to expose themselves. She had spent a lifetime hiding, concealing any breaks in the barriers she had erected. It wasn't just her fear of their judgments that kept her guarded; it was her fear of opening to herself, to the ugly wounds that festered, to the fragile whimpering child inside her. She initially decided to sit in the group meetings and hold tight to her story of being tough and uncaring. But despite her resolve, the other women's stories created a crack through which compassion leaked, for them and for herself. Many of them had lived through terrible times, they had done awful things, and they were still willing to talk about it now in the safety of the group with Glenda modeling how to listen with acceptance. Mariela felt like a little kid, terrified, broken, alone, and the only thing that was her own was the impenetrable wall of protection she had built around herself.

Then one day, as the others sat silent after listening to a woman tell of her stepfather's abuse, Glenda asked Mariela if she felt ready to talk to the group about her story. There was an option to say, "No, I'm not ready," as she had done many times before. But before she could think about a response, she opened her mouth and started to speak. "I got left on the streets of Guatemala City when I was a little kid. Then I lived in a big and awful orphanage for many years. I learned to survive but never got over being left like that," she said while looking around the room, studying the faces of the women. The women just nodded, not surprised, not horrified, just accepting of Mariela's story.

In another group a few days later, she told them about running from her burning village and living on the streets with her mother before her mother left her. In another group: "I gave up on my mom ever coming to get me from the orphanage and said I wanted to be adopted, but I didn't know how hard that would be. I got a new mom, a new family, but I had no idea how to live in a family. I didn't trust any of them and was pissed all the time. I made their life hell."

She laughed, looking sheepish.

"Yeah, I can see that," said Sheila, a Native American friend upon whom Mariela had initially lobbed many harsh words and threats until they both learned to give each other some respect.

"I got pregnant when I was fifteen and left the family who adopted me, thinking I was old enough to start my own family." She looked around the room. "I bet you guys know how that turned out." She smiled and several of the women nodded in understanding. And on it went, peeling off the layers, exposing herself, telling the truth of who she was as women listened.

"Dang," said Glenda one day, "you were one brave girl to come to the US to live in a family you didn't know, to leave your country, then come to the East Coast with no one but your little kids to start over."

The other women nodded. They accepted Mariela and even respected her, Mariela thought, amazed.

But it didn't go entirely smoothly. She opened up and trusted, then closed down and withdrew, all beyond her awareness and control.

"Where did you go today?" asked Glenda one day after the group finished.

"I don't know, but I feel like I'm done talking about myself for a while."

"It's all good. You'll know when you're ready to open up again, and we'll be here for you." Glenda smiled. Mariela liked Glenda a lot but wasn't about to trust her completely. Glenda would have to prove herself over time. Still, it felt good to have someone give her space and time and let her decide what felt safe. Mariela realized that it had been hard for Charlotte to do that. Charlotte had wanted something from her that felt impossible to give. But that had changed too. Charlotte was different and lately seemed satisfied with what they had with each other.

Months passed, and Mariela revealed herself in controlled bits and pieces. In some of her stories, she described Charlotte as a controlling bitch who put her in a psychiatric hospital; in others, she was the only person who had ever stuck with her. One rainy morning, six women, two had dropped out, were gathered again for their two-hour session. Glenda asked Mariela about Charlotte. "What does she mean to you? It's not clear if you hate her or care about her, maybe even love her?" Glenda's face was inquisitive but patient.

Mariela realized that her story of Charlotte didn't match her confused feelings about this woman who had adopted her and been there for her through all the messes of her life. Charlotte hadn't been the perfect mother she had hoped for, but Mariela couldn't deny that this woman, her adoptive mother, was the truest thing she had. The one-sided story of Charlotte's rejection, control, and betrayal was not truthful, she admitted to herself. She knew Glenda would call bullshit on that. Glenda with her attentive, piercing eyes always seemed to know what was up. Glenda has shared that she used to be all about black-and-white thinking but had discovered that the truth was somewhere in the middle. Mariela wanted to tell the truth, but she didn't know what it was.

"She really tried, I guess. That woman had me on sports teams, going to summer camps; she gave me birthday parties and bought me stuff I wanted and needed. She was good enough, but she never understood me. She thought she could just love me up and make me into something different. Eventually, after I got pregnant, moved away, yelled at her to get out of my life hundreds of times, she had enough and did what I always thought she would do anyway—she left just like my first mama." Mariela finished, feeling justified in her mixed assessment.

"Wait, I thought you said she called you a few days ago and that she was your cheerleader." Glenda's face was quizzical. Mariela looked around the circle of women, and all eyes were on her, and they were nodding like they were trying to keep up with what she was saying.

"So, your adoptive mom, was she bad or good?" asked Brandy, the thin and ragged blond who had lived in a dozen foster homes.

Maybe the simple labels of "good" or "bad" was how she had always labeled her foster homes. Mariela ignored her and looked to Sylvia, a group member she respected who looked ready to chime in.

"Wait, you're saying you got yourself adopted by a good woman who didn't abuse you; then you pushed her away, then blamed her for leaving you? Girl, you're messed up," said Sylvia in a thick accent. She had been abused by her drug-addicted mother's boyfriends for years, then by her own boyfriends, and couldn't understand what Mariela had to complain about.

"Well, I get it. Mariela got left on the streets as a kid—that sucks." Mercedes said to no one in particular, as she swung her long hair away from her pockmarked face. "My mom left too, but there were four of us, and we had each other, at least for a while until we got split up and had to go to different foster homes."

And so it went, one after another the women told of their miserably sad and scary childhoods, the abuses, the poverty, and the fighting. Finally, Sylvia looked around the circle at all the women and declared, "God, look at us. We've had it tough, but we survived, didn't we? We must have done something right to still be alive, huh?"

Glenda smiled her big, warm smile and told them they were done for the day. "Just remember, all of you, none of us is perfect, least of all me, but we're working at being the best we can be."

Mariela got up from the circle, feeling a warmth radiate through her. She was pleased with herself, an unfamiliar feeling. She looked around the room at the women with whom she had shared so much and realized she had connected with these women and cared about them. *I'm not that different from any of them,* she thought. *We've all had shit to deal with and aren't proud of what we've done, but we're just trying to get by without getting more hurt.* She smiled to herself, the feeling of connection warming her again. All these women had once been little kids dependent on adults, and those adults hurt them in various ways, but it wasn't the little kids' fault. "It wasn't my fault either," she said, a statement so obvious that it surprised and delighted her.

She returned to her bunk to be alone. In her mind's eye, she saw herself at five years old, sitting on the street with her mama, trying to be helpful and good, not complaining about the hunger and the cold. For the first time in her life, she felt compassion for that little girl. She looked down at her hands. *These hands were so little, and I took money, made change, handed tamales to adults, and would have reached for any adult's hand who would take care of me,* she thought with tears filling her eyes. *I was just unlucky, not defective. Maybe my mama didn't leave because there was something wrong with me. Maybe something else happened,* she thought, imagining a different ending to a well-known fairy tale.

"Wait a minute," she said to herself as she sat up in the bed. "Is it even true that my mom left me? How do I know that?" she inquired of herself like Glenda had taught them to do. "Maybe she couldn't come back to me. What if she didn't mean to leave me?" A small space opened in her closed heart as she imagined her poor Mayan mama trying to make it back to her, to their basket on their blanket in the market. Time and connection with others slowly stitched her deep wounds. *Maybe my mama couldn't come back, couldn't find me.* She marveled at how that sounded.

During the first months she had been in the rehab program, she had thought of leaving all the time. She missed drinking and partying, but she needed a secure place to sleep in the cold months, so she bided her time. When she managed to slip out a few times, there was hell to pay in the groups to get back in, so leaving lost its appeal. Over time, the AA groups helped her understand the consequences of impulsive actions and her addiction to numbing her pain. Drinking wasn't as fun anymore. Staying sober won her praise and a sense of belonging, but it was a constant struggle not to reach for the relief of a drink.

She stayed in the shelter for seven months, gave up drinking except for a few slips, and participated in group sessions. She met with

Glenda to sort out her thinking errors, as Glenda called them. Next thing, they asked her to go to an anger management group put on by the local mental health clinic, and at first it seemed like a bunch of crap. Without anger, how could she protect herself? How could she block other feelings if not covering them with spewing clouds of anger? Anger was the fire and fuel of her life, always smoldering, giving her energy and purpose. When she was angry, she felt most alive, most protected, most fierce.

"Think what you could do if you harnessed that energy and used it for good in your life," said Doug, the hippy guy who led the anger management group. He had kind eyes, a long ponytail, and slow and steady speech that calmed her. They practiced breathing in and out slowly to slow their heart rates, they listened to soothing music, and they learned how to stall angry reactions and ask questions about the nature of their anger. Mariela started to recognize her past behaviors in women who were new to the program. She could now identify when she became defensive or blaming, behaviors that were as natural as breathing. She learned how to stop herself most of the time.

The doctor from the mental health clinic who visited a few times a month put her on medication to help with sleep and anxiety. She started to feel better. It was a hell of a lot of work to stay sober, think straight, take responsibility, and control her anger, and she wasn't always happy doing the work. But she had nothing better to do, and for the first time in her life, she had real friends who actually knew her. And she was proud of what she was doing for herself. Her kids came on Sundays and could stay all afternoon. Maybe for the first time ever, she saw them as separate little people, with lives, and feelings, and needs. It was surprising to her that she had never thought of them that way before.

Glenda asked her if she'd be willing to see a therapist at the clinic who specialized in eye movement desensitization and reprocessing (EMDR), a therapy proven to be very helpful for patients with PTSD and trauma. "Her name is Elaine, and you won't find a nicer, gentler therapist." Mariela's first inclination was to say that she was already filled to the brim with self-examination. Then after some consideration, a new skill to slow down negativity, she declared to Glenda, "What the hell, I've got nothing to lose." Glenda had never steered her wrong, and she felt more open to things she didn't understand than she had in the past.

Elaine introduced herself with a gentle handshake and big smile. She appeared to be in her sixties, not at all flashy, but warm and easy in her approach and with eyes that shone with wisdom. After some "getting to know you" talk, Elaine said, "Let me explain what I do that makes me different from other therapists, and please be sure to ask me questions that come up. EMDR is a form of psychotherapy that is effective for treatment of trauma and PTSD. Think of it this way: When we experience a traumatic event, we store the memory of it in our brains and bodies. Any distorted thoughts, images, sensations, or perceptions of the event are stored and experienced as true. This is especially true for children who experience trauma. EMDR works by stimulating the brain in ways that lead to reprocessing those unhealed memories, which leads to adaptive resolution or decrease in symptoms, or what we call desensitization." Mariela tried to keep up with this lengthy explanation and appreciated how hard Elaine was working to help her understand. "I'll ask you to recall distressing events of your life while you follow my wand from right to left, called bilateral stimulation. This stimulates your brain and helps you reprocess your memories. You can ask me to stop anytime. You set the pace. Let's give it a try when you're ready." She smiled with tenderness.

Elaine moved a wand in front of Mariela and asked her to talk about childhood memories. The more she talked about early memories, the more memories she had, most of them coming in fragments, pieces of a puzzle, that didn't quite fit. Elaine encouraged her in a caring, patient voice to continue. New memories, like faded photos, from when she was a little kid, before the orphanage, surfaced. She had told her childhood story so many times that she believed it was true, but then she "saw" new images that filled in blanks she didn't know she had. She remembered a Latina who found her at the market and took her home. "She said she was my mama, but she was dressed like a city lady. She lied to me. My mama left to go somewhere and didn't come back; that's when the woman tricked me and took me." She breathed heavily and cried, remembering the terror of being led away. "That woman only wanted me for money; then she left me on the streets again. Policemen found me"—she was heaving now—"and took me to an orphanage. Then it's all a blur."

In the next EMDR session, she remembered being in the orphanage and being told a story over and over that she was supposed to remember, where she was from, what happened to her, and how her mother left her. "I didn't know what to believe—I was a little kid," she cried. "I just knew I hated my mama for leaving me." When the memories came rushing up from the depth of her, buried deep and hidden, because of the magic in Elaine's wand, she cried like a baby and wailed for her mama. Her mama was so young, so beautiful, so sad and scared. "I miss you, mama. I can't live without you." Mariela sobbed like the lost child she had been.

Elaine spoke softly, "You were found and taken to an orphanage; then loving people adopted you. You didn't do anything wrong; it wasn't your fault. You are safe. You are good." Elaine spoke lovingly as she urged Mariela to feel the chair beneath her, to listen to her voice and return to the present, to the office where they sat together, safe and grown up.

"Oh my God, what happened?" said Mariela. "It felt like I was back there in Guatemala, all alone and so scared." She was exhausted and shaken when the EMDR treatment was finished.

"Take good care of yourself after you leave today. That little girl inside you wants to be healed. Help her by being kind, patient, and good to yourself. Say sweet things like how brave you were, how hard you tried," said Elaine as she looked lovingly at Mariela. "EMDR can unlock memories from traumatic events that have been buried for many years. Once you feel the feelings of the child you were, you can begin to heal from them. It's all possible." Elaine continued, "I suspect that when your mama and you got separated, it was so traumatic that you blocked a lot of it; then what happened after that became a confusing blur. You were very young and so scared and hurt. The adults in your life at that time gave you a story to believe, and you were too young and traumatized to ask questions."

"Yes, the story has always been confusing, but I thought I was just a crazy kid who made stuff up," Mariela said, shaking her head in disbelief as she let in that it was the adults who had been screwed up, not her. Elaine walked her to the office door, observing her carefully, then said she would see Mariela again in a week.

At the next session, Elaine asked Mariela to try to recount what happened before she and her mama journeyed to Guatemala City. At first, she couldn't remember anything, but then the images came to her. She and her mama running through the jungle, the soldiers, the fires, her mama squeezing her hand as they ran, always scared and hungry. As she spoke, she realized they were her buried memories that now skimmed along a surface of reality. "I remember her, I remember her. She held my hand so tightly. She wanted me." Mariela cried and cried, and Elaine sat with her, speaking in soothing tones, helping her make room for new thoughts, feelings, and sensations.

Mariela caught the bus back to the residential treatment program, trembling inside like there was a seismic shift beginning, a tearing down of the scaffolding built up over the years. *A drink would help me deal with this quaking,* she thought. Just as quickly, she remembered Elaine's caring look and thought of Glenda's belief in her, and finally considered Charlotte, three thousand miles away and always rooting for her. She let the urge to stop by a bar pass by her, and before she knew it, she was standing at the door of the shelter where inside she would join her friends.

The session with Elaine turned over and over in her mind. Where had she buried the other memories of her early life in Guatemala?

Could she access those memories to discover who she was? For the first time in her life, she felt desperate to put the pieces of her early life together. Before this time, she had resisted thinking about her past or working to understand what had happened to her Mayan mama and to herself. Her history had been buried under layers of shame.

Later that same day, she felt an urgency to talk to Charlotte. The recent therapy had broken through a hard layer, unlocking her heart the way Charlotte had never been able to do. Still, Charlotte was there for her, patiently waiting. "I'm starting to remember things from Guatemala. It's amazing. I was wondering if you can tell me more about my life in Guatemala, stuff I can't remember, stuff you might have found out," Mariela said. It felt odd to make herself vulnerable like this, asking Charlotte to help her excavate who she was before their story together began. "What did the social worker tell you about me? I know you've told me, but I never wanted to hear it before."

"She told us that you were clever and intelligent and wanted to be adopted. She didn't tell us much more. I'm not sure they knew anything about you. Your history sounded similar to that of so many of the kids... Your parents died of some illness; your grandmother tried to take care of you, but she got sick and brought you to the orphanage," Charlotte said in a singsong voice, indicating the make-believe nature of all of it.

"I want to find out all there is to know about my early life, but I don't know where to start." Mariela continued, "I remember one time you told me about an adoption racket where people got rich taking kids from their families and putting them up for adoption. I didn't want to hear about it then, but I do now."

Charlotte didn't hesitate to say what she knew. "It went on for many years, especially during the Guatemalan civil war. Kids were taken or bought from poor Mayan families, then held in homes, or orphanages, until they were adopted for large sums of money by Americans, Europeans, or Canadians. Women involved in the business were often paid to take care of young kids and pretend they were either the mother or a relative, so the whole thing looked legal," Charlotte said. "Adoptive parents like us knew nothing of this illegal business and willingly paid the fees, thinking it was the cost of keeping the orphaned children healthy and safe. In reality, the people who gained from this business were the attorneys and unscrupulous people involved in the child selling."

"So, I could have been stolen from my mom when we got separated in the marketplace?" Mariela asked, her voice shaking.

"Yes, I think it is highly likely that you were part of the adoption scandals in the mid-'80s when thousands of kids were found, bought, or stolen and sold to adoptive parents who were ignorant of their kids' histories. Your poor mom probably had no idea what happened to you," Charlotte added, choking back tears.

"That's amazing," said Mariela, her own eyes filled with tears as she held tight to the phone and felt the connection to this new story and to the adoptive mother on the other end.

Mariela returned to see Elaine at the mental health clinic many more times, and each time, as Elaine mined the depths of her subconscious, more of Mariela's early life was revealed to her. Her Mayan mom had been young and scared as they ran together from the soldiers. She remembered being held tightly and comforted by her mama, the smells of her mama, fear, dust, sweat, and grief mingling. She also remembered her mama's stony silence. Elaine helped her revisit the day when her mom didn't return for her over and over until the memory lost the terror it had once held. She could talk about it without her heart throbbing.

Like thousands of others during the war, they had lost each other. Her story was sad and awful but not unique. As she allowed this fact to take hold, she let go of the personal shame she had always felt about not being good enough for a mother to stay and slowly made room for another story. Elaine had helped construct the steps to help her climb out of her past. Her mama had lost her and always grieved for her; both of them had been hurt by the cruel business of stealing kids due to war and poverty and greed. The hole in her heart where her mama had once been wouldn't heal quickly or maybe at all. She'd carry that wound inside forever, but it felt lighter, more bearable.

Chapter 21

Charlotte

"There is a voice that doesn't use words."
Rumi

We were gathered in the living room of the home of Chad and his wife, Jody. Their house was decorated beautifully and was a delight for the four small kids who played nearby. The wrapping paper that had been strewn around the room was gathered, and a small pile of gifts for each of us was neatly organized. It was time to do our White Elephant gift exchange, a tradition we were determined to continue despite the ages of Chad's and Jill's kids, all four of them between five and eight. It was a lot to expect that kids that young could unwrap a present, then willingly give it up to a family member who wanted it. We were keeping the rules flexible and fun.

We all laughed out loud as funny gifts were unwrapped for all to see and evaluate. The four cousins were beginning to understand the good-natured giving, taking, and sharing of gifts. My heart swelled with tenderness and love as I looked at my gathered family. Bill squeezed my hand tenderly when I reached to hold his. We would visit his kids and grandkids on the East Coast in a few days. I felt blessed and happy. The only thing that would have made me happier was if Mariela and her children were sitting with us that Christmas morning, but she hadn't been part of our Christmas celebrations for years. Her absence from our gathering had moved to background sadness, covered by joy and gratitude I felt in other parts of my life. I was blessed with what some people prayed for every day: good health, a loving partner, adult kids who I adored, and grandkids who were healthy and loved. It was not that I didn't still carry an ache of loss for the daughter I had once imagined weaving into our family. I had quite simply learned to carry that loss more easily.

Later that Christmas day, I called her. She was out of her long-term treatment program and holding her own with a job and a small apartment and seeing her kids on the weekends. Friends often asked me, "How's Mariela doing? Is she still living back East? Is she OK?" I knew they were demonstrating their love for me by showing concern for her. They didn't want to hear the long-winded tale of upheaval that took the conversation into the troubled waters of my adopted daughter's life.

"Actually, she is doing well enough," I answered. "She has some friends, she's paying the bills, she sees her kids." I didn't avoid the answer or make it sound better than it was. I was truly happy with how she was doing; it *was* good enough. Her successes were measured on a different scale.

And my own journey with her, while bumpy, had led me to a place where I could bear witness without making her life my problem, at least most of the time. I had become skillful at ending conversations that seemed headed to angry dead ends. Thankfully, these conversations were happening less often. I was able to remain curious but detached about her kaleidoscope of feelings. When she was critical of me, I resisted the urge to defend myself. I was learning to accept her on her own terms and feel thankful for things that were good enough, a lower bar under which most things slid. Things weren't ideal, smooth, or easy, but I discarded the belief that they should be, with Mariela or with anyone or anything. I had turned a corner, escaping from rogue perfectionism with humor and humility.

When she answered the phone, her voice was lighter than usual. "I'm spending Christmas with a friend, and my kids are coming here in a little while. Yesterday, I went to the rehab center to help put food boxes together. It was kind of fun."

"That's wonderful," I said. "Chad and Jill say hello and Merry Christmas to you and your kids."

"OK, tell them hi for me." Her voice turned stiff. I wished I knew how to heal her wound of not belonging, but she had turned down invitations to join us so many times that I had given up. Besides this way of relating from afar was easier and protected Chad and Jill and their families from her volatile moods. My love for her was unconditional, but my willingness to have her change a cherished gathering was not.

"Maybe next Christmas, you can come to Oregon for a visit," I said.

"Yeah, maybe," she said.

At the same time that I had been working to let go with love and hold on to hope without expectations, she had been in a yearlong treatment program. I hadn't been there to witness her healing firsthand, but I could hear it in her voice when we spoke on the phone. We had only talked once a month or so during that year. My previous background static of concern became almost silent as I learned to trust that whatever was happening was out of my control. A small voice inside me repeated on a regular basis, *She is moving slowly in the direction of healing.*

I now had several friends who had adopted older children from whom I received and gave support. We used humor and compassion to bolster ourselves. We were practicing skills necessary to keep our hearts open and our boundaries intact. We shared scenarios and applauded our successes, beaming with compassion toward each other and saying how much those skills had helped us with all the relationships in our lives.

One weekday evening when Mariela called next, I realized I was genuinely happy to hear from her. "Well, hello, I'm so happy you called." My fear of her hostility and my own feelings evoked by her hostility were subsiding. I sat down in a comfortable chair and opened my heart to her.

Her voice was lighter, her words less jarring; she seemed less pressured. "There's this therapist who has really helped me. I've had lots of memories of my first mom. I've cried a lot. I'm starting to see things different."

My hand held tight to the phone; I was holding my breath and tears filled my eyes. While I had stepped back and taken my focus off her, she had been healing with the help of others.

She continued, "I'm in an apartment with rent control, and my job working in a factory is boring but doesn't cause me much stress. I'm taking a few classes to train me for a better job. My case manager will keep helping me as long as I stay in the program and live by the rules. They've got me on medication that seems to help my anger and anxiety. I don't like being on meds, but I plan to stay on it and see what happens."

Oh my God, I love this case manager, I thought. "Wow, that's so great." I had wanted this for decades; it had been a long road, a terribly bumpy road. I had gotten close to giving up on her, but I hadn't. I had, however, surrendered my belief that I could affect this outcome. "Mariela, I'm proud of you. I'm here to support the hard work you're doing." I looked east out of my window as we talked. Somewhere out there, living on the other coast, she was finding her way, healing, and learning what she needed to repair her life. A weight that I was unaware of carrying lifted off my shoulders. *Thank you, thank you,* I spoke to the clouds progressing at their own pace across the sky.

Then we hung up, and I sat almost breathless with gratitude. I knew there were hurdles ahead for her that I couldn't move, but I had begun to trust that she could get around them herself. Her life was unfolding, and I was a devoted spectator.

Weeks later, we had a conversation that surprised me. "I'm thankful to be in the US. My life could have really been crap if I had stayed in Guatemala. Thank God you brought me here," she said. Vulnerability, gratitude, and appreciation, expressed out loud to me.

"Yes, I'm happy you joined our family. It wasn't easy, but we learned a lot, huh?" I said.

She agreed. There was a long pause, then: "It's taken a long time for me to forgive you for putting me in a mental hospital. Sometimes I still feel angry about it." Her voice was unsteady with emotion. "And you took Hasan's side against me. That's hard to forgive."

"I'm sorry. I didn't know what else to do. I was scared for you and Caleb, and later for all your kids," I said, realizing I had always felt guilty for the desperate act of calling the police, which led to her psychiatric hospitalization. And she was correct, I had sided with Hasan and encouraged him to be more involved with the kids. From her perspective, I had betrayed her when she needed help. From my perspective, which I had defended for years to myself and to others, I had no choice. I no longer felt a need to defend myself or justify my actions. I had done the best I could at the time. I felt compassion for both of us, and it felt good to begin processing these sad and scary times in our history together.

In another conversation, after she told me about a fight she'd had at work, she said, "I shouldn't have gotten so angry at my coworker. It just made things worse. I've been angry my whole damn life. I'm seeing that now. My anger was eating me alive, so I had to stop feeding it."

Her hardy laugh made me smile. She was taking responsibility, not shifting blame. My heart sang with gratitude for her growth. "Hey, good for you!" I said.

"Thanks."

We were both learning to keep things simple, straight, free from interpretation and agendas. She was learning from her life experiences, and my input, opinions, and beliefs, no matter how informed I thought they were, weren't useful unless she asked for them.

She called more frequently and wanted to share her thoughts and feelings. I had yearned for her to open up to me for years, and now she was calling and wanting to talk at length. "I learned a lot from you. You are good to your friends. You were good to me. You stuck by me, and that couldn't have been easy. I was a real pain in the ass." She laughed.

She'll never know how close I came to throwing in the towel, I thought. Her thoughtful words of appreciation had come unbidden and unexpected and felt like a warm blanket on our once-chilly relationship.

"Thank you, that means a lot to me." I felt myself soaring with hope, imagining a new beginning with her and a happier story than we had ever had. But I slowed my internal reverie after I hung up the phone. *That was a beautiful exchange; just stay with that,* I thought.

Mariela still seemed unstable at times, her moods occasionally volatile, her personality shifting with her internal landscape. Sometimes, I struggled to understand her perspective; I'd get hooked and want to jump in to instruct or coerce, but I was able to unhook quickly. Even she couldn't grasp the shifting sands of her inner life. I finally understood the folly of my expectation that I could. I gave up making understanding imperative. I accepted that a relationship with Mariela required me to tolerate disruptions in our connection. The trick was repairing the disruption, if possible, and not taking it personally. Our relationship had been tilled on rocky soil, and I would be grateful for whatever bloomed.

In the years that followed, Bill and I visited his two grown kids and their families on the East Coast at least twice a year. This was an opportunity to see Mariela and her kids, if she was open to a visit. Sometimes, she said she wasn't; other times she seemed thrilled to have us. Bill and I used humor to defuse Mariela's predictable unpredictability.

"Are you ready for absolutely anything from being cherished to vilified?" he quipped, as he often did, helping me relax into acceptance before the visit. He had grown fond of Mariela and saw her as a gutsy survivor. Bill's father had died when he was seven, leaving his mom with six young children. He could identify, to some degree, with Mariela's hard-scrabble early life. He had struggled to let go of control born of necessity due to an early life where he lacked it. He didn't have a history with her and took none of what she said or did personally.

The last few phone calls with her before one visit had been positive, but I kept my expectations in check and simply hoped for a brief enjoyable visit with her and her kids in New Jersey. I had coined a new phrase and way of being that I found helpful. "I've got my Teflon on," I said to Bill, meaning that whatever was said or did simply slid off and didn't stick around to mess me up. She and Yasmin and Ameer welcomed us with big smiles, and we spent two days sightseeing around New York City and playing cards on the queen-size bed of our hotel room. The visit was the best we had ever had. "Has she gotten easier, or is it me who has changed?" I questioned Bill.

"I think it's a combination of both, and you both are winners."

I still occasionally wondered what various professionals had said about her diagnosis: did she have an attachment disorder, borderline personality disorder, PTSD, depression, addiction, or a stew of psychological ailments impossible to determine? After years spent trying to make sense of her, I simply let it be and gave over to not knowing or labeling. She was a unique person with a complex history, and there was no use reducing her into a conclusive verdict. I eventually learned to let go of the occupational hazard of diagnosing, which was no longer useful.

"Hey, you seem worried; how's she doing?" Bill asked me one day after I got off the phone with Mariela.

"Yeah, I am worried. She's having trouble with her boss and a few coworkers. She tends to misinterpret then overreact."

"I heard what you said to her, and it was right on. That's all you can do," Bill said. "You said you're here for her and always available to talk. That's loving and helpful, and enough," he added.

"I know. It just makes me sad. I want her to experience happiness in her life. She had it tough from the beginning," I said, suddenly feeling very sad. That's when I remembered what a good friend said to me: "You're so used to seeing how far she has to go that you fail to see how far she's come." I had thanked her for the wisdom and swore I'd remember that perspective.

Bill and I moved on to other topics, including a summer camping trip with our kids and grandkids. The sadness lifted. I was learning to sit with the sadness, then watch as it dissipated or moved back to a contained space where it didn't needle me. Having Mariela and her kids join us on a family trip would have been a wonderful outcome, but we weren't there yet, and I simply wouldn't focus on what was missing.

In the years that followed, Mariela and I talked regularly on the phone. The pattern of her moving close then pulling away was changing. She seemed more able to maintain some closeness without the hostile pushback I had come to expect in the past. In fact, she seemed eager to talk to me, often bursting with stories that were laced with outrage at someone or something, but it was usually not directed at me, and I was thankful for that. We often laughed, even when we talked about our painful past together. We fell into a rhythm of "checking in," as she called it, perhaps something she had learned in one of her therapy groups. At times, we talked more like friends who cared about each other, rather than a mother and daughter who had struggled for decades with each other.

All the years of holding on to the notion that by sheer will, desire, and determination I would be able to turn things around for Mariela finally came to an end. I had wanted my adoption of her to be redemptive for both of us, and I had clung to my stubborn belief that I could make that happen. If things didn't turn out well for Mariela, then my story with her was a failure and my childhood script of not being good enough would be confirmed. Her life and mine had intersected and our stories blurred due to my mistaken belief that I was responsible for giving her (and myself) an ending that was satisfying and worthy of the difficult emotional journey together.

Finally, I detached from a hoped-for outcome and turned inward, living with acceptance of my own limitations. She had been perfect for me, just as I thought when I first saw her photo and imagined our life together. But not in the way I imagined.

When I read about the American mother who had returned her adopted Russian son to Russia, saying he had severe behavior problems than she couldn't handle, I hadn't known what to think. On my very worst days, which were thankfully far behind me, I could imagine the desperation to be free from the burden. The judgments of others against this mother were vicious, but I had withheld ridicule. While I wouldn't have gone to those extreme ends, I wouldn't stand in judgment of her. I had stuck with my unconscious agreement to discover a way to be with Mariela that didn't take me under, so we could both heal in ways needed. This difficult path had taken years of slow transformation to open to the gifts that patience provided.

The course of her life was set long before I arrived and didn't bend to my will. What happened to her affected me because I loved her but was not caused by me, nor could I fix it for her. Her life contained in it a tragic wound that I couldn't heal, and her problems were bigger than my ability to solve with love. Maternal love, which we are taught to believe is the salve to heal all wounds, has limitations.

My life with Mariela had felt heartbreaking for so many years, but I had begun to see that it contained a bigger story of her resilience and mine, a different kind of redemption. We were still trying to understand each other, still engaging, sometimes with delight, at times with bewilderment, more often with laughter. It was a messy, unfinished story, still revealing itself.

Mariela continued to do well enough with the support of a therapist, a case manager, and an occasional AA sponsor. Her dependence on alcohol turned out to be her biggest challenge. Periods of sobriety were interrupted with binges that threw her off course and back into self-loathing and shame. As with all the challenges in her life, it took tremendous energy to get beyond negative self-assessments and back to a belief that her life was worth salvaging and recovery a worthwhile goal. Over time, she began to understand that it would be ongoing work to stay on a path that led to a satisfying life.

Once she no longer saw herself in the roles of victim, loser, or unfortunate underdog, new roles opened to her. Along with survivor, she was a successful employee, caring mom, friend, and daughter. She spent time with her younger kids regularly, but they stayed with Hasan and never lived with her again. Her two older sons, Caleb and Antonne, lived in Oregon, and I maintained contact with them. They sometimes expressed their resentments toward her, which caused her distress, but over time they moved closer to acceptance, a journey that will probably last for years.

Working with a therapist helped her change the story of her life. She no longer saw herself as a hurt and lost child at the whim of a cruel fate. She began to tell a new story, which etched itself slowly into her being. She told me on a visit to see her one summer day as we sat in a park in New Jersey, "Did I tell you I had my ancestry done? I'm a full-blooded Mayan, and we are a proud and tough group of people who have endured hardships for generations. I'm as adaptable as they come. I was a homeless kid found on the street with nothing but a worn and empty basket, dropped off at an orphanage, taken to the US, I got pregnant at fifteen, then had years of fighting with everyone till I finally gave up on that." She laughed and looked into my eyes. I beamed back my acceptance of her. The doors between us were opening, and she was cautiously allowing me to step into the life she had begun to inhabit. Trust between us was fragile and depended on my ability to enter her life only when invited. I was learning the art of navigating around the potholes to create trust and goodwill between us.

One day, she asked me about my impressions when I first met her, what I had thought about her defiance and anger, and how Chad and Jill felt currently felt about her. Her vulnerability surprised and delighted me. She was trying to make sense of our perspective, and I wanted to tell her the truth without hurting her.

"I could see the hurt and anger in your eyes when we first met you, but it wasn't long before I loved you very much and wanted to help heal that hurt. I got carried away thinking I could. It upset me that I couldn't do it. I wish I had understood my limitations sooner and been able to love you differently." I struggled again to understand what I could have done better for her. Feelings of remorse seeped in. Then I reminded myself that the past was over and couldn't be resolved. I had done the best I could at the time. All we had was what had happened between us and what we had now. I continued to answer her questions.

"Chad and Jill have been unsure how to stay open to you. They are busy with their lives and their kids. It will take time," I said.

"I was really mean to Jill. I always felt bad about that. She really tried; she was always nice to me." Mariela sounded as if she was choking back tears.

"Yes, you and Jill were very close for a while. I always think about you two in Guatemala and on the plane when we brought you home. But the story isn't over. Things change," I added.

"How is she doing?"

"Jill is doing well. She loves being a mom and a nurse," I said. It wasn't going unnoticed that she was starting to ask about her sister and brother and to inquire about my life more than she had in many years. "Chad works hard and is a great dad, and Jody is wonderful." Then I decided to share something about Jill. I was still trying to sort out my feelings about the turn Jill's life had taken. "Jill and Brandon are foster parents to three little kids, a sibling group. They hope to adopt them. They love those kids so much and want to be their 'forever family.' It's a wonderful thing," I said, deciding this was enough information coming from me.

"What the hell?" she responded. "After all I put her through, and she wants to adopt kids?"

"Yes, she definitely does. It's a long story, and I'll tell you all about it when you want to hear it. Or you could ask Jill yourself."

"Dang, that's hard to believe that she'd want to go down that road. I'd never adopt kids; I have a hard enough time with my own." She laughed. "But I guess it's lucky for me that some people want to raise kids that aren't their own." She laughed again.

My brother Patrick called one day to catch up and ask about the progress with Jill and Brandon's adoption of the three young foster kids. It had been a long road for the court to relinquish the biological parents' rights. "It should be final fairly soon. We're all thrilled and so happy to have those kids in our family," I said. "Bill and I enjoy the kids immensely."

"Jill seems to be following in your footsteps, Char," Patrick said with a good-natured laugh.

"Not really. Jill is on her own path, and I think she's way ahead of where I was." I felt the expansiveness of love when speaking of Jill.

"How's Mariela doing these days?" Patrick finally asked. I could sense the hesitancy when family or friends asked me about her, as if talking about her was a painful subject best avoided. It was no longer distressing for me to talk about her, but I had done a lot of work, as had Mariela. Family and friends were still referencing an outdated and painful story.

"She's doing well. She's accepting help and has a job and sees her kids. She likes her therapist and has developed some insight and a sense of humor about her past and present troubles. It doesn't get any better than that!" I told my brother enthusiastically. He didn't seem overly impressed by my measurements of success, but I didn't care. I was thrilled that she was enjoying her life and not seething with anger.

She told me on the phone weeks later that her kids had started to ask about her childhood. "I've never been willing to talk about it, so they had stopped asking a long time ago. I was ashamed that I was abandoned, that I lived in an orphanage, that I was a throwaway kid. But now I tell them and other people about my childhood and talk about my first mama."

I listened with interest, wondering what she said about her mother.

She continued, "I tell them that my mother lived during an awful time in Guatemala; many people died and disappeared then. She was young and poor, and many Mayans were killed and their children taken from them to sell to foreigners. I think my mama loved me and wanted me, but she lost me during the times when villages were burned and families got separated. People wanted me to believe my mama left me, so I would forget about what really happened. My mama may still be out there," she told her kids. "And someday, I may go back and look for her."

I listened to the account she now told of her early years. She would probably never know what happened to her mama Maria, but this new story was kinder and even more plausible than the one she had always believed. She was no longer a discarded and unwanted child. Her early years were similar to thousands of Mayan children who were victims of war. The shame and hurt of being abandoned had loosened its grip on her.

"My kids also ask about you," she told me. "I tell them the truth. That you and your family found me and gave me a home, but I could never let myself love or trust you, and it never felt like my home. I expected you to trick me and leave me, and I never felt good enough for you. I tell them that I blamed you for everything and made life hell for you." Her perception landed heavy on my heart, but I recognized it as her truth.

She told me another day that she was learning to identify anger, then work to deal with it before it took control of her. "My therapist told me that anger was the only emotion I felt for years, and I loved the energy and control it gave me," she said. "I had never thought of it that way. I still get angry, but I can control it better and only use it when I need to." She laughed as she added, "Which is often in this crowded, crazy city. And everything is better when I stay away from booze. I have felt so empty for years, and I tried to fill myself up with the wrong things, the things that don't really fill you up. Now, things are starting to stay with me, inside me," she said, her voice trailing off. She had said enough for this time, she seemed to be indicating. It was more than enough.

Time has a way of transforming painful experiences and giving new ways of seeing them. I was a different person than the one who rode the bus through the highlands of Guatemala thirty years ago to adopt a traumatized child I believed I could heal. Mariela has been my greatest teacher. She needed love and compassion more than anyone I have known. She taught me to keep loving despite every fiber in my body wanting to close the door to simplify my life and guard my heart. She taught me the skill of loving with limits on what I'd tolerate to prove that love. She taught me compassion for her and for myself.

The fruits of my long labor have graced me with invaluable lessons and personal growth. The lessons I learned through my relationship with Mariela became generalized to other relationships in my life. I no longer let my expectations of others cloud my ability to really see them or create hurdles too high for them to jump. I became more tolerant of things that didn't work out the way I wanted and said much more often, "I don't know," gently shrugging with a smile. I discovered that I could hold difficult people in my heart while keeping them at a healthy emotional distance.

I learned to say no to things that didn't work for me and to deal with the mixture of feelings that arose when I disappointed others. I no longer took people's wrath and indignation personally. Mariela taught me to allow others to have their feelings without trying to solve their problems or make the negative feelings go away. She taught me to step off the paths of others so they could find their own way.

She may always search for what she lost when she was very young; a place of comfort, security, belonging, and identify, the sense of being "at home." But home is not just a place, it is a feeling, and feeling at home with oneself is a complicated process, especially for those with early loss and severed attachments. Mariela's journey to find acceptance and love within herself will be her lifelong work.

Our story is still unfolding, and the chapters ahead are uncertain in her life and also in mine. I had wanted a resolution to my adoption story that had my daughter finding a home, happiness, and connection to me, but I didn't get a story with that kind of ending. My own happy ending, which I accept with love and grace, is that Mariela and I have made some peace with each other and have created a space for our limitations and recognized that as love. We helped each other unhook from painful patterns, then we weaved an intricate tapestry of healing, hers and mine. It was our destiny to dance together to a universal rhythm not understood or easily explained, with a voice that doesn't use words.

> "I am another you, you are another me."
> Mayan saying

Epilogue

My story of navigating the rocky terrain of raising an older adopted child is not meant to dissuade loving parents from the privilege of raising a child not born to them. Rather, it is meant to encourage well-meaning parents, as I was, to keep their loving eyes wide open to the challenges of the healing journey ahead and to inform them of the patience often required to reap the fruits of their labors.

Being available for adoption, whatever the cause, means a child's life has been imbued with loss that is weaved into the fabric of their being. As an adoptive mother, I had a unique opportunity to help Mariela begin to heal. But I had to learn about the limits of a mother's love on the long and arduous journey to wholeness. I had my own lessons to learn to keep my heart open to receive the blessings that healing provides. Our journeys continue.

Mariela's children were impacted by her early loss, and as they got older, they sought answers to better understand her troubled past and to make sense of their own lives. She shared stories from her painful childhood, which helped her healing process. Her children eventually circled around to me in an attempt to appreciate who I had been to their mother, and who I was to them. My relationship with Mariela's grown sons is evolving, and I remind myself to be patient and steady. Mariela's daughter, Yasmin, now eighteen years old, came from New Jersey to visit recently. She is a freshman in college with a strong sense of herself and an uncanny ability to communicate her feelings. We talked openly about her mom, and she gave voice to both empathy and ability to set limits. She and I shared tender moments together, and I was filled with gratitude for the connection across the generations. Plans are underway for Yasmin and Ameer to come to Oregon for a summer visit.

My relationship with Mariela continues to provide practice in the skills I honed with her over years of struggle. She continues to teach me to be present and loving and to have the grace and gratitude to relax into not having all the answers.

These days, I continue my service work in Guatemala, which gives me an opportunity to give back to the country that gave me one of its children. Bill and I visit Guatemala every year, and I'm on the board of an organization I helped start, Nuevas Sonrisas (New Smiles), a dental group helping rural, impoverished children with unmet dental needs. By returning to Guatemala each year, I continue to learn about the beautiful, fascinating country to which I am connected.

I have stayed involved in Nuestros Pequeños Hermanos, the organization that caught my attention many years ago that provides a home-like setting, education, social and emotional support, and health care for orphaned children in Guatemala and other Latin American countries. I have visited the Guatemalan home for children many times, and I'm always impressed with the love and care the children receive in the country of their birth. Websites for both of these wonderful organizations are provided here:

Nuevas Sonrisas Dental Group, www.nuevassonrisas.org
Nuestros Pequeños Hermanos, www.nphusa.org

Acknowledgements

I'd like to thank my husband, Bill, whose encouragement kept me writing when it was painful to do so; and to my many friends who walked with me providing love and support along the way. I also want to thank the many Guatemalans who inspired me with their stories and all the parents I've met who are learning the fine balance of limits and self care while keeping open, loving hearts for their struggling adult children.

www.ingramcontent.com/pod-product-compliance
Lightning Source LLC
Chambersburg PA
CBHW020417010526
44118CB00010B/292